# KLEIST

# KLEIST

## A BIOGRAPHY
### by Joachim Maass

TRANSLATED FROM THE GERMAN BY
*Ralph Manheim*

*Farrar, Straus and Giroux*

NEW YORK

◇┼◇┼◇┼◇┼◇

# CONTENTS

◇┼◇┼◇┼◇┼◇

# Contents

## Illustrations

FOLLOWING PAGE 90

# KLEIST

# 1

## ORIGINS

GERMANY's greatest and most typically German dramatic genius came of an old Slavic family. "Clest" or "Klist," possibly meaning "lance shaft," was originally a Christian name and only later became a family name. As early as the twelfth or thirteenth century, the family owned large estates in the Duchy of Pomerania, and one of its members, Clest de Densin, Lord of Raddatz, is held to be the direct ancestor of our Kleist family.

Later on, the family intermarried with German knights, but as late as the sixteenth century, Slavic Christian names were still current. By the Peace of Westphalia, a part of Pomerania was ceded to Brandenburg. This made Germans of the Kleists, who retained their estates, and from then on, they were typical members of the Prussian officer-nobility. By the late eighteenth century, when Heinrich von Kleist was born, the family had already brought forth no fewer than eighteen generals.

Its coat-of-arms showed, under a white field with a red crossbar, a running fox (which may once have been a wolf) with dangling blood-red tongue; and the family crest—consisting of three hunting spears with their tips resting on three red roses— seems almost to symbolize by anticipation the work of Heinrich von Kleist. A feeling for extramilitary concerns must always have been present among the Kleists, for in their family records we find the notation: "All Kleists poets"—a rather unusual assertion in connection with a clan that had produced eighteen generals.

3

Indeed, they were not all—or not exclusively—officers or statesmen. In 1745 the physicist and canon Ewald Georg von Kleist invented the Kleistian jar, which in the following year, 1746, was once more invented by Andreas Cunaeus and Pieter van Musschenbroek of Leyden, whereupon it became more widely known as the Leyden jar.

Ewald Christian von Kleist numbered Klopstock, Lessing, and the friendship-possessed poet Johann Wilhelm Ludwig Gleim among his friends; he himself was a *guerrier, poète et philosophe,* classified in the histories of literature as an Anacreontic. He was the author of sensitive, strikingly realistic nature idylls, whose fame, especially that of *Spring,* might well have survived, had they been animated by any strong guiding idea. He, too, seems to foreshadow Heinrich von Kleist, not so much in his work as in his character, his death wish. The death of this man while fighting for Frederick the Great at the lost battle of Kunersdorf seems to have been a kind of suicide. The statue of him erected twenty years later, in 1779, by the Freemasons of Frankfurt on the Oder, shows the profile of a melancholy dreamer.

Franz Alexander von Kleist, only eight years older than Heinrich, resigned from the army as Heinrich did later on, to devote himself to scientific studies and literature, in which he achieved considerable, though transient, success by concentrating on the then fashionable themes of humanity, enlightenment, and return to nature, in magazine pieces and in books such as *Happiness in Love* and *Happiness in Marriage.* Highly respected as a man of letters, an occasional diplomat, a landowner and district magistrate, he succumbed, according to La Motte-Fouqué, who "had trembled with excitement at the prospect of meeting him," "to unrestrained debauchery in his later years." He died in 1797, when Heinrich von Kleist was twenty years of age and serving as a second lieutenant in Potsdam.

At first glance, Heinrich von Kleist's immediate family show no sign of eccentricity. His paternal grandfather, Bernd Christian, had bequeathed his estate of Schmentzien to his eldest son, and only money to the younger sons, including Joachim Friedrich von Kleist, who later acquired the estate of Guhrow and later on, after his promotion to the rank of major in command of the second battalion of the Beville regiment, the imposing house in Frankfurt on the Oder, at 542 Nonnenwinkel. The address is now 26 Oderstrasse, but the house—converted into a post office—is still standing. It then had a large back garden, bounded by the wall of a parsonage. At the age of forty-one, Joachim Friedrich married the fifteen-year-old Karoline Luise von Wulffen, who bore him two daughters, Wilhelmine, known as Minette, and Ulrique (Ulrike) Amalie, who was to play a crucial role in the life of Heinrich von Kleist. But after only five years of married life, the young woman died. The widower remarried, and his new wife, Juliane Ulrike von Pannwitz, bore him five children, the third of whom and the first son being Bernd Heinrich Wilhelm, better known as Heinrich von Kleist. Three and a half years younger than his half sister and favorite, Ulrike, he was born on October 18, 1777, though he himself cites October 10 as the date of his birth. Thus, the long list of contradictions, obscurities, and enigmas characteristic of his whole life story begins with his first day on earth.

# 2

# CHILDHOOD

FRANKFURT on the Oder was situated in a charming hilly countryside, to which Kleist attributed the beauty of a "miniature painting." Impoverished by the Seven Years' War, it was a walled provincial city of ten thousand inhabitants, with narrow streets, a handful of stately patrician mansions, and a university of no great standing. Three times a year it was the scene of a fair, on which occasion a city of market stalls sprang up; jugglers, wild animals, refreshment stands, and brass bands made their appearance, and all available rooms in the houses of the leading citizens, including the Kleists, were rented to out-of-town merchants.

Kleist himself tells us little about the childhood he spent in these unimpressive surroundings. He somewhere calls it "joyless" and speaks of "musical hallucinations" at an early age. And it is hardly more illuminating when, in recording a quarrel with one of his mother's friends, he writes: "Then it came to me how my mother felt, and my anger died down."

Considerably more informative is the first apparently authentic portrait known to us. The work of the Royal Prussian Court Miniaturist Franz Ludwig Close, it shows Frau von Kleist seated, looking kindly and dignified, and pressed to her bosom young Heinrich, aged seven. Under the long, reddish-blond hair one notes the rigidity of the forehead and the roundness of the eyes. The chin is firm and resolute, and the lips, attempting as it were to smile over clenched teeth, seem old and quite incongruous in a child. The sad little figure appears to have been "readied" inside and out, and almost reminds one of those cropped and curled little Maltese dogs often seen on the laps of courtesans in rococo prints. This picture confirms and half explains Kleist's report of a joyless childhood, resulting no doubt less from his surroundings than from his difficult character.

And of that there can be no doubt. Since public school would have been inappropriate to his station, he was tutored at home, along with his melancholy and less gifted cousin Carl Otto von Pannwitz, by the young theologian (and later consistorial councilor and rector) Christian Ernst Martini, a lifelong friend of the family. He speaks of Kleist as an unquenchably fiery spirit, thrown into a state of "exaltation" by trifles, of uneven temper, but of admirable intelligence, and "the most open, hard-working, and undemanding young man in the world." Whatever Martini may have meant by "undemanding," there was more to Kleist's "exaltation" than the forbearing tutor realized. Young Kleist and cousin Pannwitz seem to have signed an agreement to take their lives together if "anything unworthy" should fall to their lot. Thus, the thought of a suicide pact came to Kleist at an early age. But we also have early evidence of his gentler qualities, of the chivalry and generosity that stayed with him all his life. One day he asked his eldest sister for some money, which she gave him. Then the very next day he came back and asked for more. "What! So soon?" she asked in astonishment, and he replied: "Oh, Minette, I met a friend who needed it much more than I. I gave it all to him."

Otherwise, we know nothing of his relations with his brothers and sisters. But one cannot help supposing that in view of his early-manifested spirit of competition, the unquestionable charm of his brother Leopold, two and a half years his junior, must have been hard for him to bear. There is a story about a song contest in honor of a newly built cow barn on Uncle Kleist's estate at Tschernowitz near Guben. The prize of one friedrichsdor was not won by Heinrich, the future genius, but by the eight-year-old Leopold, and justly so no doubt, for it seems certain that the elder brother would have been no more capable then than later of such smiling wit. One can hardly imagine "our" Kleist penning such verses as these, which we owe to oral tradition:

> Stand, oh stand, thou solid building
> Century on century,
> Let no storm or fire ravage
> Thy so stately symmetry.
>
> Let all plague and epizootic
> Shun thy comfortable hall,
> Let the cows and bulls and heifers
> Never be disturbed at all.
>
> And when someday thou collapsest
> All at once, tremendously,
> Then let legend tell forever
> What a barn thou used to be.

What, then, do we know of Kleist's childhood? Apart from the little related here, nothing personal, only family history. His father died in 1788. His will was contested on juridical grounds; his widow appealed to the king to certify its validity, but the king—though promising favorable consideration of future petitions—referred her back to the courts; a compromise was finally arrived at after two years of bitter struggle. We cannot be sure what this litigation was all about, but it seems likely that the will favored the children of Joachim Friedrich's second marriage, on the ground that those of the first, Minette and Ulrike, would be better off financially because of their claims on the estate of their deceased mother. If so, this would account for the marked difference later between the financial circumstances of Heinrich and those of Ulrike.

Along with Pannwitz and another cousin, Kleist was sent to Berlin for further instruction. There they were lodged by the émigré Samuel Heinrich Catel, teacher of religion at the École de Charité (and later literary critic for the *Vossische Zeitung*), from whom Kleist learned to speak French so fluently that for a time he was said to have spoken it "more correctly" than German. But what went on in the young man's mind during these undoubtedly stormy years of adolescence, and whether, as has been supposed, some "indiscretion" or the "dissipated life" he led at this time was the cause of the disorders which appear some years later to have been at the bottom of one of his mysterious journeys—all this is matter for speculation, since we are without reliable, or even unreliable, information on the subject.

# *3*

## THE YOUNG SOLDIER

IT may well have been in fulfillment of the king's promise to look favorably on future petitions that in the summer of 1792 the fifteen-year-old Kleist was taken on as corporal in the king's Guards Regiment at Potsdam. Nine months later his mother died, and her sister, the widow of a Major von Massow, moved into the house on Nonnenwinkel to preside over the orphaned family. The earliest of Kleist's letters in our possession, dated March 13, 1793, is addressed to this "most gracious Auntie." Rather well written, though perhaps too rich in adventure to be entirely truthful, it gives an account of his journey to join the Army of the Rhine, which had been dispatched to beat back the armies of the French Revolution. For those were the years in which the European powers were waging war against revolutionary France, in an effort to stem the onset of a dreaded new era. The Prussian armies hardly covered themselves with glory at the time. By the Peace of Basel in 1795, Prussia was to forfeit its possessions on the left bank of the Rhine, for which loss, to be sure, in league with Austria and Russia, it was compensated by the still less glorious second and third partitions of Poland.

These battles with the French were hardly calculated to fill young Kleist with enthusiasm. "May God give us peace," he wrote, "in which to make good by more charitable actions the time we are wasting here so immorally." And no more warlike is Kleist's earliest-known poem, *The Higher Peace* (*Der höhere Frieden*), which some fifteen years later in Dresden he still thought worth publishing, though whatever genuine experience he may have been trying to express is stifled by the glitter and smoothness of the versification.

Nevertheless, apart from his occasional trouble with "musical hallucinations," young Kleist seems to have been rather carefree in his Rhineland period, unburdened as yet by painful experience. Friedrich de La Motte-Fouqué, who first met him at the end of 1794 in Frankfurt on the Main, where Kleist's corps had taken up winter quarters, describes him as a well-turned-out and lively young man with a natural gift for music. Though he had not yet learned to read notes, he seems to have composed, to have played the flute and clarinet, and to have been able to sing or play back any melody he heard.

Promoted to ensign, he returned to Potsdam in mid-1795, soon followed by brother Leopold, who had entered the service at the age of fifteen and had likewise been made an ensign after having been wounded in Poland. But Cousin Pannwitz was not to join them. He had shot himself on the way back from Poland, during the night of October 17, 1795, on the eve of Kleist's birthday, and his suicide may have been provoked in part by his memory of the suicide pact he and Kleist had concluded in childhood.

The Potsdam regiment was commanded by General von Rüchel, whom Clausewitz characterized as "concentrated acid, drawn from pure Prussianism," an utter vulgarian, who no more took to Kleist than Kleist to him. Garrison life was not at all to Kleist's liking. The eternal monotony of the barracks, the idiocy of the parade drill, the inhumanity of the war-hardened soldiers—everything bored and disgusted him.

Still, he managed to pass the time, thanks in part to his music, which on at least one occasion landed him in the lockup for neglect of duty, and in part to the social life of Potsdam and Berlin, where the "elegant young cavalier" favored the houses of certain ladies of Queen Luise's entourage, especially Frau Adolphine von Werdeck and Frau Marie von Kleist, who made her earliest recorded appearance in Kleist's life at this time. No blood relation, but allied to the family by marriage, she was to play in Kleist's life a considerable, though to this day not fully clarified, role.

It was also during this Potsdam period that he made the

acquaintance of two other figures, who were to stand by him faithfully in difficult times. In 1797, soon after his promotion to second lieutenant, he met first Ernst von Pfuel and then Otto Rühle von Lilienstern, who had both come to join the Potsdam regiment as ensigns. The son of a major general and marshal, Pfuel was later to become, first, War Minister and then Prime Minister of Prussia, while Rühle became a lieutenant general and Inspector General of Prussian Military Schools, careers which bear witness to their great talents, especially if we consider the intellectual limitations of the military nobility at that time and recall that Prime Minister Pfuel resigned in 1848 because he sided with the National Assembly against the pusillanimous and reactionary king. A deep friendship seems to have sprung up almost immediately between Kleist and the two young ensigns. From then on, they pursued their interests and pleasures together, and together they made decisions that were to affect the careers of all three.

While Pfuel was a quiet young man, prudent and somewhat phlegmatic, Rühle had an active mind and took a keen interest in music. Rühle, Kleist, and two other comrades formed a quartet, in which Kleist played the clarinet, and the praises of its excellent performances were still being sung in Potsdam fifty years later. These young officers were thoroughly imbued with the romantic spirit. At one of their gatherings, someone raised the question of how long a group of young men would be able to manage without money. The quartet replied by setting out to cross the Harz Mountains on foot in civilian clothes, without a penny in their pockets, making their way by singing and playing. Kleist was deeply moved by the kindness they met with.

He was easily moved in other respects as well, for it was then that he fell madly in love with young Luise von Linckersdorf, and years later it still stirred his heart to see Luise sitting at the window of her house and to receive a friendly nod from her. At the time, however, their romance did not go very far; its sudden end seems to have been a hard blow to Kleist, for little by little his nature began to change.

He neglected his appearance, grew more serious and thoughtful, and along with Rühle took up the study of philosophy, ancient languages, and most particularly mathematics. Their mathematics teacher was one Johann Bauer, an assistant school principal, but since Bauer merely gave them problems to do and corrected their solutions, they were to all intents and purposes self-taught. But already Kleist regarded himself as "more a student than a soldier," and since "learned officers" were a thorn in the side of their comrades as well as their superior officers, the three friends, Kleist, Rühle, and Pfuel, resolved to quit the service. Kleist immediately wrote a letter petitioning the king for a discharge, but did not send it, partly because he himself found it unconvincing and partly because he thought it advisable to learn a little more mathematics first.

Still, he was too impetuous to put up with much delay. Early in March 1799, he went to Frankfurt* to confer with his family. Obviously, no agreement was possible. His guardian, Aunt Massow—a woman "averse to all change, even from one room to another"—and all the rest of the family opposed his plans. The military career, it was pointed out, guaranteed a secure future, in comparison to which the prospects offered by the academic field seemed most uncertain, and moreover, Kleist, though not yet twenty-two, was too old to start studying. On this last point, he could not help "smiling to myself, since I foresaw that, even if I should go to my grave at a high old age, I was sure to die a student." Regardless of all the arguments brought forth, his decision had been made when he came and was not shaken when he left. He returned to Potsdam, sent the king his petition for discharge—"of my own free choice and in order to complete my studies"—and wrote a long letter, dated March 18–19, 1799, to his old teacher Martini, justifying his step.

The military career, he held, was poisoned by inequality, and hateful to his nature: "So many officers, so many drill masters, so many soldiers, so many slaves." "When the whole regiment went through its drills, it struck me as a living monument to tyranny." And on top of all this, there was the permanent question of conscience: Should he punish a subordinate's failings as

* From here on, the name of Frankfurt standing by itself refers to Frankfurt on the Oder.—Trans.

an officer, or forgive them as a human being? This inner conflict, he believed, was having a bad effect on his character. "And yet I looked upon my moral development as one of my most sacred duties. Thus, in addition to my natural distaste for the military profession, I felt it was my duty to leave it." He wrote with enthusiasm of his future goals: knowledge, happiness, and virtue. Happiness, he held, consisted in the "gratifying contemplation of the moral beauty of one's own character"; virtue he conceived rather vaguely "as a lofty, sublime, ineffable something," for which he could find neither words nor images and for which he nevertheless strove "with the utmost fervor," because in it he saw an intimation of something "higher." These ideas, elaborated in the earliest of Kleist's prose writing to have come down to us—his essay, addressed to Rühle, on "the sure way to find happiness and enjoy it without blemish, even amid life's gravest tribulations"—are hardly very original; they are the standard, then fashionable ideas of the Enlightenment. More original is the character behind the ideas, Kleist's way of taking ideas and supposed insights as absolute laws and of acting accordingly, regardless of the practical consequences.

His superior officers did their best to shield him from such consequences; General von Rüchel tried to hold him; the king wished to grant him only an unlimited leave; but Kleist stood firm, he wanted his freedom, and this may account in part for the king's resentment against him later on. On April 4 he received his discharge and trembled with joy at the thought that he now faced the future a free man. Discharge in hand, this true romantic leapt on his horse and rode to Frankfurt. Hearing that Martini was at a concert, he rode to the concert hall. As Martini was leaving the building, a figure wrapped in a long cavalry cloak stepped out of the darkness. Kleist told Martini the news "helter-skelter," embraced him, sprang to the saddle, and galloped away.

On April 17, 1799, Kleist signed a "statement on leaving the army," undertaking, on completion of his studies, "to serve my king and country in a civilian capacity," a promise which he filled most magnificently, though not in a manner welcomed by those to whom it was addressed.

# 4

## STUDENT AND FIANCÉ

**66 I** have set myself a goal that will require the unremitting exertion of all my powers and the use of every minute's time if it is to be achieved." So wrote Kleist on his return home to Frankfurt after enrolling at the modest local university, where the professors received their students not in lecture halls but in their own homes. He threw himself into his studies, chiefly mathematics, philosophy, and physics, with enthusiasm, trusting in part to his teachers and in part to his own devices. Though an excess of haste may have detracted from his method, he was undoubtedly a hard worker (his zeal was attested by his lecture notes, which were still in his possession ten years later); indeed, he himself was later convinced that he had undermined his nervous system by too much study. He took no part in the brutal, uproarious student life of the day. In short, he was a serious-minded young man, very much under the influence of Professor Christian Ernst Wünsch, a rationalist with a mystical, pietistic streak, and a compiler of scientific knowledge.

Kleist must have feared that his insatiable thirst for knowledge might lead him astray, for by way of disciplining himself he drew up a study plan covering several years, and the study plan soon grew to be a "life plan." By programming his intellectual, moral, and personal future, he hoped to safeguard it against life's hazards, for he had a strange fear of chance, holding that the incalculable and unforeseeable made a mockery of human dignity. This he felt so strongly that he urged his favorite sister, both in writing and by word of mouth, to work out a similar life plan, so as to prepare herself in mind and soul for her destiny, namely, motherhood—a destiny for which, as it happened, Ulrike felt as little inclination as he for soldiering; much to his annoyance, in fact, she seems to have had "no mark of her sex but the hips."

Meanwhile, the "serious-minded young man" was living very comfortably at the house on Nonnenwinkel, under the care of his "most gracious Auntie." "From morning to night the house rang with joking and merriment," in which he took some part, but most of the time he was grave, quiet, and absent. Immersed in his studies, he would unwittingly take up a song someone else had started and sing it to the end. Once when on coming home he wished to change his coat, he forgot what he was doing, continued undressing, and was just getting into bed when brother Leopold came in and laughingly "woke him up." He himself recognized that his interests were so different from those of the other members of the family "that they were thunderstruck when they got some inkling of them." Even his correspondence with members of his intimate family—such as his letter to Ulrike about motherhood and a life plan—hardly brought them closer; he was a stranger in his own family.

And that was not all. Not so long ago an elegant young cavalier of Berlin–Potsdam society, he now became strangely awkward; sometimes he even stuttered when conversing with those around him, and yet, always hard on himself, he sought out their company all the more, though in his opinion their "criss-crossing chatter" could hardly be called conversation. The people he sought out were primarily his neighbors, the family of the regimental commander Major-General von Zenge, whose garden was separated from the Kleists' only by a low latticework fence; a congenial family, consisting of the parents, a son, and two daughters, the elder of whom, the eighteen-year-old Wilhelmine, sometimes "listens [to me] with interest, though I do not learn much from her."

But does it not seem possible that she was the reason, or one of the reasons, for his occasional stuttering? He called on the von Zenges frequently and began to do so every day after brother Leopold was transferred to Potsdam and his social competition was no longer to be feared. The girls found Kleist a poor substitute for his lively and imaginative brother. Wilhelmine thought him gloomy and morose, but they put up with his visits and with his company on walks. Kleist availed himself of the opportunity to awaken their interest in intellectual matters and began to supervise their reading and "education."

The teaching instinct, implicit in the spirit of the Enlightenment, was strong in the student Kleist. He organized a circle of twelve young ladies, including of course the two sisters Wilhelmine and Luise von Zenge, and persuaded them to attend a private course in experimental physics under Wünsch, and one in the history of civilization given by himself. He had a lectern built expressly and proved to be a most pedantic and touchy teacher. Once, when one of his young ladies happened to look out of the window, he broke off his lecture and it was some time before he could be moved to continue. He had no sense of proportion. Dismayed by their faulty German, he made his pupils study grammar and spelling and mercilessly corrected their written exercises—all this for the sake of their "ethical improvement." Then one day, at the end of 1799, Wilhelmine opened a white envelope and found a personal letter from Kleist, along with her last essay, corrected. It was a proposal of marriage.

To judge by her portrait, Wilhelmine was anything but the ugly duckling she thought herself. It shows a well-shaped head, a childlike forehead pertly framed in curls, while blue eyes under finely drawn brows look out expectantly on the world; the face is narrow, with a long, delicate Grecian nose and an attractive, softly curved mouth, whose rather short and slightly grooved upper lip makes a somewhat rabbitlike impression. She seems to have had a pronounced personality and been well endowed with feminine instincts. She was anything but enchanted at Kleist's proposal; "not at all her idea of a husband," he was welcome as a friend, but not as a suitor. Accordingly, she declined.

He was "beside himself." Wilhelmine stopped coming to the Kleist house, but this suitor was not so easily discouraged. He tried to speak to her on walks and urged her "golden sister" Luise to intercede for him; a week later there was a second meeting, and when he pleaded "with tears in his eyes," she agreed to accept a second letter. What, he asked, was her objection to him? Wilhelmine described the husband she desired; Kleist swore he would do everything in his power to live up to her ideal, and at that she gave in.

But then (we are told) came a strange request, to which she did not accede. He wanted her and Luise to keep the engagement secret from her parents—one wonders why, since there can be no doubt of his honorable intentions. For want of a reasonable motive, we can only fall back on the strange love of mystification which was typical of Kleist's character but had never before manifested itself so blatantly. Nevertheless, when the girls refused to consider his plan, he brought himself to write to the young lady's parents asking their daughter's hand, and they gave their consent on condition that he first obtain suitable employment. Wilhelmine gave him a charming miniature of herself, enclosed in a gold-framed locket, along with a lock of her hair as a child. Now nothing stood in the way of their happiness.

But happiness with Kleist was both strange and strenuous. He plied Wilhelmine with written "thought problems" such as: "Which is better, to be good or to do good?" "May a wife inspire the affections of *no one* other than her husband?" "Which member of a married couple loses more by the death of the other?" and further hideous exercises in casuistry, to contribute to her "ethical improvement" and prepare her for marriage, motherhood, and child rearing. "He had an elevated idea of morality," Wilhelmine wrote later on. "He wanted to make me over into his ideal, and that often distressed me." One can easily sympathize with her distress. But Kleist was imperturbable, he had to "improve" her, "for that is a need with me; let a girl be ever so accomplished; if her character is *complete*, she is not for me. I myself must mold her." A modern wit has called this strange fiancé a Pygmalion in reverse, who, instead of making a work of art his loved one, wanted to transform his loved one into a work of art. He even pressed her for a written declaration of her love for him: Did she really love him? With all her heart? Oh, he was worth it. And in one of the letters that passed almost daily between the two houses, he went so far as to exclaim: "Am I not noble, Wilhelmine?"

There were also hours of less theoretical romance. One moonlit night he read Voss's *Luise* to her aloud. They went for walks in the churchyard and beside the Kellerspring, a brook which flowed "out of a grove of lindens into the Oder." He often spent mornings working in the garden, and sometimes in the evening they would sit together in the "dark little arbor" of the von Zenges' garden. He was not devoid of sensuality—they exchanged ardent kisses, he delighted in "the brownish birthmark on the soft skin of her right arm," and on the occasion of a brief separation he wrote imploring her to become his wife "soon, soon," lest unruly desires cloud his mind and soul. Yes, for all his pedantry, he was passionately and sincerely in love with her. The bottom of a cup which he gave her, and which was preserved in her family down to our own times, was inscribed with the word: TRUST.

But the question of a livelihood could not be put off indefinitely. The financial situation of the Kleist family was far from brilliant, and in the first half of 1800 they resolved to sell the Guhrow estate. Kleist's own small fortune, which probably derived from this sale, could not in itself have kept the young couple in a manner befitting their station. If he wished to marry, he would have to bestir himself to obtain a post, though he made no secret of the fact that he would much rather have gone to Göttingen for further study.

But to what sort of post should he aspire, what preparations should he make? He had no interest in law or diplomacy; a teaching position seemed more acceptable—or should he take up finance or economic affairs? He was groping in the dark; thus far, he had ignored the question of practical utility and concerned himself solely with his studies and perhaps a literary venture or two. The manuscript of an early drama shows the same careful handwriting as his first letters to his fiancée, and in October 1800 he wrote to Ulrike: "If Auntie should wish to go into my bureau because of the linen, please see to it in a tactful way that the upper part, where my scribblings are, is not opened." Of course, he may be referring to some sort of notes; such indications are not conclusive, but this much is certain: that his innermost strivings tended, not toward a practical career, but toward a spiritual development of which he himself still suspected next to nothing.

Still, he needed a position of some kind, and in the summer of 1800 he went to Berlin to prepare for one. All we know of his efforts to this end is that he entered into some vague connection, as a volunteer worker, with the office of Karl August von Struensee, head of the Excise and Customs Department (and the brother of the Danish dictator Struensee, who had been executed in 1772). Of his private life we know something more. Count Alexander von Lippe seems to have introduced him to the literary and artistic salons of Berlin, but he took root in none of them and thought longingly of his home. On reading Schiller's *Wallenstein*, which had just appeared, he sent a copy to Wilhelmine and another to Ulrike, the latter with a note observing that this was a work which should be studied rather than read. And by the same post he sent maps for Ulrike "to travel on," for she longed passionately to travel—and for the present there was no possibility of her doing so. What, if anything, he decided about the choice of a profession, we have no idea.

Then suddenly, in the month of August, he turned up in Frankfurt, with what intention we cannot be sure. He had asked Wilhelmine to "work out" her conception of the happiness she anticipated from their forthcoming marriage. One evening she handed him the first page of her confessions; he read it at once, with delight—and alarm. Visibly upset, he took it home with him. The following morning, speaking firmly though none too coherently, he announced that he must travel.

Travel? In God's name, why? He could not explain, he had no right to explain, he just needed the money, the journey was imperative, someone's happiness, honor, possibly life depended on it. The family responded with tears and supplication, but he did not give way: later—they would understand later. In the end he seems to have hinted at certain political motives, at matters which he had never mentioned before and which so terrified Auntie Massow that she exacted his solemn promise to return, come what might. Though his explanations clarified nothing, Ulrike finally expressed her willingness to finance the undertaking.

What was actually behind it? Did he himself know? Or was he merely taking flight from the painful predicament rising from the need to choose a profession into some vague fantasy purportedly connected with Wilhelmine's future happiness? Was his journey wholly, or at least in part, a flight? The frantic haste of his departure the next morning suggests as much. He barely found time to take leave of Wilhelmine and to give her a sheet of written "instructions," presumably telling her what to say if questioned about the purpose of his mysterious trip.

A romantic departure. From Berlin, his first stopping place, he wrote to Wilhelmine: "As I rode away in the gray of dawn, it seemed to me that I heard a sound at the inner window of your drawing room. The thought flashed through my mind: Could it be you? But passionately as I longed to see you once more, it was not. The coach rolled on, my body twisted round, and my eyes clung to the beloved house. The tears rose to my eyes, I very much wanted to cry, but I have too long been out of the habit." One is struck by the natural simplicity of the writing, especially by the force of the image and atmosphere evoked by the "twisting round" of his body.

But when he goes on to speak of the journey ahead of him, concerning which Wilhelmine was far from adequately informed, the old mystification sets in, and the reader is left in a state of confusion and unsatisfied curiosity: "With a matter of such importance at stake, I feel too weak to proceed alone. Before taking action, I shall therefore seek out a wise older friend, whose name I shall impart to you as soon as I find him."

This was his first opportunity to exercise his exasperating talent for mystification to the full. In an equally obscure letter to Ulrike, he bids her tell anyone who might inquire that he was in Berlin, attending to business for Minister Struensee, which was "partly true." He made Wilhelmine's elder brother, Lieutenant Karl von Zenge—with whom he was allegedly but not really staying in Berlin—promise that he would not even inquire into the aim and purpose of his trip, which may have been a mystery to Kleist himself, and has certainly remained so to all other observers down to the present day.

# 5

# THE JOURNEY TO WÜRZBURG

BOARDING the "Stettin covered stage," Kleist traveled via Oranienburg to Coblenz (near Pasewalk in Pomerania), where he sought out the wise older friend of whom he had written. This was Ludwig Brockes, a relative of the Hamburg senator and religious rationalist poet Barthold Heinrich Brockes. Nine years older than Kleist, Ludwig Brockes was then employed on the estate of his cousin Count von Eickstedt and on the point of taking on a regular post—a project which he abandoned on hearing Kleist's plea. Despite his phlegmatic nature, Brockes had a kind of pedagogic passion. After a period of study at Göttingen, he had gone into the Danish military service, but soon wearied of the drill and lack of freedom and resigned. Determined to accomplish something in the world but reluctant to accept fixed employment, he had returned to the university along with a young man whom he had hoped to benefit by his guidance. Kleist had met Brockes years before while visiting the island of Rügen with Ulrike. The hope he had set in the older man was not disappointed, for Brockes, who— "unfortunately," as he himself tells us—was motivated far more by the heart than by reason, was swayed by Kleist's fervor and convinced "that a happy outcome was probable or at least that there was no danger" in Kleist's mysterious scheme. Two days later they were sitting side by side in the diligence, on their way to Berlin.

From there Kleist wrote again to Ulrike, imploring her to abstain from "all guesses, inferences, and combinations," since they would *necessarily* be wrong, and asking her to send him a hundred ducats as soon as possible at a "secret address" in Vienna, since this sum was needed, "not to defray our travel expenses, but for the actual purpose of the trip." Departure from Berlin was delayed by the need for a conference with Minister Struensee, but on August 28 they started out. Their way led past the home of the Linckersdorfs; Kleist was strangely moved by the sight of the house, where two years before he had experienced the joys of first love. He was certain the whole family must be absent, but suddenly Luise appeared at the window of her room; he bowed low, and she nodded "most affably." He looked back several times, but then he thought of Wilhelmine and the arbor in her garden, "and I was *all* yours again."

After a stop at Potsdam with brother Leopold, they continued on through the plains of Brandenburg, "so there is nothing of interest to relate," passed through Wittenberg and arrived in Leipzig. There they called on His Magnificence Rector Wenck, and enrolled in the university—Kleist under the name of Klingstedt, son of an invalided Swedish captain; Brockes as the son of a District Magistrate Bernhoff on the island of Rügen. As Kleist reported to Wilhelmine, Wenck read them the academic statutes, gave each a printed copy of them, added a good deal of sage advice, and finally handed them their registration cards. "We went home, wrote letters, wrapped our shoes and boots in the academic statutes, and carefully preserved the registration cards." And he added the postscript: "What will Kleist say when someday he finds letters from Klingstedt in your possession?" As though to underline the adventurous character of their journey, they had—to Kleist's fiendish glee, and in fulfillment of his deep-seated love of mystification—provided themselves with false identities with which to obtain false papers.

Proceeding to Dresden, they presented their registration cards to Lord Elliot, the British ambassador, and were issued passports under the names of Klingstedt and Bernhoff. At the embassy they heard news (of what nature we do not know) which made them, from one minute to the next, change their destination from Vienna to Würzburg or Strassburg.

One would suppose that if there was a serious purpose behind the trip—a secret diplomatic mission, for example—the destination would play a crucial role. As it was, Kleist was not the least dismayed by the change; he barely mentions it in his letters home, which on the whole suggest a mounting euphoria. A romantic traveler, he enjoyed the romantic journey. Drawn by powerful horses, he sat puffing his pipe beside the good Brockes, or, when night fell, lay on the straw of their basket carriage, gazing dreamily at the sky; fragmented clouds, now dark, now bright with moonlight, passed over him, and he scarcely felt the gentle sprinkling of the fine rain on his face. When it finally got to be too much, he pulled his cloak over his head. And then in his mind's eye he saw Wilhelmine before him in the flesh, her form, her dress, the gold cross she wore, and the brownish birthmark on the soft skin of her right arm; he kissed it and kissed her a thousand times, then "I pressed you to my heart and fell asleep in your arms."

His reflections on nature lost their dry, didactic tone: "I walked along the bank of a forest brooklet, smiling at the nimble haste with which, babbling all the while, it hopped over the stones. It will not rest, I thought, until it reaches the sea; and then it will start its journey all over again. —And yet— when it stands still, as in this pool, it stagnates and stinks." Of course there was no lack, in these decidedly good-humored letters, of the usual mysterious hints and insinuations: "Someday you will learn the whole truth and thank me amid tears." —"You have become doubly dear to me since I have been traveling for your sake." —"Why, you will ask, why do I half utter such mysterious thoughts if I do not mean to state them fully? Why do I speak of things you cannot and should not understand? Dear girl, I will tell you. When I write such things, I always think of myself as two months older. Then one day, as we sit by ourselves in the arbor, leafing through these letters, I will explain these obscure passages, and you will cry out in astonishment: Ah, so that is what you meant— Adieu. The postilion is blowing his horn." Kleist's expressions of tenderness ring true, and he evidently saw no contradiction between this diabolical game of cat-and-mouse and his feelings of romantic love. Once when philosophical speculations carried his thoughts away from her, he wrote: "Then a glance at your tobacco pouch, which is always hanging from a button of my vest, or at your gloves, which I seldom take off, or at the blue ribbon you wound around my left arm and which is still tied as firmly as the bond of our love, brings me back to you." And for spoiling her with so many letters, she must reward him on his return by "giving me a kiss or putting a new drawstring into my tobacco pouch, for the old one has snapped." Undoubtedly, the company of his older friend had a lot to do with his good humor. "How fortunate I am that there is at least one man in the world who understands me perfectly. Without Brockes, my spirits and perhaps even the strength for my undertaking might fail me."

Brockes was an ideal traveling companion, quiet, not very talkative, but of so winning a disposition that he was well liked wherever he went. Kleist tells of a Pomeranian belonging to Wilhelmine's brother Karl von Zenge, "who was never very affectionate with his master or me, but frisked around Brockes with indescribable joy the moment he entered the room." And on the journey all his lovable qualities—his warmth, his delicacy, his untiring consideration—were brought into play. In the diligence he always chose the less comfortable place; if in cold or rainy weather there was not enough straw to cover both men's feet, nothing could move him to take any for himself; if Kleist in falling asleep slumped onto Brockes's chest, he remained motionless and awake for the sake of his friend's slumber; wherever they stopped for the night, he took the poorer bed, and in choosing books or newspapers, he always gave Kleist what he thought would interest him the most. Kleist could not praise him highly enough, and later on, in a letter to Wilhelmine, he wrote rather tactlessly: "Ah, if you could be among girls what he is among men."

Early in September, the friends, content with themselves and the world despite the troubled times (the armies of the French Revolution were already dangerously near), reached Würzburg and took up quarters at the splendid and expensive Hotel Zum Fränkischen Hof. Kleist had found the Saxons more cultivated than the Prussians and their country incomparably more

beautiful than his "poor Markish fatherland," but Würzburg
was not at all to his liking—neither the charming hilly countryside nor the lovely city with its heavy incense-impregnated
atmosphere, its countless priests and monks, and the frenzied
bustle of its citizens, beside themselves with fear of the French.
What got on his nerves the most was the pervasive Catholicism, for at bottom he was a heathen, and not even a practicing
Protestant. He was exasperated by the constant ringing of bells,
which reminded him every minute of the Catholic religion,
"just as the jangling of chains reminds a prisoner of his servi-
tude." There was never an end of masses and devotions, rosary
beads were in constant motion, they were "all saying prayers
for the city's salvation, but since the French are praying for its
fall, it all depends on who can pray the hardest"; processions
were held in supplication for the defeat of the French and for
the extermination of all heretics—"and that includes you and
me." The pall cast by the clergy on cultural life was "enough
to make you laugh or cry"; neither Wieland nor Goethe nor
Schiller was to be found in the library, all were forbidden;
"nothing but chivalrous romances, on the right with ghosts,
on the left without ghosts." All this infuriated him, and he felt
impelled to write Wilhelmine a long letter on the subject, to
which he appended an essay. Man's first concern, he wrote,
must not be his lot in eternity but the conduct of his earthly
life. Only one thing really matters, the performance of our duty
as we ourselves conceive it, and nothing else: "I have no fear of
hell-fire to come; what I fear is my own conscience."

That was all very well, but Würzburg, however Catholic,
was the goal of Kleist's journey, the projected setting for whatever he had resolved to do. Strassburg had been eliminated
from his plans, on the ground that he was not "permitted" to go
there. But what *did* he do in Würzburg? Well, he saw the
sights, especially the Julius Hospital, from which, though it was
endowed by the bishopric and operated (with impressive toler-
ance, it seems) by priests and nuns, he could not entirely withhold his admiration. Some two weeks after their arrival, the
friends moved from the expensive hotel to private quarters on
the New Market. Joseph Wirth, their new landlord, took them

in without a billeting order, for which he was reprimanded by the town council.

By then they had seen all the sights. The two stayed home a good deal of the time, standing idly at the window commenting on the passers-by, but more often reading and writing. It was then, no doubt, that Kleist acquired the first of the notebooks which were by turns named Journal, Magazine of Ideas, and Fragments, and which, there is reason to believe, he kept up until 1807 at least. They contained reflections on life and nature of the kind already known to us, and like the letters themselves (had he not instructed Wilhelmine to keep his letters and to jot down her own impressions?) were designed for literary exploitation. Apart from these brief reflections "full of profound meaning," the notebooks may have included, as was reported after his death, the beginnings of a few short stories, which, in view of the above-mentioned dating, seems likely but not certain. Since Kleist never hesitated to repeat once-formulated passages word for word, the phrase "for literary exploitation" is definitely applicable to any of his notes.

But what else was he doing in Würzburg? In a letter to Wilhelmine he speaks of wishing to describe to her the wife who might now make him happy; this, he declared, was a great undertaking to which he intended to devote every free moment left by his future situation; it would give his life new charm. "In five years, I hope, the work will be finished." Did he mean by this that he was planning a literary work, perhaps something on the order of Rousseau's *Emile?* And did he actually begin such a work? We simply do not know.

What we do know is that Joseph Wirth was a surgeon, and that according to the records of the Würzburg town council, one of the two students lodging with him was ill.

Yes, Kleist was sick in bed for a time; in a letter written later on he tells us that when the doctor was visiting him, Brockes, out of delicacy, left the house regardless of the weather; we also learn that unbeknownst to Kleist the light of the candle in his room shone through the open door and kept his poor companion awake night after night: "Oh, and something else that I will tell you one day but not now—another sacrifice of which

I knew nothing at the time, which obliged him to walk the length of the cold corridor with only a coat thrown over his shoulders."

But were this illness and this medical treatment, as has sometimes been supposed, the sole purpose of his mysterious journey? Was the purpose of his journey a painful treatment designed to enable him to perform his conjugal duties? This theory is not entirely without foundation—unless we choose to interpret certain passages in his letters to Wilhelmine as wild exaggerations. Referring to the day of their separation in Frankfurt, he wrote: "Then I was not worthy of you; now I am . . . Then I was tormented by the realization that I was unable to fulfill your most sacred needs, and now, now—but hush!" And elsewhere he writes that this whole long journey was nothing "but one long thought of you." Still, one is startled to find him tormenting himself with the thought that she might abandon him, that he might harvest ingratitude from her "for whose happiness he was risking his *life*."

But what is one to think when, speaking again of Wilhelmine's possible infidelity, he cries out in a paroxysm of vainglory: "How you would humble yourself if I were to rise up before your eyes, adorned with the laurels of my deed!" And after a brilliant description of the sun rising over the mountaintops he goes on: "I promise you something of the kind, when the sun will rise over your inscrutable lover." And how does it fit in with all this that he somehow feels guilty and even begs her forgiveness? "Give me hope that you will forgive me, and I shall have the courage to tell you all." In the last letter from Würzburg he even underscores his plea for forgiveness.

Back in Berlin after a hurried five-day journey, Kleist mentions the trip to Würzburg several times in his letters to Frankfurt. His entire fortune, he wrote, was as nothing to him beside what he had acquired on that journey. Clearly referring to Wilhelmine and himself, but without further explanation, he speaks of an "unparalleled deed and equally unparalleled forgiveness," and relates how, beclouded by dread intimations of death, he had gone for a walk in the country before the "most important" day of his life: "Looking inward, I passed through the vaulted gateway, my thoughts turning back to the town behind me. Why, I thought, does the vault not tumble down, since it has no support? It stands, I replied, because all its stones want to tumble down at once." In these thoughts, he tells us, he found indescribable comfort which sustained him "up to the crucial moment." And then, under the influence of new cares, torments, and impressions, the memory of his mysterious undertaking pales, making way in his letters and writings for other experiences.

No fully satisfactory explanation of the mystery has ever been put forward. We have before us an equation with too many unknowns. The one thing the episode makes clear is to what lengths Kleist's mystification mania could go and with what virtuosity he manipulated it. Otherwise, we must accept the fact that the concrete truth is beyond our reach and will probably remain so. Still, considering Kleist's life as a *whole*, the most plausible hypothesis would seem to be that his main if not his entire purpose in taking the trip was to treat a disorder of the kind that would no doubt be termed psychosomatic today; more specifically, some sexual deficiency. It also seems likely that his sexual drive, deprived of its natural outlet, was converted into creative activity. But none of this can be proved.

# 6

## CRISIS IN BERLIN

AT the beginning of his stay in Berlin, Kleist was happier than he had been in a long time, but he had no desire to go home to Frankfurt, because of the intolerable questions that he would be "absolutely unable to answer." For the great secret, the secret of the journey to Würzburg, had not been disclosed, not even to Ulrike, his most trusted intimate, who had repeatedly helped him out of his financial difficulties and whom alone he may have confided in later on. In this period, at all events, he thought optimistically of the future, nourished hopes of something resembling "normal" happiness, and even took a cautious step in the unpleasant business of choosing a profession; that is, he obtained permission from Minister Struensee to attend the sessions of the Technical Deputation—but only to attend them, without actively participating —by way of judging whether "commerce and industry" might provide him with a congenial career. This question was answered only too soon; before two weeks had passed, he informed Wilhelmine in no uncertain terms that he would not take any post, that it would not be right of him to do so, since he despised the kind of happiness such employment might give him, "and if I find my place nowhere on this earth, perhaps I shall find a better one on another star."

But what of the marriage he so longed for, the marriage which made employment a necessity; what of his life with Wilhelmine? Far from giving up hope, he had suggestions of his own. If the two of them pooled the little they possessed, would it not suffice for a modest sort of happiness? Yes, modest it would be, not at all in keeping with their station; but what was "such trumpery"—rank, honor, wealth—to them, since all they wanted was to love each other? If their funds should not suffice for even such modest happiness, the prospects would indeed be "dark, oh very dark," but not yet hopeless. He could go to Paris, for instance, and offer the latest philosophy, that of Kant, to the curiosity of its citizens; Wilhelmine would only have to give him a little time, a few years, "six at the most," then he would surely be earning money. If only she trusted him, she would someday garner glory with him; he was preparing for a literary career, the Magazine of Ideas was expanding day after day, he could go to the South of France or to French Switzerland and keep afloat by giving German lessons—"Wilhelmine, wait ten years, and you will embrace me not without pride."

These offers could not have been very attractive to Wilhelmine, who had no desire to leave her family. Why, she suggested, couldn't they move in with Aunt Massow on Nonnenwinkel and share the housekeeping expenses? No, Kleist wouldn't hear of it; at the most, he himself might take over the house on attaining his majority, and apply for an academic post in Frankfurt. At all events, he declared, there were still numerous possibilities, he was still attending the sessions of the Technical Deputation, and the minister had offered him a post in writing; or if she insisted, he would travel for two or three years and then take a post, which would no doubt bring them money and honor, though little domestic happiness . . .

Thus, he made no secret of his increasing unwillingness to take a government post, and not only Wilhelmine was displeased but the king as well. At an audience in Potsdam, he received Kleist coldly, but the effect was lost on the young man, since "it would not be difficult for me to find another king, whereas he would have difficulty in finding other subjects." Nor was he swayed when the minister made it known to him that if he should not deign to accept a post at the present, his chances for the future would be meager. He merely replied that he would make up his mind in the spring.

In November, Brockes had arrived unexpectedly from Dresden and taken up quarters in the apartment shared by Kleist and Karl von Zenge; undoubtedly, his presence had contributed to Kleist's comparatively cheerful and even mood. In January, however, he departed, having finally overcome his distaste for gainful employment, and accepted a post at the court of Mecklenburg. Brockes's decision and the loss of the only friend who fully understood him were a source of torment and confusion to Kleist; the change in his mood was immediately reflected in his letters to Wilhelmine and Ulrike, and above all in his mode of life, which now became almost hysterically active.

There is no doubt that he began to look "outside" for a refuge from his inner dilemma, for little by little he had come to realize that all his suggestions to his fiancée had been absurdly unrealistic, and that the hateful decision to take a government post offered the only possibility of securing their future together.

His frantic attempts at flight did not help him much. Professor Huth of Frankfurt introduced him to the learned circles of Berlin, which appealed to him no more than the unlearned ones had done. Everyone, he said, sits on his special field as a caterpillar sits on its leaf, which it looks upon as the only beautiful and important thing in the world, because it never gets to see the whole tree. Altogether he was not cut out for society; in him there was a "sad clarity," which, unasked, revealed to him "the thought behind every look, the meaning behind every word, the motive behind every action," which in short showed him everything, even his own nature in all its wretched nakedness. In addition, perhaps as a consequence of this clarity, there was his constant embarrassment, which often brought on stuttering and made him, when in a drawing room, feel inferior to the silliest of women and the most fatuous of men.

Still, he did not shun society entirely, and sometimes attended the artistic salons of the younger romantic generation, chiefly those of Rahel Levin and Henriette Herz. It was these Jewish salons that he liked best, if only they had not been "so precious about their culture." But nowhere did he feel really at home, and he came to the conclusion: "I am not suited to human society; that is a sad truth, but a truth; and the reason, to put it bluntly, is that I do not like people." But since he could not spend all his time alone with his gloomy thoughts, he led an impersonal sort of social life, went to the theater or to cafés, but could not throw off his depression. On the contrary, it deepened—he even began to doubt his love for the sciences, for he could not hope to study them all, and the thought of burrowing into any one of them, as a mole burrows into the ground, was repellent to him. An inner voice whispered: "Knowledge cannot be man's highest goal."

And then something happened which, though trifling in itself, suddenly clarified and sharpened his dilemma. At a session of the Technical Deputation attended by Kleist, someone produced a recent French work on mechanics and suggested that it might prove to be of interest. The chairman of the Deputation turned to Kleist and said: "This looks like something for you. Take it home, read it through, and bring us a report." Taken by surprise, Kleist nodded—and in that same moment resolved *not* to plow through this tome, which, he estimated, would demand a whole year of study. He was cornered; on the one hand he was unwilling to sacrifice so much time and trouble, on the other he was aware that to decline was to abandon all thought of a post now or in the future.

The time had come. He would have to make a decision. He shut himself up in his room, resolved to stay there until he had answered the fateful question once and for all. But after tormenting himself for an entire week, he left his room as undecided as ever. How was he to explain his indecision? And to whom? To Ulrike? To Wilhelmine? "Ah, there is no way of making others understand one *fully*, man is doomed by nature to have no other confidant than himself." Nevertheless, in the hope that Wilhelmine might console him, he then went to Frankfurt for a week. From there he wrote to Ulrike, who had just gone away on a trip: "The inside of my head looks like a lottery bag, one big winner and a thousand blanks."

And then he was back in Berlin, still with the same anguish, still tormented by the same question, which was unanswerable yet had to be answered one way or the other. At length the answer came in an unforeseen, prophetic way.

Since boyhood, Kleist had cherished the mystical belief that after our earthly death the truths we gather on earth would redound to our benefit on another star and there help us to perfect ourselves. But now in studying Kant he learned that our senses are anything but reliable, that they are incapable of apprehending the truth, the "thing in itself"; he learned that there would never be any way of knowing whether what we apprehend *is* the truth or only *seems* to be—and that consequently there could be no question of acquiring eternal truths that would stay with us beyond the grave. Regardless of whether this interpretation tallied exactly with Kant's teachings, it pierced Kleist's heart like a poisoned arrow and sent him staggering. All his striving, his most sacred endeavor, his insatiable thirst for knowledge—everything had been in vain, it had all been a pious delusion. The path he had chosen with so much ardent hope ended in dense, impenetrable fog and led nowhere. If the truth did not exist, he was left with nothing at all, for that was his nature: all or nothing. His spirit would not content itself with anything less: "My sole and highest goal has vanished; now I have none."

But does it seem possible that so intelligent a young man had never reflected on the relativity of human truths? What was the "sad clarity" of which he himself had spoken other than a kind of skeptical realism? Does it then seem possible that he had never harbored doubts? We think not. What seems more likely is that the mystical truth-cult carried over from his boyhood served him as a crutch and that now, with the sudden removal of his crutch, he had only his two feet to stand on. He had conceived timid doubts about the sciences at an earlier date, and his crutch had never entirely satisfied him or given him happiness. But now that he was deprived of the comfort of the half-mystical, half-rationalistic life plan which he had carried around with him since his earliest student days and which now, along with his belief in "the truth," dissolved into nothingness, his head reeled. He found himself in the midst of a trackless wilderness, with no idea where he was going.

The sky over Berlin was as gloomy as Kleist's view of the future. The rain was coming down. But he could no longer bear to remain alone with his anguish. At this juncture he thought of Potsdam and his old friends there: his army comrade Karl von Gleissenberg, brother Leopold, and most particularly Rühle, who was intellectually closest to him. Braving the rain, he walked to Potsdam, where he arrived drenched to the skin and embraced them all. After that, he felt a little better and was able to unburden himself. As expected, it was Rühle who understood him best; to distract him a little, he gave him a novel, *The Man in Chains* (*Der Kettenträger*, presumably by F. M. Klinger). Kleist read a little of it; it all seemed so familiar, so hackneyed; he leafed impatiently through the book, banged it shut, threw it on the table, and sank back exhausted on the sofa cushions. Was he to return to Berlin as he had come, without consolation, without a decision, without an aim in life?

Oral tradition has it that ten years before his death Kleist went with Rühle, Pfuel, and other friends to the shore of the Wannsee, where he later killed himself; that while there they discussed the various ways of committing suicide and came to the conclusion that the surest method would be to fill one's pockets with stones, row out into the middle of the lake, sit down on the gunwale of the boat, and shoot oneself . . . It seems not unlikely that this somber tradition harks back to that rainy day in March 1801; it is undoubtedly in keeping with the state of anguish he was in, and always when his anguish was more than he could bear, he took flight—to another town, another country, some new activity and adventure—but what tempted him most was death. For his innermost feeling told him that the evil which poisoned his life would end only with his life, because it was inside *him:* "For this forever tormented heart gives me nothing but pain."

The day of ultimate flight was still far off, but how was he to escape the torment of the present moment? A skillful and original letter writer, he wrote to Wilhelmine on his return to Berlin, first in calm, easy sentences, then with mounting urgency, describing the impossible situation he was in, the collapse of his spiritual world, his futile excursion to Potsdam, his intolerable aimlessness. Not a word about what must have been on her mind, the question of choosing a profession, which in his present distress had lost all meaning for him. "In this state of anguish a thought occurred to me. Dear Wilhelmine, let me travel." Travel? What for? He himself half realized that he was only trying to run away from himself. But since he was too upset to work, he concluded with a kind of brilliant irrationality that it would be preferable "to see the world."

True, he asked Wilhelmine's permission, but in a postscript to the same letter he took it for granted and announced that he would probably go to France, adding that he would ask Ulrike to go with him, as he had promised to do in the event of a trip abroad.

He would undoubtedly have preferred to go alone, as anyone but Ulrike would have gathered from the cold tone of his invitation. He pointed out that the journey would be costly, that if they both went they would need their own carriage, horses, and servant; that he himself could not contribute more than one reichstaler a day, and that if his offer seemed too sudden, she might just as well wait until the following year. And in conclusion: could she help him out with three hundred reichstalers? This as soon as possible, since he wished to start in a week.

Wilhelmine cannot have been very enthusiastic about her fiancé's new travel plans, and yet, with touching devotion, she tried to refute his (or more properly Kant's) skepticism about the reliability of human truths, and asked him to reply at once. He rejected her arguments amiably but firmly: "Dear Wilhelmine, it is by my own fault that I have fallen into error, and I alone can lift myself out of it." Moreover, he would feel happier among strangers than among friends "who look upon me as mad when I dare reveal my innermost soul."

Ulrike, on the other hand, was delighted; her old wanderlust took hold of her and she agreed to everything, though she had one or two suggestions for reducing the expense. She announced her imminent arrival in Berlin, and this was unfortunate, for now Kleist could no longer recoil, and in the meantime sober reflection had confirmed his instinctive reluctance to take Ulrike with him. Traveling alone by stage, he would have needed no other identification than his student card, but to go abroad with his sister, a servant, and his own equipage, he would need passports, and for these he would have to apply to Herr von Alvensleben at the Foreign Ministry, adducing a plausible reason for the trip. Obviously, he could not state the real reason —that he wished to "flee from all science" and hoped that a change of scene and atmosphere would bring some illumination. The only convincing motive he could put forward was the exact opposite; namely, that in the interest of his country, so to speak, he was eager to deepen and broaden his knowledge through a period of study in Paris. This design so delighted not only Herr von Alvensleben but also Kleist's professors and academic friends that they showered him with advice and even with letters of recommendation to French scholars. So there he was, cheated by "blind fate," driven not into freedom but once again "into association with the cold, dry, one-sided men," whose company was so utterly hateful to him. Circumstances had played him a nasty trick, and indeed he would have preferred to call off the whole undertaking, but that was no longer possible. He had *wanted* to travel, and now he was *obliged* to travel. The prospect depressed him more from day to day and aroused dark forebodings; he felt as though he were going to his doom.

It was in this frame of mind that Kleist sat for the painter and engraver Peter Friedel, whom he had engaged to do a miniature of him as a farewell gift to Wilhelmine. To please her, he found the strength to smile "conscientiously" while sitting, and when, on completion of the portrait, he expressed the wish that Krüger might have rendered him more "truthfully," the model may well have been more at fault than the painter. In any case, the little painting provides a welcome addition to our knowledge of Kleist's appearance. We know that he was rather short and thickset. In addition, the miniature shows a small, round head, with short, reddish-brown hair. There is an air of defiance in the rigid stance of his head and neck. His face, with its somewhat bulbous nose, is half averted from the viewer, so that the blue eyes peer at us from the corners of the lids, their flashing cheerfulness looking just a little foolish in conjunction with the forced smile and clenched teeth. Contemporaries speak of a distinct family resemblance to

Ulrike; she, too, was short, with the same thick neck and slightly potatoish nose. And she resembled him also in character, in her generosity, her energy, and the mysterious restlessness which drove her from place to place on the meagerest pretext (and later on, in her abomination of Bonaparte, whom Kleist hated far beyond the requirements of patriotism—a brief family chronicle cites Heinrich's name without comment and Ulrike's with the characteristic gloss: "Ulrike, most determined, wanted to murder Napoleon").

Kleist sent Wilhelmine the miniature—unframed, because he needed every penny he had—in a case which he asked her to return, since it belonged to the picture of her that he was taking away with him. He bade her have his likeness framed at her expense, he would return the money to her "*someday*" (underlined by Kleist). On April 12, 1801, he wrote to Privy Councilor Kunth, informing him officially that "higher considerations" prevented him from pursuing the career he had entered upon with his participation in the sessions of the Technical Deputation, and two days later he wrote a last letter of farewell to Wilhelmine: "Forgive me this journey—yes, *forgive*, I have not used the word by mistake, for I myself now feel that what brought me to it was first of all an excess of impatience." For though he still had no clear idea of what to hope for or fear from the future, he sensed that neither honors nor riches nor learning could really satisfy him, and that his only unmistakable desire was for her, for Wilhelmine, with whom he was now obliged to part. O irony of fate! But from this fate, he went on, he would, regardless of the cost, wrest the utmost good, in *his own way* he would learn, and above all he would try "to forget the accursed quibbles and sophistries that are to blame for all my confusion." So saying, he took leave of the "happiness that was close at hand." "Adieu, adieu, be my good *strong* girl. Heinrich K."

Did he suspect that this might be a parting for all time? Thus far, his life had consisted of one leave-taking after another—from the army, from the glitter of the salons, from the sciences, from a career that might have secured his livelihood, and finally from the programmatic rationalism instilled in him by the wan-

ing Enlightenment. He was now terrifyingly free, with no
other inducement to prepare himself for a "serious" career than
his dream of marriage to Wilhelmine.

Yes, his dream was still very much alive, and yet Wilhelmine
had good reason to feel afraid. Kleist himself was aware that
love had given her few of its joys and much of its sorrow, since
she had tied her fate to that of a young man whose "strangely
restless spirit" drove him this way and that, but always toward
the remote and unattainable. Did he expect too much of her
"strength"? She was a simple, charming, undemanding young
lady, with all the instincts of a good wife and mother and no
taste at all for adventure. How much further would she be able
to follow this impetuous young muddlehead?

# 7

## TRAVELING WITH ULRIKE

I	T was not until the travelers reached Dresden that they bought a carriage and horses—with the help of young Herr von Einsiedel, a relative by marriage, and of Johann, the servant whom Karl von Zenge had put at the young people's disposal for their journey. But the travelers, Kleist in any case, were in no great hurry to go on. True, his first and only letter to Wilhelmine from Dresden sounds sad. "Circumstances," he reports laconically, have prevented them from starting for Leipzig as quickly as they had hoped. But subsequent statements by Kleist, and more particularly Ulrike's remark about the impossibility of "prying him loose" from Dresden, throw a different light on the matter.

Einsiedel had introduced them to the widow of a Judge von Schlieben and to her daughters, Caroline and Henriette. The von Schliebens were poor, and the two girls were obliged to do needlework to eke out the family's resources. Even so, Caroline, who was engaged to the painter and engraver Heinrich Lohse and who was very much interested in the arts, found time now and then to copy paintings in the museums. Kleist saw a good deal of her; she took him to see the great art collections; they went walking under the dark linden trees of the Schloss Park, stood on the Elbe Bridge watching the sun set behind the blue mountains, and sat together on the sloping Brühl Terrace, where the young lady plaited a good-luck wreath for herself, with Kleist holding the blades of grass and handing them to her as she needed them. This strange relic of the romantic age, dry, firmly knotted, but still green, has been preserved. After Caroline's death it was found in a white envelope with the inscription: "I plaited this wreath with my dear friend Kleist on May 16, 1801."

And he was charmed by Henriette as well. She was a pretty young thing with short curly hair and lips that tended to crinkle and give her the look of a saucy, good-natured boy. Kleist praised her kind heart and her looks as well. Her figure, her face, the color of her hair and eyes, he thought, would make her a perfect model for a foreign painter wishing to paint a German woman. He would bring such a painter to her and say: "This is a *real* German girl." It is hard to say how close he was to her at this time; to Wilhelmine he spoke of the Schlieben girls with reserve, and when he writes that, in leave-taking, "one of them wept from a full heart," we are at a loss to say which one.

In any case, Caroline and Henriette were sympathetic friends in trying times; the same could not be said of Ulrike. He could speak to her of anything—except what was closest to his heart. "Her cheerful disposition and adventurous restlessness" were hardly what he needed just then. And as she herself once said, she failed to see how "lascivious poems or paintings" could arouse anyone's interest. That was the crux of the matter, for it was during this period in Dresden that Kleist first experienced the sensuous charm of painting. And this was the main reason why he could not be pried loose from this city.

Here was a new experience. Without his days of despair in Berlin, without his break with his science cult and programmatic rationalism, he would not have been open to it. But now he savored it to the full. He could not tear himself away from the Greek gods and heroes standing silent in the great halls, from the Sistine Madonna "with her silent grandeur, her noble gravity," from the many other masterworks of Italian painting, from the countless portfolios of engravings, or, last but not least, from the music in the Catholic church. "All these are things one can enjoy without the intellect, which speak directly to the heart and senses. This was my first entry into a new world of beauty, and I was very happy." On his walks, he saw young artists sitting with a drawing board on their knees and a pencil in hand, tracing the beauties of nature, and he envied these happy men, "troubled by no doubts about the truth that is nowhere to be found, living in the world of beauty which, sometimes, if only as an ideal, discloses itself to them." So fascinated was he with the immediate yet enigmatic impressions which met his eye for the first time that he once asked one of these demigods whether a man of twenty-four without previous training could possibly become an artist. In Würzburg he had detested Catholicism; but now, recalling the sound of the music, the splendor of the altars, paintings, and vestments, and the fervor of the worshippers, he was filled with yearning: "Ah, just one drop of forgetfulness, and with joy I would turn Catholic." The virtue that had been taught him and that he himself had pedantically expounded, the truth which he had so desperately pursued—all this had paled to insignificance beside the richness of his new experience, which made him at once drunk and clear-sighted, and aroused still undefined hopes and dreams for his own future. After virtue and truth, beauty had come into his life, stirring his innermost depths.

It came as no surprise that this call of fate should at first have bewildered him as much as it lured him. How could anyone foresee whether or not this early enthusiasm would develop into creative genius? And it was not in Kleist's character to content himself with less. No wonder he had misgivings about the future and would gladly have prolonged the present. In the course of a farewell excursion through the Dresden countryside, he and Ulrike went for a boat ride on the Elbe. He saw the huts of the small vintners, saw the fishermen at work on the river, and thought he would gladly forsake glory and ambition, everything "that lies over the mountains," for such modest happiness. "To live for the future—ah, that is a boy's dream, and only one who lives for the moment can live for the future." He was a disciple of Rousseau, whom he passionately loved, but the "back to nature" creed, which he was later to embody in so splendid and surprising a way, namely, in his art, was still a spontaneous, unreflecting yearning.

Stirred by such scenes of simple happiness, he took hold of Ulrike's hand—which was cold. All in all, she was not the right traveling companion for him. She did not share his enthusiasms, and she distracted him with her constant need for activity. After the boat ride, as their carriage was approaching Töplitz, where the country resembled "a storm-tossed sea of earth," their road was blocked by a heavily loaded wagon. Hemmed in by the fence at the side of the road, they could move neither forward nor backward. "The fence must go!" cried Ulrike—a sensible suggestion, but not content with suggesting, Ulrike, "forgetting her sex, seized the rail with her weak hands; it did not move." The disproportion between her will and her strength, her contradictory nature, exasperated Kleist; perhaps he saw her as a caricature of himself, for if she had had his sensibility and intelligence, they would have been very much alike. She, too, was utterly fearless; well he remembered the storm that had blown up while the family were boating on the lake at Fürstenwalde; the others had wept and wailed in terror, but she had only muttered: "Why complain? This will get us into the newspapers." No one can be as irritating, especially in a moment of great decision, as a companion who resembles us in large part but differs in the qualities that matter. Such considerations, along with his vexation over the travel plan that was forcing him, late to be sure but too soon for his liking, to leave Dresden, added to his annoyance with this "hero's soul in the body of a woman."

They resumed their journey, and after the warm, happy, intoxicating hours in Dresden, his spirits flagged. Not that the journey was lacking in distractions. Wherever they went, they sought out "the teachers of mankind," the most illustrious men of learning. Their first stop was in Leipzig, where they called on the mathematician Karl Friedrich Hindenburg and attended a lecture by Ernst Platner, the well-known physiologist and anti-Kantian—Ulrike "in disguise," that is, dressed as a man, a costume she liked as much as Kleist disliked it and which little by little became habitual with her.

In Halberstadt they went to see the aged poet Johann Wilhelm Ludwig Gleim, who in his youth had sung the glories of the Seven Years' War. They arrived with no other recommendation than their name, but they could have had none better, for such was Gleim's devotion to his old friend Ewald Christian Kleist that "anyone named Kleist" was dear to him. He took them to his study, which was lined with paintings of his many dearly beloved friends, and said: "Each one of these wrote a great work or performed a great deed; Kleist did both, and Kleist is at the very top." He went on to tell them how long years ago he had visited the wounded Kleist in the hospital and had read him one of his humorous poems. Kleist had laughed so hard that the bandage had slipped off his wound— luckily for him, because, unbeknownst to all, dry gangrene had set in. And so, once recovered, Kleist had dedicated his life to the poetic art which had saved it—an anecdote which, as told by the eighty-three-year-old poet, went straight to the heart of the hero's youthful descendant.

In Wernigerode the travelers were befriended by the family of the Counts Stolberg; in Goslar they went down into the old mineshafts of the Rammelsberg and climbed the Brocken. In Göttingen they were invited to a ball, and Kleist wrote: "My feet will hop while my heart weeps." And everywhere Ulrike's matter-of-factness weighed on him. "In Kassel a stone satyr played the flute with streams of water. It was a pleasant song, I listened in silence. She asked: How does it work?"

It was when they stopped to feed the horses in Butzbach near Frankfurt on the Main that their most perilous adventure occurred. They stayed in the carriage while the stable boy unbuckled the bridle. Suddenly an ass brayed loudly behind them; the horses took fright, reared, and went racing over the cobbles. Kleist seized the reins, but to no avail, for they were hanging down loose. The carriage collapsed, a wheel and an axle were broken and the harness badly damaged, yet the travelers climbed out of the wreckage, miraculously unscathed. "Can it be that a human life hung on the braying of an ass? If it had been cut off then, is that what I would have lived for? Is *that* the end the heavens would have decreed for my dark, enigmatic earthly life, that and nothing more?"

Some days later, with Mainz as their base, they went for a

boat ride on the Rhine, and again they were in danger when a storm arose unexpectedly. Everyone on board, concerned only with saving his own life, clung to some brace or cable, and though appalled at his uncontrolled fear of death, Kleist did likewise. Was *this* life worth it? he asked himself later. "This mysterious something that was given to us, we know not by whom, that leads us we know not where—it belongs to us but we do not know whether we have the right to dispose of it; it is a worthless possession though it has worth for us, something that is all contradiction, shallow and deep, barren and luxuriant, precious and contemptible, rich in meaning yet unfathomable."

In Mainz, Kleist was seized with a painful nostalgia for his boyhood. Only six or seven years had passed since then, and yet how utterly lost it was! When quartered in nearby Biebrich, he had wandered about this beautiful countryside deep in poetic thoughts, and as he strolled along the bank of the Rhine, the lapping of the waves had mingled in his hearing with his musical hallucinations. He had heard an entire symphony, "melody and accompanying chords, from the tender flute to the resonant double bass." His spirit had flitted this way and that, as lustingly as a butterfly browsing over honey-scented flowers; he had dreamed so much and hoped so fervently for so many things that his hope in itself had almost been a fulfillment . . .

And now? What was left of all these hopes? Gloom, inner conflict, mental anguish. While formerly his best hours had been spent in seeking self-awareness, now he shunned it, for he could not reflect on his situation "without horror." He shrank back from any attempt to clarify his ideas in writing and had neglected his journal entirely: "Ah, just one drop of oblivion!" His thoughts were in utter disorder, "like threads of flax in a distaff," life "nauseated" him, he no longer knew what to wish for, what aim to pursue, he trembled to think that he might choose the wrong one, and so wreck his whole future. One thing he felt strongly, that only work could bring him peace—but what work? And now this journey with Ulrike, whose companionship, much as she had to offer in other respects, could not give him peace—oh, why had he not clung to his solitude? "A ruthless fate drives me to this place and that place, when I have no other need but peace." Peace, release from the eternal flux of phenomena, from the multitude of images that come and go; his heart was too small, it was sickened by the unceasing round of impressions, it no longer had the strength to take them in, and he was seized with clearsighted horror at the thought that the emotion which so tormented him should be so short-lived. "Ah, how bleak and empty and sad it must be to outlive one's heart."

Such was his frame of mind when he arrived in Strassburg with Ulrike. At first they planned to continue on to Switzerland. But then they heard such glowing accounts of Bastille Day, the Fourteenth of July, which was to be celebrated this year with special pomp in honor of the Peace of Lunéville, that they changed their minds and proceeded directly to Paris.

The horses Herr von Einsiedel had purchased stood up excellently; one had only "to fill them up with oats and tickle them gently behind the ears, and they performed splendidly." In eight days Kleist and Ulrike, hardly stopping to rest, spent 120 hours on the road and reached Paris in plenty of time, on July 10, 1801.

# 8

## WITH ULRIKE IN PARIS

T HE travelers rented lodgings on the rue Noyer, an ancient street that has since disappeared; it branched off from the rue Saint-Jacques not far from the Seine and the present-day Boulevard Saint-Germain. Looking out of his window, Kleist could see the gables of the Tuileries in the distance. In the foreground there was nothing to be seen but irregular slate roofs with their unshapely chimneys, and at his feet a never-ending swarm of humanity, which left him indifferent at best; for he did not understand these people. And though his keen eye often saw true, his view of life led him to misinterpret what he saw.

These people struck him above all as frivolous. Look at what they made of this Fourteenth of July celebration, this national holiday supposedly dedicated to the blessings of peace and freedom. Oh, not that there was any lack of obelisks, triumphal arches, decorations, illuminations, and gun salutes! There were also merry-go-rounds, street theaters, jugglers, and tightrope walkers, the people amused themselves royally, all Paris was one enormous noisy fairground. And this was how the French people celebrated peace and freedom, the most sacred gifts of the gods to humankind! Good Lord, what sort of humans were they, what were they worth? In a city of eight hundred thousand people, what could a few individuals matter? That night a balloon was sent up into the sky; attached to it was a great iron hoop, supporting a firework which was supposed to set fire to the balloon; and so it did, the sight was impressive, the only drawback being that when the balloon

48

took fire the enormously heavy hoop fell to the ground, killing several onlookers, "nothing more." Kleist was too much of a Prussian to understand these people with their knowing enjoyment of life. And he was horrified by the contempt of the French bourgeoisie for the French soldier, whom they praised for his heroism but would not hear of admitting to good society, holding that he was neither refined nor entertaining enough, and was deficient in "*éducation.*" And all they seemed to care about was pleasure: they stopped at every square to gape at the capers of the comedians and jugglers; after the theater or opera, they flocked to the cafés and hotels to sip their sophisticated drinks and marvel at the illuminations and fireworks. "For a Frenchman likes nothing so much as to be dazzled."

They desecrated everything—love with their immorality, the human spirit with their frivolity, even nature, which they were capable of enjoying only in the silliest imitation. At Chantilly they would pay admission to spend a day in patriarchal simplicity at the *hameau.* In the morning they would stroll arm-in-arm in an alder-shaded meadow "a hundred paces long, as far as the wall, where anti-nature begins"; at midday, they would repair to the huts of fishermen, hunters, or shepherds, where disguised lackeys would serve them exquisite dishes and fine wines in wooden bowls; in the afternoon they would go rowing on a sixty-foot pond to the sound of rustic music; in the evening they would conclude the romantic festival with a ball; after which they would return to the anti-nature of their city. This was what they had learned from their Rousseau!

One would have expected him to appreciate the plain Frenchman's love of art and beauty, but even this meant little to him. He found the Louvre crowded at every hour of the day, and once he saw a water carrier setting down his buckets at the entrance, "to gaze for a while at the Belvedere Apollo"; for a moment the water carrier had stood beside him and asked: "*Tout cela, est-ce fait à Paris?*" The charming naïveté of the man left Kleist cold, and in reporting the incident he only remarked dryly that the French still had much to learn. But sometimes, for all his disparaging intent, he hit the nail on the head. With a dash of malice he compared the quick and varied conversation of the Parisians with the heavy thoroughness of his compatriots: "The German speaks with intelligence, the Frenchman with wit. The conversation of the former is like a business trip, that of the latter like an excursion for pleasure. The German goes round and round the subject, the Frenchman catches the ray of light it casts upon him, and passes by."

Gleim had implored him not to return home a Frenchman; there was no ground for concern: this thickset young man with the small round head, the flashing blue eyes, and reddish-brown hair was in little danger of being infected by Gallic charm and elegance; he was too German even to fall under the sensuous spell of this unique city. With a few exceptions, he found everything he saw absurd or hideous: "the long, narrow, winding streets, covered with muck or dust, giving off a thousand repellent smells"; the tall narrow houses, "six stories high, as though to multiply the space they occupy"; the swarms of people, "who shout, run, pant, push and shove; jostle and are jostled without taking it amiss." And when a passing Frenchman struck up a polite conversation with him, they were both quick to weary of it, there was no flow of sympathy. In short, Paris was too big and too densely populated for the "poor crackpot from Brandenburg"; it seemed to him that the Seine—"pure and clear on entering, saturated with every kind of filth on leaving, like many a young man who has come here for a visit"—would do well to pass through this foul place in a straight line and as quickly as possible. Life in this city was not at all the same as in Potsdam; Kleist read the news of the day and exaggerated its implications: a father committing incest with his daughter, a son with his mother, poisonings, murders among friends and relatives, swindles, robberies, burglaries—here all these were "mere trifles that upset no one."

He sought warmth in art, in the masterworks of paintings, in idealized figures such as the Belvedere Apollo and the Venus de Medici; but in the long, somber galleries of the overcrowded Louvre he found the paintings poorly framed, badly hung, lined up as in a storeroom, while silent old gods and heroes stood in rooms with wooden walls painted gray in the hope "that the viewer would mistake the wood for eternal stone"; the sky of France lay heavy upon the ancient statues, and it seemed to Kleist that they yearned like exiles for the soil of their classical home. Yet, for all his carping, the art collections were his favorite refuge. He spent happy hours in an old monastery which had been converted into a museum; in times of stress, innumerable French artworks threatened with destruction had been brought here; centuries later, they had been disposed in several rooms, in the cloister, and in the courtyard, where in the shade of an ancient plane tree stood the urn containing the ashes of Abélard and Héloïse. In the gallery of Versailles he studied the development of French painting, and discovered the genius of Eustache Le Sueur, who died in 1655, poisoned, it is believed, by his jealous rival, Charles Lebrun.

Of course, the museums could not be a home to him, and he often yearned for his native land, to which, so he said, he would "probably" never return—for Dresden, Potsdam, and Frankfurt on the Oder. He wrote to Caroline von Schlieben: Did she remember the poor little man who, when the skiff of his life was storm-tossed on the high seas, cast anchor in the peaceful port of Dresden among kindly new friends? "Leaf through your album—when you find a word as warm as a heart and a name that sounds as fair as the name of a poet, you will make no mistake; for surely it is Heinrich Kleist." In detail, with the fine aptness of expression characteristic of his letter writing, he related his Paris adventure to Wilhelmine and even to Frau Adolphine von Werdeck, whose home he had frequented more than five years before, when as a lieutenant in Potsdam he had nourished a romantic passion for Luise von Linckersdorf. What blessed days, and yet he made no mistake, even then there had been yearning and inner unrest, no present could satisfy him, for an "inborn flaw has made me incapable of seizing the moment; I am always living in a place where I am not and in a time that is past or has yet to come."

In Paris, this was as true as ever. Nothing that came his way could please him, least of all the sciences. Wilhelm von

Humboldt and Prussian Ambassador Girolamo Lucchesini had introduced him to French scientists and he attended some of their lectures, increasingly repelled by the one-sidedness of these men of science and convinced that in viewing a girl's bosom even a great scientist like "Newton would see nothing but a crooked line and find nothing of interest in her heart but its cubic content." They spoke of acids and alkalis, whereas "an all-powerful thirst" consumed Kleist's innermost soul. What was his heart to do with all this? "I *will* not bind and rend it any more, it shall move its wings in freedom and fly unbridled around the sun, even if its flight be as dangerous as that of the moth around the flame."

Little by little he stopped going out, avoided libraries, theaters, and cafés, and gave himself up to his thoughts in his room on the rue Noyer. He hinted at his preoccupations in a letter to Wilhelmine: in a solitary hour he had "worked out an ideal," and he was guarding it anxiously, for he failed to understand "how a poet could deliver the child of his love to such a crude lot as human beings are." A short time before, he had spoken coolly of a literary career; now the thought of writing books for money sickened him. He knew by now that he was incapable of "any conventional relation to the world."

We would gladly tell the reader what sort of "ideal" it was that he had conceived in his solitude, but we do not know. Possibly he was working on a first version of his *Schroffenstein* tragedy, originally titled *The Thierrez Family (Die Familie Thierrez)* or sketches for *Robert Guiscard (Robert Guiskard)*, which may have been inspired partly by an article in *Horen* and in part by his stay in Paris (for the city was still full of the fame of the Egyptian campaign, and Napoleon's dream of founding a Turkish empire had been shattered by an outbreak of the plague among the troops besieging Acre, just as Guiscard's dream of founding a Greek empire was shattered at the siege of Constantinople). But all this is speculation, and none of the sources reveals the truth.

In any event, his stay in Paris, detestable as it was to him, helped to clarify his plans for the future. "Yes," he wrote to

Wilhelmine at the time, "perhaps a time will come when I shall bless this trip to Paris, which I cannot justify even to myself." And there had been changes in his way of thinking; now he was able to speak half in jest of his old rationalistic moralizing: "Let no one say that a secret inner voice tells us clearly what is right. The same voice that tells the Christian to forgive his enemy counsels the South Sea Islander to roast him, and he piously eats him up."

And in his thoughts he had gone further than his feeling would ever go—until shortly before the end. He had ridiculed the thirst for glory which was secretly undermining his peace of mind: "Fame! What a strange thing it is, that one cannot begin to enjoy until one is no more! . . . Who, after thousands of years, will speak of us and our fame? What do Africa and America know of our geniuses?" And he had also come to appreciate the richness of his emotional life as a young man, the value and strength of his early joys and fears: "If youth is moved by every impression and destroyed by the first violent one, it is not because youth offers no resistance but because its resistance is *strong*. The dead oak tree stands firm in the storm, which topples a verdant tree because it can take hold of the crown."

But was he happy? Not at all! He had many talents, but a talent for happiness was not one of them. And the circumstances were not propitious. Still, he felt that he would not always be unhappy, because he did not deserve to be, and he knew that, to an eye which has looked into the sun, all earthly objects look black. And despite the secluded life he was leading he had acquired friends; in particular, Caroline von Schlieben's fiancé, the painter Heinrich Lohse, who was then in Paris and of whom he had become very fond. But his constant companion was Ulrike, whose character and behavior exasperated him more and more. True, she was "noble, wise, and generous," but everything about her conflicted with him and his ideas. With her undisciplined willfulness, she was either too free or not nearly free enough: cool and collected in the face of danger, she would start trembling like a leaf because a dog had suddenly appeared on the scene. But what annoyed him most of all was her habit of going about in men's clothes. (On one such occasion, a blind flute player recognized her and addressed her as Madame—and this little incident seems to have inspired a scene in Kleist's first play.) He described her as a person who "writes and acts orthographically, who plays and thinks in step." She was without understanding for his inner conflicts, for his restless searching (and she suspected no more than he did that her travel mania was only a different expression of a similar inner drive). Her highest ideal was unruffled calm, and when someone told her about a man who, on hearing the news of his dearly beloved daughter's death, had not even risen from the gaming table, she thought him enviable and worthy of emulation. Her brother's gloom and unrest were beyond her; she advised him to drink less beer— "a materialistic interpretation" of his sorrows which so offended him that he never forgot it. She was a straightforward, open, robust character, and in the end, all appearances to the contrary, always veered toward what was sensible, bourgeois, and commonplace, toward the conventions which repelled him in every fiber of his being and which he was then engaged in ruthlessly shaking off. That he loved her all the same made matters worse rather than better; he hated himself for harrying her with his ill humor and scenes and scoldings, when in his heart of hearts he had to admit that her only real fault was "being too big for her sex."

He was less and less able to control his sullen irritability; for it was part of his being and had far deeper roots than his dissatisfaction with Ulrike and Paris. Regardless of his inner calling, he faced the necessity of choosing some sort of outward framework for his life. This was an incessant torment to him, but he felt that he must not be in too much of a hurry. "If I make another mistake, it will be the last—for then I will despise either my soul or the earth, and I will separate them." Once again, as so often with this high-strung man, it was a question of life and death. And he wanted so much to be happy. The heavens owed it to him, and he owed it to himself. What stood in the way of his happiness? His unquenchable thirst for fame! He must overcome it. All he wanted was peace, a simple, inglorious life, far from all striving, envy, or rivalry. "For only *in* society is it painful to be a nobody. Not outside it." What, then, was needed for happiness? "To till a field, to plant a tree, to beget a child." That was a venerable truth which he, too, recognized. In sublime antithesis to the corrupt big-city life around him, Rousseau's "back to nature" message took on more and more seductive colors in his mind, and at last he arrived at a decision: he would buy a piece of land in Switzerland and become a peasant.

He wrote to Wilhelmine: "I bear an inner commandment in my heart, beside which all others, even if a king had signed them, would be void"—thus, he would never be able to adapt himself to any conventional mode of life. It was no longer thinkable that he should take a government post; he had definitely given up the sciences; he could not return to his native land, for he would inevitably disappoint the expectations that he himself had aroused; and to write books for money— oh, not another word! Quite possibly he was some sort of "shipwrecked genius"; in any case, he was resolved to kill the ambition within him—that vice which poisons all joys—and this meant tearing himself away from everything that could provide it with nourishment. Moreover, his small fortune would not suffice for a life befitting their station at home, but might enable him to buy a modest farm in Switzerland and to support them both if he himself worked in the fields. Oh, well he knew that he could not demand such a sacrifice, that he could not command her to become the wife of a peasant, nor would he interpret it as lack of love if she declined—but what other solution was there? None, most likely, and he would therefore await her favorable answer with yearning. He was planning, he concluded, to spend the winter "in this dismal city" and go to Switzerland in the spring.

Two and a half weeks later, in another letter, he assured her that her consent was all-important and that he would not think of making a decisive move without it. But on the other hand, the circumstances, especially his financial situation, were pressing; winter, after all, was as good as any other season for preparatory steps and the gathering of general information, and even if nothing should come of the whole thing, he would be glad to leave this city, "which, it is hardly too much to say, is loathsome to me." Accordingly, he would set out soon— she should write to him in Bern.

Was he not, despite his resolution, again acting overhastily? His attempt to make the peasant life attractive to Wilhelmine on the ground that there was no other in which a woman can so fully enjoy her husband's love seems almost infantile. After barely mentioning the fact that Ulrike was opposed to his project, he adjures Wilhelmine to say nothing to her parents, who should hear of his plan only after it became a reality.

Ulrike was indeed opposed; she had no more use for the Rousseau cult than she had for poetry; moreover, she wisely doubted whether the plan was practicable and whether, if carried out, it could make her brother happy. But resistance only reinforced Kleist's resolution. He clung more and more obstinately to his idea, and the longer he argued with his sister, the more determined he became.

Their departure was soon arranged. Lohse would join them, and the two young men would accompany Ulrike to Frankfurt on the Main, whence, for the most part on foot, they would make their way to Switzerland, while Ulrike would return home alone. On their arrival in Paris they had sold their horses with a heavy heart but for a good price. They now acquired new ones. Their departure was set for November 17. But then unforeseen complications arose. On the 15th, the servant Johann, whom Karl von Zenge had lent them for their trip, ran away, leaving them in the lurch "most disgracefully." Kleist was stunned: "If he had been half as fond of me as I was of him, he would have stood by me. Is there no loyalty in the world?" And on the morning of their departure he received a letter which provoked the same question.

It came from Wilhelmine and was a half refusal. Of course she wanted to follow him; but to leave her country and family, her father and mother was more than she could bear. Nor was she born to be a peasant woman; she hadn't the strength and the sun gave her headaches. She therefore favored a suggestion made by Luise, her "golden sister": that he should come home to Frankfurt, where they would talk the whole matter over and decide what to do.

Kleist would not hear of it. Hadn't he clearly stated his will? For the moment he forgot that he had left the decision up to her. Resistance exasperated him and increased his obstinacy. He was indignant and deeply offended. And now, with the disloyalty common to all mortals, his servant had run away. He himself was obliged to harness the horses, and what with his bad humor and his lack of practice, he went about it very clumsily. Amid the guffaws of the "mob," he worked himself into a sweat, and they might never have got started if a good-natured tailor had not come to his help.

And so they left Paris, that city for which he could find no word of gratitude, though he had learned a great deal there, thrown off the burden of science for good, "worked out an ideal," purportedly devised a plan for happiness, and actually taken an essential step toward the freedom he so urgently needed. Indeed, his freedom was almost complete, his relationship with Wilhelmine and his dream of marriage and peasant life were a last tie, a last attempt at a "sensible" conventional life—but of this the prospect already looked more than doubtful. For a man of his stamp was not likely to give in to a little girl in Frankfurt on the Oder.

# 9

## IN THE TRACES OF ROUSSEAU

ULRIKE was uncommonly kind and considerate during their journey. This and the passage of time helped to appease Kleist's anger. He answered Wilhelmine's letter only on reaching Frankfurt on the Main, two weeks after receiving it; his reply was unyielding, but brief and rather good-natured. He still had faith in her love; "though it is not a lofty sentiment, it is warm and sincere, and in spite of your letter it can still make me happy." In response to her objections to his "peasant plan," he argued that the Bible enjoined young girls to leave father and mother and cling to their husbands; the work of a peasant woman, with two or three maids to help her, would improve her health and strengthen rather than exhaust her; "all will be forgiven if you can make up your mind with *joy* and *serenity*—Heinrich Kleist." In short, she should obey cheerfully, or all was over. In any event, he would carry on with his plan and await her reply, which would tell him whether it was to be with her or without her. But does a man gamble so lightly with the love of a woman he seriously cares for? Of course not—unless something in his unconscious bids him get rid of her.

The last word had not yet been spoken, but Kleist proceeded with his plan. After taking leave of Ulrike, he set out on foot with Lohse. In variable weather they reached Darmstadt and passed through the beautiful Bergstrasse country to Heidelberg with its ruined Schloss. Near Durlach they stood on a hilltop and watched the sun set on the Vosges beyond the Rhine;

they visited Karlsruhe, that star-shaped city, "as clear and luminous as an everlasting principle," crossed the Rhine at Strassburg and made their way through French Alsace to Basel, where they arrived in mid-December. "It was dark night when I entered my new homeland. The rain was pouring down. I looked for stars between the clouds and gave myself up to mixed thoughts. For near and far, everything was so dark. I felt as though I were entering on a new life." And when day broke over the silent, almost deserted city, he saw snow on every hillside, and nature looked to him like an eighty-year-old woman who may have been beautiful in her youth.

Still more disappointing was the absence of his old friend Heinrich Zschokke, who had resigned his post as government commissioner and moved to Bern. Aged thirty, this native of Magdeburg had won a reputation as a popular writer and a political figure. In Kleist's army days he had studied and served as an instructor at Frankfurt on the Oder, and it was then no doubt that Kleist had made his acquaintance. Later he had gone to Switzerland, collaborated with the famous educator Pestalozzi in operating a school for poor children, helped to found *The Honest and Astute Swiss Messenger*, a journal devoted to popular enlightenment, and championed the public welfare in several difficult and responsible posts, in compensation for which, in lieu of other payment, he had been awarded Swiss citizenship and lastly been appointed government commissioner for Basel. Now he had retired to private life from this illustrious career, apparently out of dissatisfaction with the political orientation of the government headed by his personal friend Aloys Reding.

The political situation was indeed anything but gratifying. The patriciate, the clergy, and the landed gentry had long been oppressing the population of town and country alike, but in the last decade a French-inspired resistance had sprung up. No end to the conflict was in sight, because on one side the Austrians and on the other the French backed their favored party with funds or intervened more directly in their behalf. The French had grabbed a certain amount of Swiss territory and were determined to keep the Swiss in a state of dependence. French pressure had forced the Swiss authorities to proclaim a Helvetian Republic, but of late they seemed to be slipping back into their old patrician-conservative ways. Furthermore, the country had become a battlefield, ravaged and plundered by passing troops and ruthlessly starved by such French generals as Masséna, who barred anyone but themselves from importing grain and sold their shipments at extortionate prices.

Altogether a confused situation. Without fully understanding it, Kleist realized that Switzerland was going through troubled times and that its citizens were locked in irreconcilable strife. He almost began to doubt whether the quiet, withdrawn existence he was looking for would be possible in this country. In addition, he had his irritable, violent, untractable nature to contend with. Even for himself he was a difficult companion.

No, he was not an easy man to get along with. In Metz he had quarreled so violently with Lohse that Lohse had fled; when Kleist came to his senses, he had searched the whole town before finding him, and then they had made up. Now, from their base in Basel, they embarked on an expedition into the snow-covered countryside. In Liestal they quarreled again, about what we do not know. Kleist obstinately refused to give in and once again Lohse fled, saying he was going back to Basel. The next day Kleist thought matters over and sent his trunk key to Basel so Lohse could retrieve his belongings. The key was accompanied by a letter in which he laid his heart bare, a letter at once vicious and affectionate, hostile and conciliatory. Thereupon he went back to his quarters in Basel, where key and letter were returned to him—Lohse had not arrived. Frantic with worry, Kleist searched the whole town as he had done in Metz, but did not find his offended friend. In desperation he went to Bern, where Heinrich Zschokke was living. Zschokke welcomed him affectionately at his home on Gerechtigkeitsgasse, and informed him that Lohse was in Bern, alive and well. So Lohse had lied to him! Though glad to be relieved of his worry, Kleist was indignant, and in this frame of mind he appended a postscript to the letter that had been returned to him. Two days later he saw Lohse "under the arcades," and unable to understand how he could have hated him so, he added a second postscript, asking Lohse to come and see him so they might part without hard feelings.

Characteristic as it was, this incident would not in itself merit such detailed treatment, especially since the two were reconciled and remained friends. What seems more important than the quarrel itself was Kleist's reaction to it, his three-part letter to Lohse, with its misleading warmth, its abrupt transitions from stroking to clawing, its gently cruel game of cat-and-mouse, its utter disregard of Lohse and his feelings. It has no parallel among the letters Kleist had written up until then.

"I beg your forgiveness," Kleist wrote. "I know I have been guilty, not of an odious offense, to be sure, but guilty nevertheless, in failing to honor your good conduct according to its deserts, because it was not the best possible conduct. Oh, forgive me! It is because I am so absurdly overwrought that I can never take pleasure in what is, but only in what is not. Do not say that God will forgive me. *You* forgive me, your forgiveness will become you divinely . . . I do not believe you have given much thought to what I have done for you. Yet I have done a great deal, a great great deal . . . Think of it now and then, and think of Metz, I need only remind you . . . I am sure you are not even aware of *what* grieves me . . . What was it we were seeking on our beautiful journey? Was it not peace from passion? Why you? Why did it have to be you—? Everything in the world was so indifferent to me, even the highest was so indifferent; how was it possible that I should attach myself to something unworthy, as if it had been a matter of life and death? Oh, it is horrible, horrible, I feel so bitter, so hostile, so hateful— And yet you could have coaxed the sweetest sounds out of the instrument, but all you have done is shatter it . . . Oh, do not despise a warning. It is the last, it comes from a pure source. Do not trust the feeling that tells you it is too late to change any part of you. There is a great deal that you *should* change and a certain amount that you *could* change. Also you must learn delicacy . . . And now, what I wanted to say—it is so hard for me to say this last—we were such good friends in Paris, such good friends—are you not unspeakably sad?" And then in the first postscript, after seeing Zschokke, Kleist wrote: "So you did not go to Basel? Damnation! How easy it is to deceive gullible people! I looked all over for you, I was frantic, it was Metz all over again. So you're here in Bern, alive and well? Well, I'm glad, I *am* glad. But God knows, I bear you a bitter grudge, never again shall I be able to embrace you with all my heart."

Then a few days later he seems to have thought they should part as friends. Why, then, could he not have left this letter unsent? Instead, he added a second postscript, containing an apology of sorts for the venomous body of the letter: "At that time I still took pleasure in hurting you." But was this not a new expression of animosity; in saying that he no longer took pleasure in hurting Lohse, was he not disparaging his one attempt at conciliation? Was this not tantamount to saying: Hurting you is no longer worth my while? But if it had ceased to be worth his while, why, by sending the letter, did he do it nevertheless? Cat-and-mouse. Caressing and clawing with the same paw.

And while we are on the subject of "caressing"— isn't there something strangely ambivalent about this entire letter, a note, not usual between men, of rebuffed affection taking its revenge? If we did not know that Kleist's letter was written to a man, we might easily suppose its addressee to be a woman who had spurned Kleist's love. True, people coddled and indulged their emotions in the romantic age, but here Kleist goes further. He was by nature immoderate in his feelings; there was a secret sadism in his love for man or woman, and no one could ever know what to expect of him. Did he himself know?

In the belief that he as a foreigner had nothing to fear from the political turmoil of Switzerland, he clung to his "peasant plan." Establishing himself in Bern, he moved about, looking at farms that were offered for sale, studying books on agriculture, and learning what he could from conversations with country folk. He wrote to Ulrike, asking her to settle his debts and to make the rest of his capital available to him. And if necessary would she add some money of her own? There was a property to be had for 3,500 reichstalers on Lake Thun; it looked good to him, especially as the owner had agreed to stay on for a year as his tenant and teach him everything he needed to know. And besides, Lohse—yes, believe it or not, Lohse!—would live with him and help him. She could not lose if she went in with him, for her contribution would be guaranteed by a first mortgage: "Whether or not you will make any profit, I mean, apart from the interest, remains—? My dear little Ulrike, with you I must keep silent about certain things, for I am ashamed to speak at cross-purposes with one who acts." But as for Aunt Massow and his brother Leopold and his other sisters, who, he felt, were angry with him, since they did not even send him their regards, he pressed them to his heart, desolate "that fate or my nature—but is that not my fate?—should have created a gulf between them and me."

The gulf was wide and deep; his family had little idea of the motives behind his Rousseauist dream, or of the life he was leading while waiting to fulfill it. It was the life of a nascent writer, and the men among whom he was living were literary men.

Heinrich Zschokke, historian, journalist, and writer of popular fiction, was by far the most gifted. It is true that while stopping in Leipzig on his way to Würzburg, Kleist had been able to sit through only two acts of Zschokke's play *Aballino* and had thought it abominable; but personally he was fond of him, and Zschokke returned his affection. "Kleist," he wrote later, "was one of the best things in my life, one of those men whom one loves for themselves and never stops loving. Even when in a cheerful mood, he seemed to bear some secret sorrow within him. That is what attracted me most; more perhaps than his rich talent and noble ethical sense. That is what gave his companionship its true charm."

A friend of Zschokke was Heinrich Gessner, son of Salomon Gessner, the celebrated writer of idylls, who had also been a painter, engraver, and etcher, and had illustrated his own pastoral verses. The younger Gessner gave himself the title National Book Dealer of the Helvetian Republic, though he was far from being an outstanding book dealer or publisher, but was more of a literary hanger-on.

Related to him was Louis (or Ludwig) Wieland, the worrisome son of the aged Christoph Martin Wieland, who was then engaged in translating and commentating Greek and Latin authors, for whose texts he wrote introductions of great wisdom and beauty. To the old man's displeasure, young Louis tried his hand at every known literary genre, all with equal incompetence; he had spent a short time in the government service and was now making himself useful in Heinrich Gessner's business. Gessner was his brother-in-law, for he was married to the elder Wieland's daughter Charlotte, familiarly known as Lotte, and at his father-in-law's request had taken the revolutionary-minded young man under his wing.

These three, now joined by Kleist, were the core of the group which met sometimes at Zschokke's lodgings on Gerechtigkeitsgasse, not far from the Hôtel de Musique, where Kleist took his meals, and sometimes at Gessner's home. Zschokke, a great admirer of Schiller, knew nothing of the romantics, the moderns of the day; he had barely heard the name of Friedrich Schlegel, whom Kleist had met in Potsdam, or of Tieck. But young Wieland was so devoted to romanticism, and so enthusiastic about Goethe as the Messiah of art, that he held his father's poetry in low esteem. One can imagine their impassioned discussions, especially if we bear in mind that young Wieland, a great man's son determined to strike out on his own at all costs, had the mocking, supercilious expression so often found among untalented literary men, and a comical way of grimacing which, according to Zschokke, could make the saddest man on earth laugh.

It was about this time that Kleist must have changed the title of the play he was working on from *The Thierrez Family* to *The Ghonorez Family;* either then in Bern or soon afterwards somewhere else, he read the play aloud to his friends and earned a most unexpected success. Provoked by the preposterous accumulation of ghastly misunderstandings, chance encounters, and mistaken identities, and no doubt abetted by Wieland's jokes and horrified grimaces, a storm of merriment arose; the laughter, in which the dramatist joined, finally became "so uproarious and prolonged" that he had to stop reading—but it should not be thought that the strange creation went unappreciated. On the contrary, Gessner offered immediately to publish it (which he subsequently did, though the fee agreed upon was never paid). Wieland advised Kleist to transfer the scene to Germany, and that was how *The Schroffenstein Family* (*Die Familie Schroffenstein*) finally came into being.

In Zschokke's living room there was a copperplate engraving by Jean-Jacques Le Veau, after a painting by Jean-Philibert Debucourt, representing a village court of justice: a judge, solemnly enthroned, is roaring at a peasant boy, who is feebly defending himself; in front of the judge stands an old woman, demonstratively holding up a broken jug; between her and the young man, who is already half convicted, stands a young girl looking guilty and toying with her apron, and at a table to the other side of the judge sits a clerk, eyeing him suspiciously. The picture bore the title *Le Juge ou la cruche cassée*. The four friends discussed possible interpretations and finally decided on a contest in which each would put his conception into literary form. The result was just what one might have expected. Gessner simply copied the lame hexameters into which the hack versifier Karl Wilhelm Ramler had squeezed his father's idyll *The Broken Jug: A Faun's Lamentations over His Shattered Wine Pitcher*; Wieland wrote his feeble comedy *Ambrosius Schlinger*; Zschokke turned out his more or less acceptable short story *The Broken Jug*; and Kleist produced a first version of his comedy *The Broken Jug* (*Der zerbrochne Krug*), which in its final form, as completed five years later, was to occupy a place of honor beside Lessing's *Minna von Barnhelm* as one of the few great comedies in the German language.

For he was a slow, dogged worker, who thought well only of his conceptions, never of his accomplishments. The contrast between splendid conception and inadequate achievement left him no peace; whether in the mood or not, he drove himself unceasingly, devising variants, working and reworking. The force of his imagination, the strange tenacity of his memory, which, once he had caught hold of an image, could make him hold it fast for years and invoke it on a variety of occasions— in short, an almost pigheaded attachment to a motif, once he had hit on it—deprived him of the freedom of movement enjoyed by less rigorous talents.

Nothing could distract him from his work. In January, Wilhelmine had written him a letter, once again setting forth the reasons why she could not become a peasant woman, and once again urging him to come home and talk things over. Kleist did not even answer.

Other developments were more disturbing. The political outlook was dark. Under Aloys Reding, the government had sunk deep into the old conservative bog, the patrician party had won control. Zschokke, as a liberal, was no longer in good odor, and his German friends became suspect to the authorities. One evening Zschokke invited a few friends, among them Kleist, Wieland, Gessner, and Pestalozzi, to dinner; as the guests were leaving, they saw a man loitering outside the house. They seized him and questioned him severely. In the end he admitted that the police chief had sent him to find out what sort of people Zschokke had invited to dinner.

The atmosphere in Bern had become intolerable. Zschokke, too, wanted to leave. Kleist had his eye on a piece of property near Thun, and resolved to go there at once.

In Thun he felt happy and "in good spirits," for he was getting on with his work. His life there was almost entirely solitary; he visited properties in the region but was in no hurry to buy. On his way out of the town, he passed a house with an appealing old inscription over the door: "I come I know not whence. I am I know not what. I am going I know not whither. I am surprised to be so cheerful." And then he went out into the snow-covered countryside, where he would roam around for hours, "for here, as you know, nature was fashioned with spirit, and that is a pleasing sight for a poor devil from Brandenburg, where, as you also know, the artist seems to have fallen asleep at his work." A highly significant image for a nascent master, who was getting into the habit of looking at everything, even God's creation, critically, as a product of art: little by little, art and nature were merging in his mind, and what could be said of one could be said of the other.

He would have been perfectly content in Thun . . . if it hadn't been for Bonaparte, that "damned consul," who was doing everything in his power to foment strife in Switzerland, for what purpose it was not hard to see. Sooner or later he was sure to burn his fingers, for once they saw through his intentions, all parties would unite "against the common wolf"—but for the present Zurich was in a tumult and no one could foresee what the immediate future would bring. Under the circumstances, Kleist thought it would be irresponsible to risk the money for which he had asked Ulrike and which she would no doubt send. He wrote again, asking her to keep it and to send him only as much of his own money as could be made available in cash. His plan to purchase property had to be postponed to a more favorable moment.

But that moment never came. On the contrary, the situation grew more and more alarming; peasant riots broke out only a few miles away, a French general marched into Thun with his troops, and Kleist watched their arrival "not without bitterness." He had wished to become a Swiss citizen. Was he now to be turned into a Frenchman by sleight-of-hand? Horrified at the mere possibility, he abandoned all thought of settling permanently in this unfortunate country, which, one way or another, he felt certain, would fall "a victim to French brutality."

Unfortunately, his letter to Ulrike had not reached her in time, and she had already sent the money. What was he to do with it? Oh, why was he always so hasty?—though on this occasion it was not he, but fate, which had proved inconstant. Ulrike's check had arrived, he had not yet cashed it, and, if possible, the money would remain far from his "unreliable hands" until she decided what was to be done with it; still, if she could repay herself out of his share in the Frankfurt house, he would be glad to keep the money, which could come in handy at any time.

Ulrike could hardly have been ignorant of what would happen to her money. True, Kleist thought he would be able to support himself sooner or later by his literary efforts, but in the meantime he had to live and to make some sort of practical arrangements. Was he to stay in Thun under the French occupation, which filled him with rage and horror? Zschokke was in the process of renting the castle of Bieberstein near Aarau, a romantic refuge from the troubled times. In the end, Kleist rented a small but well-equipped house on a small island in the Aare River, which flowed into the Lake of Thun. There he lived and worked for the next six months and waited to see what would happen in the outside world.

But what of his "peasant plan"? It was abandoned, along with his engagement to Wilhelmine. He had now cast off all his fetters and was able to live entirely for his work. It remained to be seen whether he would prove worthy of his freedom.

# 10

## ISLAND IDYLL

IT was in April 1802 that Kleist moved to Delosea Island, as it was called. The only other house on the island was occupied by a fisherman named Stettler and his family. Stettler sent one of his daughters, Elisabeth Magdalena, known as Mädeli, to keep house for Kleist. She was pretty and affable, the same age as Kleist, and he grew very fond of her. While he sat working or pacing the floor in his room with the grandiose view of the Alps, he could hear her moving about in the kitchen; she grew flowers in the garden and picked them to decorate the table at which they ate together. Apart from the painful feelings which were so deeply rooted in his nature that even this idyllic life could not dispel them entirely, he was without cares. He seems even to have earned a bit of money with his writing, though of course it was spent in no time. One day Kleist, who had never in all his life been able to save, thought it necessary to ask Mädeli to run the house more economically; but she did not understand the word, and he tried in vain to explain his meaning. After a while they both burst out laughing, and nothing was changed.

It was a truly idyllic life. The days were devoted to work. At night he would often go out on the lake with old man Stettler to help him cast his nets and pull them in; on Sunday, he and Mädeli would row the quarter of a mile across to Thun, where she, in the charming Swiss costume he had bought her, would go to church while he went for a short walk in the mountains. After church, they would row back together to their refuge. He was as happy as he was capable of being, and had no other wish than to die when he had created three things: "a child, a beautiful poem, and a great deed." To die— yes, even in happiness he was haunted by the thought of death, now longing for it and now fearing that it might overtake him before he had completed his work.

What work was it that he was afraid of not completing? *The Schroffenstein Family* was as good as done, requiring only the finishing touches; it was published by Gessner of the National Publishing House in the following year, 1803. Or had he already begun to put *The Broken Jug* into its final form? We do not know. Earlier biographers speak of a tragedy, *Leopold of Austria (Leopold von Österreich)*, the first act of which he supposedly wrote at this time and later destroyed. His old friend Pfuel remembered a gloomy scene in which Leopold's knights threw dice in their tent to see how each would fare in the next day's battle, and for one after another the dice foretold death. The relevance is obvious, for this was the battle of Sempach, in which in 1386 the Swiss won their independence from Austria. But it is most likely that during his island idyll Kleist was struggling with *Robert Guiscard*, a unique literary conception, which was giving him the utmost difficulty.

In any event, he worked for hours on end, not even taking the time to read books or newspapers. When he had to write a letter, he felt that he was stealing time from his work, and indeed he seems to have written very few between April and August 1802. But he did not begrudge the time when Zschokke, Gessner, or Wieland came to see him, for when he read aloud to them, they had only the most flattering comments to make, and their enthusiasm encouraged and inspired him. Wieland, in particular, was quite carried away by these readings and wrote to his father that Kleist was an extraordinary genius, from whom "in the dramatic field something far greater may be expected than has been seen in Germany up until now"; and the elder Wieland replied that he would welcome further news of his son's new friend.

Only once was Kleist's seclusion disturbed by a call from the outside world—a letter from Wilhelmine. Writing after a long silence, she had sad and touching news to report. Her brother, Karl von Zenge, with whom Kleist had lived in Berlin, had died of inflammation of the throat; she herself had been gravely ill; when she asked her little sister Emilie: Where is Kleist? the child would kiss his picture in Wilhelmine's locket; Kleist's sister Auguste, who had always objected so sternly to any display of affection on the part of betrothed young ladies, had married Kleist's cousin Wilhelm von Pannwitz, and was extremely affectionate and happy; she, Wilhelmine, had suffered a good deal, but she dared to "*hope*," though without saying what she hoped for. Kleist hesitated, then replied that he had been silent because he had wished to spare her and himself long-winded explanations. "There is one word in the German language that you women do not ordinarily understand. That word is *Ehrgeiz* [ambition]. There is only one possibility of my going home: if I can live up to the expectations that I myself foolishly aroused by my boastful behavior. Such an eventuality is possible but not probable. In short, if I cannot return to my country covered with glory, I will never return. This is as certain as my nature." A horrible uprising, he went on, had upset his plan of buying property in Switzerland; now he had withdrawn into solitude and for better or worse begun to write; he was spending his small fortune and would probably have gone through it in another year. "In addition to the sorrows I share with you, I have very different cares that you are not even aware of, and in this situation your letter reaches me, reviving my memory of you, which had happily, happily, paled just a little—Dear girl, don't write to me any more. I have no other wish than to die soon. H.K."

Not a word about the early death of Karl von Zenge, who had after all been his close friend, not a smiling word of tenderness about little Emilie kissing his picture. No digressions, just one terse, irrevocable statement, scarcely softened at the end by a faint breath of melancholy. Yes, he could be a hard man when he felt the need to be.

But Wilhelmine took this brusque dismissal rather well: she would always feel for him and take an interest in his career;

she was returning his picture. With her previous letter, Wilhelmine, who for all her simplicity was not without a certain shrewdness, had merely wanted to sound him out one last time; in the meantime, she had made the acquaintance of Dr. Traugott Krug, a professor of philosophy. They were well suited to each other, and that same year, after receiving Kleist's letter of farewell, she became engaged to him. Kleist's letter, she said later, had indeed shaken her, but she had felt sorrier for him than for herself: "I saw that I could never become his wife, and had long ceased wanting to." But she thought of him without bitterness and looked upon him as "a sublime instrument, by which the kindly Creator wished to ennoble me."

With his engagement disposed of, nothing seemed to stand in the way of Kleist's work. But in June or July 1802 he fell sick and hurried off to Bern, where he was treated by the physician and pharmacist Dr. Wyttenbach, a friend of Zschokke's. We do not know the nature of his illness, Kleist himself does not tell us, and there is no record of Dr. Wyttenbach's diagnosis.

In general, Kleist's ailments and breakdowns defy interpretation from a purely medical point of view. He would complain of persistent pains in the abdomen, of fever, constipation, hallucinations, of feelings of pressure, raging headaches; something or other was always torturing him, laying him low, and vanishing as suddenly as it had come; no physiological explanation was ever found or any treatment worth mentioning given. Since there was nothing wrong with his organs, one can only suspect his psyche as the source of his troubles. What with his immoderate demands on himself, he was under a constant strain, and when the strain became more than he could bear, he seems to have fallen sick. This is a phenomenon well known to modern psychology, which has aptly termed it "flight into illness." Though all artists seem to indulge in such flights now and then, none has ever shown greater talent for it than this dramatist, whose most impressive heroine dies an utterly unexpected and purely psychogenic death—a conception unprecedented in world literature. Flight into illness was Kleist's way of reacting to situations that struck him as hopeless, and most likely the illness that drove him away from his island was just such a flight.

Contemporary gossip—which, in view of the many gaps in the record of Kleist's biography, cannot be totally ignored— offers a psychological explanation of sorts for Kleist's sudden departure from Delosea Island. The story is that he had been having an affair with Mädeli, that he had got her with child, and that she was deceiving him with a French officer. But there is no proof whatsoever that they were having an affair, or, if they were, that it ended badly. On the contrary. Forty years later, Wilhelmine's "golden sister" Luise von Zenge visited Switzerland with a friend. Obliged by an accident to her carriage to spend some time in Thun, she found that the "nice young German" had left behind him a memory unclouded by any suspicion of scandal. And Luise's stay in Thun yielded something more than this gratifying report; namely, what was for a long time our only authentic portrait of Kleist, the locket miniature, which Wilhelmine had returned to him in June 1802 and which he had thoughtlessly left in his drawer. The pastor, to whom Luise applied for information about Kleist, handed her the picture; he had inherited it from his grandfather, to whom the Stettlers had given it for safekeeping. And Kleist's nieces, Auguste and Friederike von Pannwitz, who in September 1834, in the course of a trip to Nice, visited "that island, where Uncle Heinrich had lived some thirty years ago," were also given a friendly welcome.

"Kleist's island" was bought by a Swiss industrialist in the 1930's and is still in the possession of his family. Today there is no sign of Kleist's house or of the fisherman's hut, but a tablet has been put up with the inscription: "The author Heinrich Kleist lived on this island from 1802 to 1803."

There can be no doubt that Kleist had other troubles, unconnected with Mädeli. He was not getting on with *Leopold of Austria;* he finally put it aside and never went back to it. *The Broken Jug* was still unfinished, and *Robert Guiscard,* the most alluring of his projects, was resisting all his efforts.

And so, since it was not in Kleist's nature to accept defeat when in good health, he appears to have sought relief in illness. And the theory of a flight from his troubles is rendered more plausible by the desperate tone of a letter written to his cousin, brother-in-law, and occasional financial adviser Wilhelm von Pannwitz. Having lain sick for two months, he wrote, he besought God for death and Pannwitz for money. It seems likely that the family had already begun to worry about him. Pannwitz passed the letter on to Ulrike; Ulrike, never one to procrastinate, borrowed money on the Nonnenwinkel house and set out for Switzerland to see what was going on.

We have a record of this journey from the pen of Ulrike herself. Accompanied by a lackey, she traveled day and night by diligence as far as the Swiss border. Switzerland was in a turmoil, but as a foreigner she had no idea what to make of it. When she stopped in Soluthurn to change horses and rest, she was told that all available rooms were occupied by officers who had been taken prisoner. She went to her carriage and thought: Why worry my head over nothing? If anything happens, I can always turn back. And on she rode in the midst of marching troops, who saluted her politely. At six in the afternoon she made her entry into besieged Bern with a column of provisions wagons. Hearing that the streets must be cleared by seven o'clock, she quickly found an inn and got one of the servants to take her to Dr. Wyttenbach. The astonished doctor assured her that Kleist was in good health, but regretted to say that he did not know his address. At that, the hotel servant exclaimed: "Why, Herr Kleist, he takes his meals with us." And he knew where Kleist lived. Dressed exactly as she had been when leaving him the previous December in Frankfurt on the Main, she walked into Kleist's room. He was seated at his table, writing. Clapping his hands over his head, he cried out: "Ulrike, you look as if you'd just gone out the door and come in again." She asked him to escort her back to the inn; Kleist said no, he couldn't, he had promised friends to help defend the city (for General von Erlach was on the way to Bern with his army corps). "Never mind that," said Ulrike. "Let them defend themselves. Now you're coming with me." And she dragged him away with her.

It was Ulrike's realistic good sense that persuaded Kleist to leave this unhappy country in all haste. The Reding government had fallen, giving way to a regime of arbitrary tyranny. Zschokke, the honorary Swiss citizen, thought it advisable to take a holiday in the Black Forest; Gessner's National Publishing House had been closed and was under seal; Wieland was suspect for having been employed for a time by the preceding government; and Kleist was known to be the friend of all these dubious persons. Brother and sister decided to travel via Neuchâtel to Jena and Weimar, and to take young Wieland with them. They had not yet finished packing when Kleist and Wieland were summoned to police headquarters; the moment they stepped in, the police chief handed Wieland an order to leave Bern within twelve hours. On the way out of the building with Kleist, Wieland laughed and put on one of his comic acts as a kind of protest. Whereupon he was ordered to leave in two hours, then in one hour, and was issued a pass valid only for Basel. Since he was totally without funds, the Kleists would not hear of his traveling alone; Ulrike stored her trunks and clothes at Gessner's, and within the prescribed hour they drove out through the city gate. This was in October 1802.

# 11

## AT THE WIELANDS'

K LEIST and Ulrike were in Weimar. There had been an unwelcome delay in Erfurt, where Louis Wieland found an old love with whom he was in no hurry to part. In the end, Kleist had grown impatient and they had gone on without him.

It has been supposed that while in Weimar the Kleists paid their respects to Goethe and Schiller, but of this there is no adequate evidence. They did, however, call on old man Wieland on his nearby estate of Ossmannstedt. Ulrike appeared in man's clothing, and the old gentleman was not aware that she was Kleist's sister. He was probably too fascinated by Kleist himself, this short, broad-shouldered young man with the small round head and the over-alert eyes. Louis had spoken of him so enthusiastically in his letters, and there was indeed something irresistible about him, for Kleist could be very charming when he chose. And in this case he chose, not so much, perhaps, because Wieland was an important writer as because he had been famous for many years, and in Kleist's eyes fame in itself was a desirable quality. Sometimes aging fame and budding fame enter into an alliance, for while the former cannot help wishing for recognition from the rising generation, the latter requires the recognition and favor of established authority. Apart from personal sympathy, this was the foundation of the fine friendship that developed between the almost septuagenarian Wieland and the just twenty-five-year-old Kleist.

His period of rest with Dr. Wyttenbach, the journey with

Ulrike, and now the warm reception given him by his influential new friend had restored Kleist's strength and prepared him for a new siege of work. Ulrike set out for home, and Kleist went back to his main preoccupation, *Robert Guiscard*. He rented lodgings in Weimar, where he could have prepared his own meals, but this he found too distracting, and instead he spent whole days in Ossmannstedt, where a room had been made available to him. Actually, Wieland had wanted to move to Weimar and had bought a house there, but was deterred from moving by fear of losing his servants. The new house was next door to the Dowager's Palace, which was haunted by the ghost of Johann Friedrich IV, sometimes in the form of a little white bird and sometimes of a gray, paper-thin little man, the "blotting-paper prince," as the people called him. And naturally the servants didn't want to be mixed up with such spooky doings!

Kleist was made to feel very much at home in the house at Ossmannstedt. Respect for creative work was traditional in the family, and the young guest was left to labor undisturbed. He was very much in need of the kind consideration and soothing atmosphere that surrounded him here. *Robert Guiscard* was as intractable as ever; the difficulties were inherent in the grandeur of Kleist's underlying idea, which amounted to combining classical tragedy with Shakespearean drama, or, one might say, to psychologizing myth. But he could not seem to sound the depths of the human soul in the elevated style to which he aspired. Success alternated with failure, euphoria with despair. He could barely find time for a short conversation or a terse word of greeting to Ulrike: "You know what a letter from me means. The time may come when a *blank page* from me will make you shed tears of joy."

But with the obstinacy of the possessed he persevered in his labors and was occasionally rewarded with a bit of recognition —and then he would burst out in jubilation: "My dear Ulrike, the beginning of the poem, in which I try to explain your love of me to the world, has won the admiration of all those to whom I have shown it. Dear Lord! If I could only finish it! If heaven will only grant this one wish." We do not know to whom he showed it, definitely not to old Wieland, though he already felt so much at home in Ossmannstedt that he not only spent the Christmas holidays with the Wielands but decided in January 1803, "despite a very pretty Wieland daughter," to move in.

Once again he was living in a place where, as he supposed, his fate would at last be decided, "happily in all likelihood." It goes without saying that he worked, and since his work never left him entirely free, he was rather an odd guest. Son-in-law Gessner had spoken in his letters of Kleist's "uncontrolled genius"; ordinarily, the old man was repelled by eccentrics, but this one was so charming, he seemed to honor and love him like a father, and, though nothing could bring Kleist to behave with "simple familiarity," he had a certain "irresistible something" that made one tolerate his oddities. His behavior at the noonday meal was particularly strange. At the head of the table sat the kindly, wise, and illustrious head of the family; on either side, his three lovely daughters—among them the "very pretty" one, Luise, the youngest, who was his favorite because she resembled his late wife—his son Louis with his grimaces and witticisms, and finally Kleist. Kleist would sit there mumbling something between his teeth "almost like a madman," looking as if he thought he was all alone in the room. For a moment he might join in the conversation, but then he would suddenly fall silent when a word, spoken at random by one of the company, started his mind off on some chain of associations, which so absorbed him that he would lose sight of the world around him, even of little Luise, who could not tear her eyes away from this strange table companion.

Once when they were alone, the old gentleman spoke, ever so circumspectly, of his young friend's exasperating ways. Kleist offered an embarrassed apology and finally admitted that he was working on a tragedy that left him no peace. A word spoken by chance, he explained, would associate itself in his mind with his recalcitrant work and suggest some new solution. Yes, recalcitrant it was, and though he had already written whole scenes, he kept having to destroy them because they were so far from measuring up to his conception. Wieland suggested that Kleist should write out the whole play as best he could and then rework his sketch in every detail until he was satisfied with it. But Kleist could not work in this way; the slightest imperfection confused his train of thought and blocked the flow of ideas, the chain of associations indispensable to all creative work. Greatly as he esteemed the old man, he could not take his advice; when it came to his work, he could recognize only one authority: himself.

Fortunately, he met with understanding in Ossmannstedt. More than was good for him, in fact—had his instinct not warned him about the "very pretty daughter"? There were three daughters at home, all unmarried, and all three, each in her own way, felt strongly about Kleist. Amalie, perhaps because she was afraid of succumbing to his charm, "hated" him; Karoline had a crush on him; but Luise was really in love with him. She was only fourteen, but precocious, sensitive, and indeed "very pretty," with her long, finely shaped nose, the fine curve of her lips, and her large, dark, knowing eyes. She probably understood Kleist better than anyone else in the family; she felt that he was in some way endangered, and that made him all the more worthy of being loved. Of course, it was unwise to give her heart to Kleist, she was sure to be disappointed, for he belonged entirely to his daemon. But even if Luise had some inkling of this, she was in love and only too willing to be deluded. Any number of "seeming trifles" convinced her that her love was reciprocated. We do not know to what degree Kleist was to blame for her misapprehension, but it is clear that he did little if anything to correct it, though he was well aware that her advances to him had gone beyond the bounds of seemliness, unless he meant to return them. Sooner or later he would have to leave this house, and he might have done so, but quite apart from the charm of being loved half in secret, how could he run out on such kind friends without an explanation? Moreover, Wieland had begun to dictate the story of his life to him (the manuscript, unfortunately, was lost); and the old gentleman would undoubtedly be deeply offended if he were to drop this work without an acceptable reason. He might have left even so, but then something happened which attached him to that house more strongly than ever.

One afternoon as they sat alone by the fireside, Wieland was so successful in breaking through Kleist's usual reserve that he not only spoke at length of his work but went to his room for the manuscript and began to read it aloud. A number of accounts bear witness to the power of Kleist's reading. At first his delivery was feeble and halting, but once he gained confidence, he read with fire and passion, and the effect was overpowering.

Wieland had preserved his youthful capacity for enthusiasm; his aged face glowed with excitement; he was so moved by what he heard of *Guiscard*, so carried away, that when the dramatist had finished reading, both men were speechless and Kleist, as he tells us, prostrated himself before Wieland, "covering his hands with hot kisses." Nor was Kleist's account exaggerated; some months later Wieland described his impressions as follows: "If the spirits of Aeschylus, Sophocles, and Shakespeare were to collaborate in creating a tragedy, the outcome would be equivalent to Kleist's *Death of Guiscard the Norman*, if the whole proves equal to what he then read to me. From that moment on, it was clear to me that Kleist was born to fill the wide gap in our dramatic literature which, at least in my opinion, even Goethe and Schiller have failed to fill." Small wonder that such admiration from a man of such prestige, assigning him a place not side by side with but above the greatest names in German literature, should have held him in Ossmannstedt. What with his total concentration on *Guiscard*, he could hardly have been expected to realize that such encouragement might have its harmful side; he could only seize upon it and make use of it for his work, which was dearer to him than life. This house was the place for him. Even if little Luise was falling more and more hopelessly in love—he had to stay if at all possible, he *had* to finish *Guiscard*.

Beside it, nothing else mattered, not even his own earlier writing. *The Schroffenstein Family* was published by Gessner in Bern; it appeared anonymously, and of that he was glad. He had come so far since then; "wretched trash," he called it in a letter—but then he crossed the words out, for the play was *his work* and it meant something to him after all.

We share his mixed feelings. *Schroffenstein* is the story of a senseless and cruelly destructive feud between two noble houses. It relates how this furious quarrel, born of a misunderstanding, takes in more and more people; how, nourished by accidents, misunderstandings, mistaken identities, and the temperaments of the various protagonists, it poisons the hearts even of lovers and drives them to self-destruction, death, or madness. The concatenation of events, each releasing the next with the automatism of fatality, shows great talent. But it is all too schematic, the design shines through the fabric, the gruesome, theatrical effects are sometimes merely unpleasant and sometimes unintentionally funny, and though many passages are powerful and true to life, a good deal of the play is so improbable and grotesque that one cannot help laughing. Still, it should be remembered that Kleist was only twenty-four when he completed this strange play. For all its faults, one cannot help admiring its originality, not so much in the plot or in character portrayal as in its language, which, whether tender, brutal, or passionate, always rings true.

*I puzzle you,*
*Do I not? Take comfort, God puzzles me.*

*Just that is the curse of power, that*
*The revocable will so quickly grows*
*An arm which acts*
*Irrevocably.*

*His very thought*
*Hatches disaster and the least*
*Of his servants has this advantage over him,*
*Of being entitled to will evil.*

*The diseased, dead oak tree stands*
*Up to the storm, which lays the sound one low*
*Because it can seize hold of the crown.*
*—A man should have to sustain every blow,*
*And if God seizes hold of him, I think, it is his right to fall.*

Indeed, there is much to catch the ear, much to admire in this strange drama, and soon after its first performance, it found admirers, first Schiller's and Körner's friend Ludwig Ferdinand Huber, who in Kotzebue's journal *The Liberal* published a review of it under the heading "A New Dramatic Poet Makes His Appearance," in which he terms Kleist "a genius of truly Shakespearean spirit"; then a hardly less enthusiastic critic reviewed it for the *Journal for the Fashionable World*, and a year later Joseph von Görres for the Munich *Aurora*.

But Kleist himself, when he received a copy of his first published book, was not impressed; on the contrary, he found it so embarrassing that he didn't even want Ulrike to read it and dreaded that strangers should learn of its authorship. Something incomparably finer would bring him fame. He *must* finish *Guiscard!*

But the situation at Ossmannstedt became more and more untenable. Louis Wieland seems to have sided with Amalie, the sister who "hated" Kleist, and to have been put off by Kleist's apparent disregard of his youngest sister's passion, and Karoline, despite or because of her crush, was also being made unhappy by Kleist's presence. Their father did not intervene. According to Ulrike (in whom Kleist must have confided), the old gentleman favored his darling's love and would have welcomed a marriage between the two young people. And why, indeed, would he have objected to a man of Kleist's promising talent, upright character, and noble antecedents as a son-in-law? But then, perhaps as a result of gossip by servants or occasional guests, the rumor spread that something not quite right was going on at the Wielands'. And in the long run, precisely because Luise was really in love, the presence of a man who did nothing to discourage her, but never frankly responded to her advances, could not but be a source of suffering to her. Preferring to give up her love, rather than prolong this painful situation, she joined Karoline in a conference with Kleist, at which they begged him to restore their peace of mind by going away.

How gladly he would have stayed on! And how sorry old Wieland, who was not told of this conference, was to let him go. But the decision had been made; it was no longer possible to stay. "In tears," he left the house where he "had found more

love than the whole world can provide." Uncertain where to
go, he spent a few desolate days at a hotel in Weimar and then
—without knowing why—set out for Leipzig.

The Ossmannstedt episode was ended (as it would have been
in any case, for in spite of the "blotting-paper prince" the
Wieland family soon moved to Weimar after all). But Kleist
had won old man Wieland's heart and little Luise continued to
love him. She never stopped worrying about "that unspeakable
man" and urged her brother Louis not to break off his friendship with Kleist entirely. And eight years later, in a letter to
her elder sister Charlotte Gessner, she spoke of the unforgettable impression Kleist had made on her from the first moment
she laid eyes on him. Their encounter may have destroyed her
emotionally; in 1814 she married another man, and a year later
died in childbirth.

# 12

## THE STRONGER

I<small>N</small> Leipzig, Kleist, renewing a friendship from the year before, went to see the mathematician Karl Friedrich Hindenburg. Hearing he had been in Paris, the professor asked: "Well, what have the French been doing in mathematics?" Kleist had no idea. "Oh, so you were just touring?" said Hindenburg, visibly disappointed. Touring indeed! . . . Kleist hastened to inform him that he had not been idle but had been working on *something*. "On what?" Hindenburg asked, but quickly answered his own question: he had been told that Kleist had spent the winter with Wieland—so, naturally, he knew what to expect. At that, Kleist fell on Hindenburg's neck and embraced him, whereupon the startled mathematician had to own that every man must cultivate what he feels to be his dominant talent.

This Kleist did in every conceivable way. To draw profit from his rather pointless stay in Leipzig, he took lessons in declamation from a university instructor by the name of Kerndörffer, allegedly because he believed that the tragedy on which he was working would be more effective if he learned to recite it properly. But he may also have believed that declamation would lend new impetus to his work; for *Guiscard* was giving him as much trouble as ever.

He even toyed with the idea that the work might benefit if he were to spend a few months with his family in Frankfurt— if only Ulrike and the others didn't drive him crazy with their worrying over what was to become of him. "O ye Erinyes with your love!" And yet how dearly he loved them all! Especially here in his loneliness. "And as they stand there like organ pipes, kiss them all from the tallest to the smallest, the little mouse carved from an apple core! A single word from you, and before you know it, I will be gurgling with joy in the middle room."

But instead of returning to the warm nest in Frankfurt, he finally chose Dresden, where he would be undisturbed but not alone: Rühle, Pfuel, and La Motte-Fouqué were all there at the moment, and of course he went to see the two sisters he was so fond of, Caroline and Henriette von Schlieben; and though their first meeting was somewhat strained, because of his quarrel (long since patched up, to be sure) with Caroline's fiancé Lohse, Kleist's "great warmth" soon won them over and everything was as before.

Yet they were not the most cheerful companions. They were poor, they wore themselves out with their needlework, which to spare the family's sensibilities they secretly sold for a song to a friend who tried to resell it. And then the worry about Lohse, who never wrote. Caroline lived in terror that something had happened to him, that he was ill, that he was being unfaithful to her. "If this goes on," she said one day, "I shall go mad." Kleist sat beside her on the sofa, deep in thought, strumming a guitar. "You're right," he said. "That's the best thing you can do. And if you ever recover your reason, I'll take a pistol and shoot us both dead. Why shouldn't I do you the favor?" Did he, after these terrible words, give her a questioning look? In any case, the words had been spoken calmly and gravely, they were anything but empty talk. Caroline was terrified. Instantly cured of her melancholy, she shuddered at the abysmal gloom of this man who had made an inseparable companion of death. From that day on, she felt that Kleist was "a strange being," whom she would never understand.

But what of Henriette? Was Kleist, for her too, "a strange being," or was there an intimacy between them? Here, as so often in Kleist's biography, there is an area of uncertainty. But there is one startling hint. We have seen that the good-luck crown which Caroline had plaited "with dear friend Kleist" on May 16, 1801, was found among her effects after her death.

Along with it there was a sketch of a young girl with a pretty, curly-haired, boyish head and a rather saucy mouth, and below it, written in Caroline's hand: "Henriette von Schlieben, Kleist's fiancée." Caroline, one would think, must have known whether or not her sister was engaged to Kleist. On the other hand, this is positively the only indication that they were engaged, unless we wish to put such an interpretation on imponderables such as: Kleist's prolonged (several months') stay in Dresden; the rather intimate present Henriette gave him when he left, an "exceptionally handsome" embroidered "half-shirt"; and the letter he wrote her a year later from Berlin, speaking of his "cruel fate" and asking her forgiveness for "so utterly failing to fulfill the promise he had made on parting." But all this admits of other interpretations, and if not for the inscription on Henriette's picture, it would never have occurred to anyone that she was engaged to Kleist. Could it be that, like Luise Wieland, Henriette—and Caroline as well—had let herself be deluded by Kleist's "great warmth" and overflowing charm? Perhaps in his association with Henriette he really did toy with his old idea of marrying—when his work was completed and he had achieved fame and fortune.

But that was far in the future; *Guiscard* resisted his efforts, and he sat over it day and night, torn between hope and despair. And when he despaired, he carried despair to its logical conclusion, urging the rather phlegmatic Pfuel to put an end to the shameful torment of his life by joining him in suicide. The idea became an obsession with him; he repeated his suggestion over and over again, and Pfuel would always reply good-naturedly: "Suppose we sleep on it. Plenty of time for that." And after a while they would both start laughing. Undoubtedly, Pfuel, with his keen but unpresuming intelligence, his even temper and unfailing friendliness, was the best companion Kleist could have had. A trifling example may show the helpful interest he took in his friend's work. By pretending to doubt Kleist's gift for comedy, he provoked him into dictating the first three scenes of *The Broken Jug* to him. In the end, however, Kleist's self-torment became more than even Pfuel could bear, and he suggested a solution, a walking trip to Switzerland, confident that, buoyed up by the change of surroundings, Kleist would be able to finish *Guiscard*.

But Pfuel was not a rich man; Ulrike, on the other hand, had plenty of money, and she was, after all, Kleist's sister. Accordingly, Kleist wrote to her that his money had all been spent and that Pfuel had suggested a trip to Switzerland; would she lend him enough to live on until he had fulfilled "his great destiny and gathered the laurels of immortality": "One day your friend will thank you, as will art and the world"; he would welcome an affirmative answer, but better still: couldn't she come to Dresden to talk things over?

Ulrike was never one to resist an invitation to travel, and before long she arrived in Dresden, apparently accompanied by one or more relatives. She gave little evidence of the family's supposed anxiety over his future—that was a relief—and as usual she was generous. She did not think much of the Swiss plan, but since nothing on earth meant more to her brother than Pfuel's companionship, she raised no objection. Once the financial arrangements were settled, she wished her brother a pleasant journey and started back to Frankfurt on the Oder.

Ulrike had hardly gone when a letter came from Wieland—a message of heartfelt enthusiasm and encouragement which Kleist took as a good omen for the present and a talisman for the future. Nothing in his present crisis could have given such reassurance as these words from the illustrious old man: "For the genius of the sacred Muse who inspires you, nothing is impossible. You must finish your *Guiscard* even if the whole Caucasus and more weighs you down." Kleist's first thought was that Ulrike must read this, then she would be thoroughly convinced that the man she had helped was not unworthy. He sent her the letter, asking her to return it promptly, for he wished to have it with him to console him in times of stress.

There is a story to the effect that Kleist took hurried leave of the Schliebens, assuring them that the sole purpose of his trip was to see Lohse (to whom he had already written on the subject of Caroline) in Italy, so as to form a picture of the situation and report back to Dresden. If this were true, it would lend support to the theory that his intimacy with Henriette was such as to require him to spare her feelings—why otherwise would he have told the sisters a story so misleading? But all indications are that he did nothing of the kind. The sisters knew that he was having difficulty with his work; he had taken Ulrike to see them, and she could always be counted on to blurt out the truth; moreover, Henriette must have known well in advance that he was leaving, or she would not have had time to make him a fine embroidered "half-shirt" as a farewell present; and finally, he himself was hardly in a mood for comedy. He may have said something about seeing Lohse just to make the parting easier for all concerned; and the above-cited letter he wrote to Henriette a year later from Berlin argues that he found time before leaving for a good long talk with her.

And then he was on the road again, this time with Pfuel. They stopped in Leipzig, hiked through Switzerland, visited Bern and Thun. For a time they stayed on Delosea Island, where Kleist worked—a strong indication that he had parted on good terms with the Stettlers and Mädeli the preceding year. He struggled with *Guiscard* and, insofar as it left his fancy free, enjoyed the companionship of Pfuel, whom he truly loved. "Often in Thun," he wrote later, "when I saw you going down to the lake, I contemplated your beautiful body with truly girlish eyes . . . Your small curly head set on a stout neck, two broad shoulders, a wiry body, the whole an exemplary picture of strength, as though you had been modeled on the most beautiful young bull that ever bled for Zeus . . . You restored the age of the Greeks in my heart, I could have slept with you, my dear boy."

But even the idyllic island failed to help Kleist with his work, and the friends resumed their travels. One night, when Kleist and Pfuel stopped at an inn, their voices were recognized by the occupants of the adjoining room (after Kleist's death, Ulrike was to experience a gruesome companion piece to this little incident); they were old friends from Potsdam, Christoph Wilhelm Werdeck and his wife, Adolphine, who were members of Queen Luise's coterie and were feared at court for their wit. The couple were on their way to Italy and France. Kleist and Pfuel joined them. The four of them crossed the Saint Gotthard

Pass together and went to Varese near Como. There Kleist met Lohse, but Lohse's affairs were in a tangle and he spoke in riddles. Kleist could not get much out of him and started, but did not complete, a report to Caroline von Schlieben. On one occasion the four traveling companions took the painter (who, as it happens, soon married Caroline and died shortly afterwards, in Milan) with them on an excursion to the monastery of Madonna del Monte, and this beautiful place, especially its heady wines, induced a fine state of euphoria in the whole company, including Kleist, though *Guiscard* had by then become an affliction that "was gnawing away at his heart."

The Werdecks had no difficulty in persuading him to go to France with them, and Pfuel, himself quite uncertain of his plans, raised no objection.

But in Geneva, in a clear-sighted moment, Kleist sat down at a table and wrote the magnificent letter in which he abandoned his painful and hopeless struggle with *Guiscard:*

Heaven knows, my dearest Ulrike (and I wish to die if this is not literally true), how gladly I would give a drop of my heart's blood for every letter of a missive starting: "My poem is finished." But you know what happens to those who, in the words of the proverb, do more than they can. I have now put half a thousand consecutive days (including most of their nights) into my attempt to add one more to our family's laurel wreaths; and now our sacred tutelary goddess calls out to me: enough! In sympathy she kisses the sweat from my forehead and comforts me by saying that if each one of her beloved sons did as much, our name would not be wanting a place in the stars. So be it. The fate which determines every cultural advance of the nations does not yet, I believe, wish art to prosper in this northern clime. In any event, it would be folly for *me* to expend my powers any longer on a work which, I must at last confess, is too hard for me. I stand back for one who has not yet come and bow, a thousand years in advance, to his spirit. For beyond a doubt the invention I have conceived is a link in the chain of human inventions, and somewhere a monument is in the making for the man who will someday bring it forth . . .

But is it not ignominious that fate should stoop to leading so helpless a creature as man by the nose? And what else is one to think when it seems to give us fool's gold in mines which we dig without ever finding genuine metal. It was hell that gave me my half talents, heaven gives a man whole talents or none . . .

Farewell, my greetings to all—I cannot go on.

HEINRICH

*Geneva, October 5, 1803*

P.S. Do send me Wieland's letter.

*The portrait of Juliane Ulrike von Kleist (1746–1793)
and her seven-year-old son Heinrich,
painted by Franz Ludwig Close*

*Kleist at the age of eighteen*

*Kleist and (facing page) his half-sister Ulrike (1774–1849)*

*Wilhelmine von Zenge (1780–1852)*

*The miniature portrait by Peter Friedel, painted in*
*April 1801, when Kleist was twenty-three*

*Chalk drawing after the miniature portrait by Friedel,
commissioned by Wilhelmine von Zenge, probably in 1831*

*Ernst von Pfuel (1779–1866)*

*Otto August Rühle von Lilienstern*
*(1780–1847)*

*Rahel Levin ( 1771–1833 )*

*Henriette Vogel ( 1777–1811 )*

*A life mask of Kleist; its authenticity is disputed*

# 13

## THE SHADOW LINE

I N his moving letter to Ulrike, renouncing his struggle with
*Guiscard,* Kleist had written that he was on his way to
Paris, where, "without making any great decisions," he
would seize upon whatever came his way. But what could possibly take the place of a work that had been his whole life?
Now he was in Paris, living with Pfuel, in a frenzy of anxiety
over his fate. Again he immersed himself in his *Guiscard* manuscript; but to his despairing eye it had lost all its radiance, he
wanted nothing more to do with it. He tore it up and burned
it—and then he really had nothing more to live for. Descending
from megalomania to deepest despair, he could think of only
one way out—death—and he wanted Pfuel to die with him.

Pfuel responded in his usual easygoing way—yes, yes, it was
worth considering, they'd think it over, there was plenty of
time. But Kleist could no longer be made to laugh, Pfuel's
resistance infuriated him, he screamed and raged, his outbursts
became more and more violent. And under his calm surface,
Pfuel himself was inwardly torn. He had left the military service along with Kleist, but since then he had hit on no occupation giving promise of a satisfactory future; his family belabored him with reproaches, demanding that he cease his aimless wanderings and resume the ordered, secure life of an officer.
He found it increasingly painful to look on as Kleist destroyed
himself, and one day this ordinarily phlegmatic man lost his
temper. "This is intolerable!" he shouted. "It's not possible to
live with such a man." Had Kleist's ears deceived him? He

stared at Pfuel for a moment, turned on his heel, and left the house, slamming the door behind him.

Pfuel, too, went out; when he got home again and found their rooms empty, he was seized with alarm, and his alarm turned to terror when Kleist failed to appear the next day. Where in God's name could he be? Unable to endure waiting any longer, Pfuel ran to the Werdecks. After a brief confer- ence, the friends notified the police and the Prussian embassy, which were also without news. Where in this huge city were they to look for him? His friends looked in the most likely place, a gruesome search: every day they went to the morgue, but they did not find him.

He was no longer in Paris. "As though driven by the Furies," he made his way through northern France, craving the one thing that would give him peace—death. The "damned consul" was raising an army to invade England. A golden opportunity; Kleist would find death on the seas. On October 26, he wrote to Ulrike from Saint-Omer: "Heaven denies me fame, the great- est of this earth's treasures; like a stubborn child I am rejecting all the others it has to offer me . . . hurling myself to my death. Be easy in your mind, O Sublime One, I shall die a beautiful death in battle . . . I rejoice at the prospect of an infinitely glorious grave." Side by side with his obsessive death wish, he was racked by a headache so violent that in the end he would have "reversed the earth's axis" to be rid of it.

Then one day he saw a troop of conscripts marching down the road. He approached them, struck up a conversation, and offered to change places with one of them; but tempting as such an offer may have seemed, none took it up, they didn't trust him, God only knew who the fellow was, and what he had up his sleeve. Bitterly disappointed, Kleist watched the conscripts march off.

The episode might have had very serious consequences for Kleist, but as it happened, his whole insane escapade ended harmlessly enough. A French army doctor with whom he was acquainted ran into him near Boulogne and, alarmed at seeing him so wild-eyed and exhausted, asked him where he had come from, where he was going, and if he had a passport. No, Kleist had nothing of the kind. Was he blind, the Frenchman asked, to the danger of his situation? Not long ago, a German nobleman had been arrested under similar circumstances and shot as a Russian spy. Since Kleist had come looking for death, one might suppose that this would have been just what he wanted, but not at all—being shot as a spy was a far cry from the glorious death to which he aspired, so in the end he listened to reason. Entrusting himself to the Frenchman's protection, he followed him to Boulogne as his "servant." Then, though he persisted in his *idée fixe* of joining the army, he let himself be persuaded to apply to the Prussian ambassador in Paris for a passport and for authorization to join the French army. Prepared by the Werdecks and Pfuel, Lucchesini, the ambassador, replied by return mail; four days after sending his petition, Kleist received a passport, valid for only one purpose: immediate return to Potsdam.

Once he realized that this was an order, his resistance collapsed. Almost mechanically, he started on his way. Pfuel had left Paris by the time he arrived, but Adolphine von Werdeck was still there. He continued on his way in a kind of trance; the motives for his recent actions had become more and more uncertain to him. All he knew was that he was returning willy-nilly to those whose expectations he "had aroused with all his boastfulness." And here he was, defeated, his head uncrowned, a total failure; he had not even succeeded in committing suicide. So much bitterness was too much for him, and in Mainz he collapsed.

Help came from a friend of Wieland's, an eminent physician, the Baron Dr. von Wedekind, who—as Ulrike tells us—liked Kleist so well at their first meeting that he immediately invited him to stay at his house, where he could keep him under observation, for at the moment he did not see what there was to cure. Kleist's ailment proved as stubborn as it was mysterious. For months, he left his bed only to sit in his room. Wedekind consulted Wieland, who in his reply praised Kleist's genius, but explained that he had always behaved oddly. Kleist himself had no doubt that his trouble was psychological; recognizing the need of adjusting to everyday life, he had hit on the idea of hiring himself out to a carpenter near Koblenz, and Wieland thought the idea must have been suggested by his "guiding spirit." Nothing came of it, or of Dr. Wedekind's attempt to have him employed in a friend's office. For a time he lived at a parsonage near Wiesbaden and it was then—to judge by the vague hints at our disposal—that he may have made the acquaintance of the canoness Karoline von Günderrode, a wildly romantic poet, who two years later killed herself for love: with a knife in her bare breast and a towel weighted down with stones around her neck, she was found in a willow thicket on the bank of the Rhine near Langewinkel. Kleist did not remain at the parsonage for long; the parson's daughter fell in love with him, and he was obliged once again to leave a hospitable house.

He was a sick man; but when at last he summoned up the strength to continue his journey and stopped with the Wielands in Weimar, he was still "that enchanting Kleist" in little Luise's eyes. "Composing [herself] with difficulty" for her meeting with him, she found him unchanged—his thoughts, his gentle modesty, his charm, which had so captivated her the preceding year. He stayed only a few days.

And now, after an absence of many months, he returned to his home and native land, which he had resolved not to see again until he had covered himself with glory. One June evening in 1804 he arrived in Potsdam and appeared in Pfuel's room like a ghost. Pfuel had already gone to bed. It was not a happy reunion—Pfuel was about to eat humble pie, to resume his military career under pressure from his family, and as for Kleist, what was to become of him?

It seems that when news of his arrival reached Ulrike, she hurried to Potsdam and forced him to take the "exceedingly painful" step of returning to Frankfurt. A family council ensued and, as might have been expected, it was decided—Ulrike concurring—that Kleist must give up his aimless wanderings once and for all, convert himself into a normal hard-working member of his class, and embark on a career befitting his station. This, of course, meant obtaining a government post, and once he had done so, the family would help him—with a monthly income of twenty-five reichstalers.

In obedience to family orders, Kleist went to Berlin in search of employment, and, with what feelings it is easy to imagine, started by taking the most indispensable step, calling at the royal palace in Charlottenburg. Karl Leopold von Köckeritz, the king's aide-de-camp, a short fat man, received him with a frown. When Kleist asked if he had the honor to be known to Köckeritz, the reply was a curt: "Yes." Kleist set forth his business. He started by admitting that while in France he had written Marquis Lucchesini a rather odd letter, attributable, he assured Köckeritz, to his state of depression at the time. He inquired whether he might count on His Majesty's sense of justice to grant his petition for employment. After a moment's thought, Köckeritz asked if he had really, that is *fully*, recovered. And when Kleist gave him a puzzled look, he expatiated: "I mean, have you really recovered from all the silly ideas that were in fashion not so long ago?" As calmly as possible, Kleist replied that he had been physically ill, but that except for a slight weakness, which the baths would undoubtedly soon relieve, his health was satisfactory. Köckeritz blew his nose and, taking a somewhat friendlier tone, observed: "Young man, you are in our bad books": he had left the army, turned his back on the civil service, wandered about foreign countries, considered settling in Switzerland, written "verses," tried to enlist in Bonaparte's expedition against England, and so forth and so on. The tears welled up in Kleist's eyes. Controlling himself as best he could, he replied that he could provide explanations for everything he had done, that there had been no political motive behind his attempt to join Napoleon's army, and that his actions were more the province of a physician than of a court of law; would it not be the height of cruelty to hold a sick man, driven half mad by his suffering, responsible for his acts? Köckeritz, who was as good-natured as he was limited in outlook, showed his frowning face again. The king, he informed Kleist, was not set against him; Kleist could try, he could write him a letter, but in anticipation of a refusal he should append a request for permission to seek his fortune abroad. "No!" Kleist cried. He wanted to live in his own country. Perhaps, said the other, somewhat mollified, *per-*

*haps* His Majesty would change his mind, and if so, he, von Köckeritz, promised not to stand in his way. Kleist thanked him for this "favor" and prepared to take his leave, whereupon Köckeritz went so far as to beg his pardon if he had offended him, cursing his position, which forced him to antagonize everyone. With the assurance that his only sentiment toward him continued to be one of veneration, Kleist bowed and left the palace.

So that was how they treated him, that was how they felt about him! Kleist's only consolation was Wieland's letter, which he carried about with him everywhere. He drew it from his pocket, read it, heaved "a deep sigh," and so comforted himself for the humiliation he had suffered. On his return to Berlin, he wrote to the king in a tone which, as he reported to Ulrike, would give him no cause for regret, regardless of how the matter turned out. And now there were any number of unpleasant steps to be taken. Oh, how he loathed every one of them. "I cast myself at your feet, my big girl; perhaps the wish I cannot utter will touch your heart after all."

But Ulrike's decision was firm; she had hardened her heart and had stopped listening to unuttered wishes; she did not even answer her brother's letter. Yet in the end things were not made as unpleasant for him as he had expected. He bore the name of a respected old family, he belonged to the best society, friends who were not put off by his youthful errors had influence at court and elsewhere; Adolphine von Werdeck and Marie von Kleist were close to the queen; Marie von Kleist's brother-in-law, the amiable Colonel von Massenbach, had excellent connections with various government offices, and her brother, Major von Gualtieri, had recently been transferred to the Foreign Ministry, where his prospects for the immediate future were bright: he was soon to become ambassador to Madrid, not because Count von Haugwitz, the Foreign Minister, wished it, but because the influential privy councilor, Johann Wilhelm Lombard, had intrigued in his favor. This Major von Gualtieri, formerly the king's aide-de-camp, was a witty eccentric. He took an immediate liking to Kleist. Since Kleist's petition for employment, despite repeated calls on Köckeritz, remained unanswered, Gualtieri offered to apply to the king for permission to take Kleist to Spain as an attaché, and assured him that in three years at the most he would rise to the rank of legation secretary. Gualtieri was indeed infatuated with Kleist; more and more often, they took their meals together at the Stadt Paris restaurant on Brüderstrasse, and Gualtieri felt certain that his Madrid plan would go through. But Kleist was far from sharing his enthusiasm. He appealed to Ulrike: Did she really want to "banish" him to Spain? If so, God alone knew if they would ever see each other again. But Ulrike was adamant, and again he received no answer. He had no recourse but to go about his "unpleasant tasks."

But it should not be supposed that all his time was spent in the antechambers of highly placed gentlemen likely to advance his petition to the king. Through it all, he never entirely forgot his literary and artistic interests. He renewed his acquaintance with Ezechiel Benjamin Cohen, a Dutch-born merchant devoted to the arts and sciences, and frequented his salon, where he met a number of young writers: probably Rahel Levin; certainly her brother Ludwig Robert and her future husband, Varnhagen von Ense; La Motte-Fouqué's friend the young jurist Julius Eduard Hitzig, who, years later, would be instrumental in publishing Kleist's work; the taciturn Friedrich Wilhelm Neumann; and the crusty Adelbert von Chamisso, scion of a French noble family which had fled the storms of the Great Revolution. These young people, most of whom belonged to the Northern Star Association, were then engaged in publishing their *Green Almanach of the Muses*, as Chamisso was later to recall in dedicating his immortal *Peter Schlemihl* to Hitzig. Hitzig, he wrote, must surely remember the hero of his little book and how, in the "springtime" of their youth, he—that classical, legendary embodiment of the homelessness of every diaspora and emigration—had run through their sonnets.

In his dealings with his literary friends, Kleist, as Varnhagen von Ense wrote, "was vivacious and affable," but neglected to mention that he himself, if only anonymously, had published a literary work which had not been really unsuccessful but had had the typically German sort of *succès d'estime* that makes authors feel like total failures. *The Schroffenstein Family* had found enthusiastic readers, such as Charlotte von Kalb, who had read it twice "with respect and profound admiration," and Jean Paul, who in his just published *Introduction to Aesthetics* mentioned it, along with works by Novalis, Zacharias Werner, and Clemens Brentano, as giving promise of a new poetical flowering. The play had even been performed in Graz, where it was well received, especially by the press, whose enthusiasm was tempered only by two unfortunate reservations: the actors had not learned their parts properly, so that the voice of the prompter was heard almost uninterruptedly; and the text (much to its disadvantage) had been rendered from verse into prose. But, of all this, Kleist was probably unaware. As is so often the way with early literary success, it had happened behind his back, so to speak; in any event, he said nothing about it. Moreover, he could not become too deeply involved with his friends from the Cohen salon, because he had promised his family to give up literature and take up a respectable and remunerative career.

And then the dreaded goal seemed to be within reach; his prospects for obtaining a post were beginning to look up. Perhaps Adolphine von Werdeck and Marie von Kleist had influenced Queen Luise and she in turn her husband, King Friedrich Wilhelm, on his behalf. On Kleist's fourth visit, Köckeritz received him most amiably, informed him that his petition was under favorable consideration, and implored him not to risk the royal displeasure a third time, but to do all he could to hasten the still outstanding royal decree. Relieved to drop the Spanish project, Kleist complied. Gualtieri went to Spain without him and died a few months later, perhaps by his own hand, perhaps of a fever, which carried him off quickly since he refused to have anything to do with doctors or medicines. In any case, the circumstances seemed suspicious to the populace, who stoned the foreign Protestant's hearse.

While waiting for the royal decree, Kleist lived first in expensive private quarters on Spandauer Strasse, then at the far more expensive Golden Star Hotel. Thrift was not one of his virtues. A free spender, he borrowed heedlessly and, despite the poverty that plagued him all his life, never learned to handle money. It seems indeed an irony of fate that the post which presented itself should have been in the field of finance. The royal decree was handed down, Marie von Kleist's brother-in-law, Christian von Massenbach, recommended him to Karl August von Hardenberg, the Foreign Minister, and Hardenberg referred him to Finance Minister Baron von Stein zum Altenstein, who then became his patron. Kleist went to work in von Stein's office; on one occasion, it appears, he worked almost without interruption for eight days and nights, evidently to show his goodwill, the quality in which he was most lacking.

Of course, such activity could not satisfy him. He wrote to Ulrike: "I am very sad. I know you no longer have much sympathy for me, but really I am suffering enormously . . . I know you love me and want me to be happy, it's just that you don't *know* what would make me happy." And in a letter to Pfuel he sadly recalled the glorious enthusiasm which seemed a thing of the past, but which in fact never left him: "How we leapt into each other's arms a year ago in Dresden! The world lay open before us like an immeasurable race track, we were vibrant with eagerness for contest! And now, both fallen, our eyes completing the race to a goal which has never seemed so desirable, we lie in the dust where we fell! Mine, *mine* is the guilt, it was *I* who involved you, oh, I cannot say all that I feel. —Ah, dearest Pfuel, what am I to do with all these tears? . . . Never again shall we embrace each other as we did then. Someday we shall recover from our fall—from what does one not recover?—but it will not be the same when we meet on crutches . . . I shall never marry, may you be wife, children, grandchildren to me! Go no further on the path you have taken. Don't throw yourself under the boots of fate, it is merciless and will trample you. Let *one* victim suffice . . . I should like to say more, but it would exceed the dimensions of a letter."

Clearly, Pfuel, too, was unhappy. He had finally resigned himself and applied for reinstatement in the army, and a few months later was assigned to the 23rd battalion of fusiliers at Johannisberg in East Prussia. At the same time, Kleist's old army comrade Hartmann von Schlotheim attempted suicide. Marie von Kleist was "sick with fear and grief," in good part because of worry for Kleist, whose death wish she sensed and who alarmed her by sitting for hours at Schlotheim's bedside and by defending his desperate act.

This occurred in April 1805, and not long after that, Kleist's immediate problem was solved. By then he had been in Berlin for about nine months. Yielding to family pressure, he had taken the necessary steps to obtain employment "worthy of his station" and had worked hard in Altenstein's office. Everywhere well liked, he had associated with nobles and Jews, frequented aristocratic and artistic salons. But that was not all. One is startled to read this little sentence in a letter of April 1805 to Colonel von Massenbach: "At last *The Jug* is coming along." What can be meant but *The Broken Jug*? In other words, despite all his official and social exertions, he had not given up writing.

And one day Kleist was faced with an astonishing choice: either to accept immediately a post at an annual salary of 1,200 reichstalers or, if he aspired to a career in the government service, to spend a year in Königsberg at state expense, studying under Christian Jakob Kraus, the leading Prussian economist, whose former students included almost all the high officials of the land. But was there really a choice? Kleist did not hesitate for one moment. This year of study was a way out of his dilemma; when it was over, he would see. Perhaps he was deceiving his superiors and his family, but it is equally possible that he truly thought he would become a civil servant at the end of the year—in any event, there was no need to do so at the moment. He would merely take some trifling part-time post to eke out his income and otherwise enjoy a postponement and holiday, which in the end might bear some fruit.

As stipendiary of the Royal Chamber of Crown Lands with an annual grant of six hundred talers, Kleist left Berlin. He was delayed for two days in Frankfurt on the Oder for needed repairs to his carriage and arrived in Königsberg on May 6, 1805.

# 14

## KÖNIGSBERG

I N a first report to Altenstein, Kleist termed the half-official, half-academic activity imposed on him in Königsberg his punishment for an unwisely spent youth. The punishment was a mild one, and he accepted it willingly. On the very day of his arrival, he called on Hans Jakob von Auerswald and Herr von Salis, respectively president and director of the Chamber of Crown Lands, who both gave him a friendly reception and promised to draw him into all affairs likely to advance his education. In the days that followed, they introduced him to several members of the university faculty and took him to the offices of the Chamber. Thus, no sooner arrived, he found himself at the center of activity. The very first week he attended a session of the Chamber of Finance; promising to keep silent, he sat at a separate table with some officers of the Königsberg garrison, merely listening and looking on. But soon he was allowed to participate, to take the minutes, to read an occasional paper dealing with problems first of rural, then of urban taxation. He was quick to realize that a thorough study of the financial administration, not to mention the crown lands, in which he was supposed to specialize, would be most time-consuming. He therefore wrote Baron von Stein a letter pointing out that one short year would hardly suffice for all this work—a precautionary measure by which he sought, more or less unconsciously, to postpone as long as possible an irrevocable decision about his career.

Early in his second week, he attended a lecture by the celebrated Christian Jakob Kraus. A protégé of the late Immanuel Kant, Kraus, who had come to the university as a philosopher and mathematician, was now the leading economist and political scientist of the kingdom and one of the spiritual fathers of the political reform movement that was then remaking Prussia. He was a gaunt, pale, sickly little man, whose utter devotion to his work did not detract from his generosity and friendliness. He would welcome his new students, among them the sons of the highest Prussian nobility, with the question: "Well, my dear boy, what have you got to offer me?" Kleist was immediately fascinated by his lectures (which were often held at his home behind the Mint). There sat the gray little man at his desk, "with tightly closed eyes, gesticulating as though tortured by labor pains," bringing ideas into the world and dispensing them with the largesse of a rich spendthrift. He lectured without book or manuscript. When Kleist came to him, the course was far advanced and would have been too hard to follow, even though he would not broach his central topics—industry and political economy—until the winter term. This gave Kleist time to attend other classes, in law and the natural sciences, and to look around.

And look around he did—in offices and in society. He soon became a welcome guest at the home of Hans Jakob von Auerswald and his wife, the Countess zu Dohna-Lauck. Finance Councilor Friedrich August von Stägemann, the future co-editor of the *Berliner Abendblätter* and co-author of Baron von Stein's reform program, was reputed to love only "himself, his family and his country," and yet Kleist was on friendly terms with him, though perhaps even more so with the beautiful and gifted Frau von Stägemann. A third Königsberg acquaintance, Johann Georg Scheffner, Councilor for Military Affairs and Crown Lands and a member of Kraus's circle, reports in his *Memoirs* that there was "something somber and strange about Kleist" and that a certain peculiarity of speech made him, when carried away by an argument, seem hard and stubborn, qualities that were probably (or so Scheffner thought) foreign to his nature.

In any case, as an interesting young bachelor (he was then

twenty-eight) he was everywhere received with open arms, and all went well, or might have, if he had not, once again, been assailed by a variety of ailments—rheumatism, "intermittent" fever, and assorted aches and pains, especially in the abdomen, which kept him in bed for half of his second month in Königsberg and plagued him on and off during his entire stay. He himself seems to have diagnosed his illness better than any doctor—the source of his ill health, he once said, was an insuperable heartsickness. In other words, his trouble was psychological. But even illness has its advantages; it freed him from his official and social obligations and gave him time to read. It was then that he seems to have read Molière's *Amphitryon* and Montaigne's essay on drunkenness, in which the following anecdote occurs: One day a virtuous widow in a village near Bordeaux discovers that she is with child; she has an announcement read from the pulpit to the effect that she will forgive the unknown man who confesses responsibility for her condition and marry him; a young farm worker comes forward and explains: one day, when she had drunk too much of her wine, he found her sleeping so soundly and in such an indecent posture that he was able to have his way with her without waking her. Whereupon the marriage actually takes place. This anecdote and Molière's comedy are the sources of two important works that Kleist began at that time—the short story *The Marquise of O. (Die Marquise von O.)* and the comedy *Amphitryon.*

But it should not be imagined that illness or official duties cut him off from all human contact. True, he was to write later on that he was as much alone as he had been in Königsberg. He may have felt lonely there, but this does not mean that society shunned him or he society; any number of houses were open to him, he visited new friends and renewed his acquaintance with old ones. One evening at a ball he caught sight of Wilhelmine and Luise von Zenge, his former betrothed and her "golden sister." An embarrassing situation. His parting with Wilhelmine had been so dry, so abrupt, and now she was married to Wilhelm Traugott Krug, Kant's successor as professor of logic and metaphysics at the university. She was sure, Kleist thought, to be angry with him, to bear him a grudge. After three years of silence since her love had been spurned, this meeting could hardly be welcome to her. But there was no help for it. Pulling himself together, he approached Luise, asked her to dance with him, and consulted her. Would Wilhelmine wish to have anything to do with him? The "golden sister" had not changed, she comforted him and introduced him to Wilhelmine's husband, who invited him to his home.

Wilhelmine bore him no grudge; perhaps because she had never loved him, or at least not as she loved her husband. She had preserved her old feelings of admiration and gratitude, which were known to the good-natured Krug but did not trouble him. As she herself said, she could never become indifferent to Kleist, and now, when he came to see her in her comfortable, well-ordered home, he met with the friendliest of receptions. After a brief moment of embarrassment, he felt more at ease than he had years before when he had made impossible demands on her in trying to link her fate to his. The sisters found him "calmer and more serious" and enjoyed his frequent visits. Wilhelmine was no longer upset by his presence. Now that she was happily married, the quality which had proved so upsetting to many women, the wholehearted enthusiasm he put into his momentary attentions (his "childlike devotion," as Wilhelmine called it), had ceased to be a threat. At the most, she may have felt flattered at still being thought worthy of his interest, and their past love cast a glow of tender melancholy on their hours together. The sisters were enchanted by the "spark of fantasy" in everything he said and by his way of reading aloud. He seems, among other things, to have read them passages from his works in progress. And playing just a little with fire, he wrote for Wilhelmine his charming poem *The Two Doves* (*Die beiden Tauben*), after La Fontaine's fable. The allusion to "the dear girl's arbor" is transparent, and the poem ends with the poignant question: "Are the days of love then ended?"

As we see, he was not entirely alone. In addition, Ulrike turned up in Königsberg, though we do not know exactly when, and stayed with him for a time. It is to their life there together that we owe his brilliant essay dedicated to Rühle von

Lilienstern, *On the Gradual Formation of Ideas in Speech* (*Über die allmähliche Verfertigung der Gedanken beim Reden*), which shows remarkable psychological insight and throws considerable light on the author's thought processes. In it he tells how, while trying to solve a certain problem, he would fix his eyes on the brightest point in his surroundings—namely, the lamp—and without stirring from the spot start discussing his problem with his sister, who was sitting over her needlework behind him. Thus, he would feel his way out of his perplexity, little by little raising to consciousness the solution that had lain darkly dormant within him. What lent wings to his thought was not so much the questions his listener might ask as her expectation that what he had begun as a question would end as an answer, especially if she made a movement suggesting a desire to interrupt him, for this encouraged him to reward her impatience with a crowning conclusion. Of course, Kleist was not the first thinker to have this experience, but the lucidity and thoroughness with which he described it, advancing from the subjective to the universal, illustrating the process by historical and other examples, showing step by step how speech and the development of ideas go hand in hand, and coming at last to the conclusion: "It is not *we* who know, it is primarily a certain *state* we are in that knows"—all this is highly original and modern enough to do honor to any Freudian.

The essay shows us one charming aspect of Kleist's life with Ulrike in Königsberg; but their life together had another, less gratifying side. There was constant friction and no real harmony between them; their quarrels were often stormy. Their conflicting temperaments made it impossible for them to live together for any length of time, and Kleist, as he later admitted, was "violent, uncontrolled, and unjust." Ulrike can hardly have failed to notice how, for all his good intentions, her brother kept backsliding into literature, thus sabotaging the family's plan for a respectable career in the civil service. *The Broken Jug* was almost finished, *Amphitryon*, *The Marquise of O.*, and another short story, *The Earthquake in Chile* (*Das Erdbeben in Chili*), were coming along, new plans were waiting in the back of his mind; in short, he had many irons in the fire, and though occasionally weakened by fatigue and all manner of ailments, he had no cause for self-doubt. Undoubtedly, his ill health, that "amazing linkage of the mind with a bundle of bowels and entrails," as he called it, was closely related to his struggles and difficulties with his work, and consequently little more than the shadow side of his productivity. If he nevertheless felt "unhappy," it was not for any tangible reason, but because of "something fundamental" to his nature. In any case, he was far from holding his current circumstances to blame, for toward the end of the stipulated year he applied for an extension of his stay in Königsberg, which Altenstein willingly granted.

Meanwhile, in the outside world, the waves of history were surging high. That "damned consul" had made himself emperor; his plan for invading England, in which Kleist had hoped to find liberation and death, had been frustrated once and for all by the destruction of the French and Spanish fleets at the battle of Trafalgar; reports that the Austrians and the Russians were busily preparing for war diverted the newly crowned emperor from further designs on England. Marching swiftly against the Austrians, he surrounded their main army near Ulm, forced it to capitulate, and inflicted a crushing defeat on the remaining allied armies under Kutuzov at Austerlitz. This phase of the war ended with the Peace of Pressburg and the founding of the Rhenish Confederation under Napoleon's protection. Thereupon, the "common wolf" flung himself on Prussia, which, to be sure, had countenanced his march through Franconia, but, as Kleist puts it, was standing armed and menacing at the gate through which he would have to pass on withdrawing from Austria. Prussia was at war.

Nothing could have discouraged and infuriated Kleist more than Friedrich Wilhelm III's lukewarm pursuit of this war, keeping his army in a state of almost total passivity when it was not in winter quarters, thus virtually inviting the enemy—and what an enemy!—to further aggression. "How," he cried, "can a mighty force provoke so mediocre a reaction?" The king should long ago have convened the Diet and informed the princes of the realm in no uncertain terms that this was a matter of life and death, that no other course was open to him than to seek an honorable death unless they helped him to increase the strength of his army by three hundred thousand men. Was that so impossible? "Suppose he had had all his gold and silver plate melted down for coin, got rid of his chamberlains and horses, suppose his whole family had emulated him, and he, after setting this example, had ascertained the will of the nation! I do not know how much or how little he enjoys the food he eats off his silver plate, but I am sure the emperor in Olmütz is not enjoying his meals." He took a gloomy view of the future; these times, these tumultuous times, would sweep away everything that was old and venerable (and, true enough, the Holy Roman Empire was soon to breathe its last), and a federation of half-baked principalities subservient to the Corsican adventurer would take over all Europe—how was it possible that someone, a refugee perhaps, did not put a bullet through the brain of this "evil genius of the world"!

As for Kleist's friends, Pfuel was in the field with the army, and Kleist knew he was one to give his last breath to save "the lost honor of his country"; nor would Rühle, though not yet in active service, hesitate, when the time came, to seek a glorious death: "For, as things stand, we can count on little more than a beautiful end." And he himself? Well, he was on his way to becoming a civil servant, meanwhile busying himself with all sorts of important questions, in particular those connected with free trade, which was his favorite field—insofar as any aspect of government service could be called a favorite with Kleist. His heart was not in it, his heart belonged to art, "and perhaps the times have never been right for art; art, so they say, has always gone begging; but nowadays it is left to starve."

As we have seen, he had many irons in the fire, both plays and stories. It was at this time, most likely, that he set to work seriously on a theme he had been toying with for some time: *Michael Kohlhaas*. It seems that Pfuel had called his attention to the story, and that he had then read the details in the *Märkische Chronik* of Peter Hafftiz, which relates how in the year 1540 the merchant Hans Kohlhaas was publicly executed in Berlin along with his apprentice, Nagelschmid, for having pillaged, robbed, and murdered to avenge himself on the Elector of Saxony, whose officials had trampled on his rights. Clearly, this was a subject made to order for Kleist; it fell in with his excessiveness, his insistence on absolutes, and provided a magnificent illustration of the maxim he had formulated in *The Schroffenstein Family:* "For the sense of justice outweighs all else." How far he got with this story in Königsberg, it is hard to say; dating of this sort is always a difficult and thankless task with Kleist, in view of his unorthodox working methods and the scanty information at our disposal. Suffice it to say that *Kohlhaas* was a new item on his program, and one which he never abandoned. In any case, he could not complain of any lack of material, and had it not been for his quality of dogged perseverance, his "resignation," as he called it, he might easily have been intimidated by the magnitude of the tasks ahead of him.

He did, however, begin to ail, and it was then that he first considered the possibility of jettisoning all unnecessary ballast; that is, despite his promises to his family, of giving up the studies that were supposedly preparing him for government employment. Ulrike must have been furious, and this may well have accounted for the breakup of their household in Königsberg. Be that as it may, we know that in the spring of 1806 she went to Schorin, the Pomeranian estate of her brother-in-law Philipp von Stojentin, where she may have considered buying property and settling.

A few more months were to pass before Kleist applied to Altenstein for his discharge. Making no secret of his reasons, he wrote, employing an image of which he had only recently made literary use: "I am sitting on a precipice, my noble friend, my spirit perpetually overlooking the abyss, where the hope of my life has perished: now winged by the desire to pull it up by the hair, now dejected by a feeling of insuperable incapacity." And it is even more psychologically revealing when, speaking of his inadequacy at a session of the Finance Committee, he says: "All through the winter I have been flustered when it came my turn to report: the subject I am to report on vanishes from my mind and it is as if I had a blank page before my eyes." These words speak for themselves. Utterly possessed by his writing, he was not available for anything else. Without even waiting for Altenstein's reply, he petitioned von Auerswald, president of the Chamber of Finance, to relieve him of all duties, and when a few weeks later Altenstein's answer came, offering him a six months' leave instead of a definitive discharge, he was quite satisfied; he had gained time and that meant everything to him. Again he was free, freer in fact than ever before, since the road back to captivity was now effectively cut off. In a letter to Rühle, he made it clear that he had accepted Altenstein's leave of absence only so as "to disengage myself more gently."

Financially, to be sure, things would be somewhat difficult; but now that he could devote himself unhindered to his literary work, that would keep him above water, and his salary, which would soon stop, was at least in part replaced by an "honorarium," which under the seal of secrecy Queen Luise sent him from early 1806 on—through Marie von Kleist, the kindest of all friends, who may, there is reason to believe, have taken the money from her own pocket, though she was far from wealthy. Kleist felt deeply grateful to her, and it was to her that he first sent his comedy *The Broken Jug* as soon as it was finished.

He had probably completed it in Pillau, where he went in the late summer of 1806 for a five-week cure. According to his own testimony, he spent two days out of three in bed and took the baths only a few times. In short, there was no improvement in his condition, but he worked. Small wonder that his "nervous system" was "wrecked," for he constantly overtaxed his strength. Referring to his obsession with his work, he spoke quite matter-of-factly. To Rühle he wrote: "If I write, it is only because I cannot help it . . . I am determined to support myself by my dramatic works . . . I can always write a play in three or four months; even if it brings in no more than forty friedrichsdor, that is enough for me to live on . . . Now I am working on a tragedy." True, the tone soon becomes more elevated: "I hear, my dear boy, that you, too, are busying yourself with art. There is nothing more divine. And nothing simpler. Yet, why is it so difficult? Every first move, everything unwilled, is beautiful, but once self-conscious, it all becomes crooked and perverse. O reason! O unhappy reason! Don't study too much, my dear boy." In the light of this declaration, what did he mean by saying that his conception of his artistic faculties was "a mere shadow of what it had been in Dresden"? In Dresden his conception had defied fulfillment, and it continued to do so; he would never be able to fulfill it. His dream and his temperament outran all satisfaction. And in the same letter he seems to groan under a burden too heavy for him: "Come, let us do something good and die in the process. Two of the millions who have already died and are yet to die. As though we were passing from one room to another."

But what of the "tragedy" he was working on? He was referring to *Penthesilea*. The subject, the most Kleistian he ever dealt with, was taken from a late Greek legend recorded in lost tragedies and extant vase paintings. After hard battles before Troy, Achilles kills Penthesilea, Queen of the Amazons; then, contemplating the beauty of his dead victim, he is so overwhelmed by pity that the cynical Thersites scoffs at his softness. Whereupon Achilles strikes him dead. In a variant in Benjamin Hederich's *Mythological Lexicon*, presumably Kleist's principal source, Penthesilea first kills Achilles but, moved by the pleas of his mother, Thetis, restores him to life, whereupon he slays her. At first sight, this half-forgotten tale and its variants seem of no great interest, mere words about a savage and more or less pointless fight. Actually, it was the vagueness and barbaric impassiveness of the accounts that gave them their appeal for Kleist. His imagination, with its deep atavistic roots, was just what was needed to weave the contradictory strands of the old tradition into one and make something unique out of them.

The war, as Kleist had foreseen, turned out disastrously. On October 14, 1806, the Prussians under Prince Hohenlohe-Ingelfingen suffered a crushing defeat at the hands of Napoleon at Jena and Auerstedt; two weeks later, the victorious French army marched into Berlin, the king's ministers swore an oath of fealty to the emperor, all except Baron von Stein, who escaped with the state treasury, so giving the court which had fled to Königsberg the possibility of holding out in the eastern provinces and mustering forces for new struggles. The horrors of this war were further exaggerated by rumor; it was whispered that Napoleon had promised to let his soldiers loot the larger cities, and even if Kleist refused to believe in such extremes of malignance, he took a dark and anguished view of the future. "How frightful if this madman were to establish his empire! ... We are the subjugated peoples of the Romans"—this is the first glimmer of the idea which two years later found expression in his play *The Battle of Teutoburg Forest* (*Die Hermanns-schlacht*). This was a difficult period for Kleist. If only Ulrike had been there to sit by his bedside and hold his hand. If she had been there, "alive to the misery all about us, we would sink into each other's arms, we would forgive and forget and love each other, the last remaining consolation in such terrible times." But she was not there, he was alone; he was without news of his brother Leopold; all he knew of Pfuel and Rühle was that they were members of the Hohenlohe Corps and had possibly been annihilated along with forty thousand others. And Marie von Kleist, whom he showered with affectionate letters—for months she had neither written nor forwarded his "honorarium" from the queen. Quite apart from the money, was she alive? And the manuscripts (which ones we do not know) he had sent to Berlin to be sold—no payment had reached him, nor even any assurance that they had been received. On every side uncertainty, doubt, and gloom.

But, as he discovered to his astonishment, trouble had one good side. Whether the historic turmoil around him had really or only seemingly improved his health, it is certain that he felt "lighter and more at ease," he found people—as though taught by misfortune—"wiser and warmer, more magnanimous in their view of the world." And he could not think without tenderness of Queen Luise, who was now living here in Königsberg. "She calls this war a misfortune, yet through it she has gained more than she would have in a whole lifetime of peace and enjoyment. She is visibly developing a truly royal character. She, whose mind seemed until recently to be concerned with nothing more than the impression she made while dancing or riding, has learned to understand the whole vast cause that is now at stake. She is gathering around her our great men whom the king neglects and who alone can bring us salvation; yes, it is she who sustains what has not yet collapsed."

But the very fact that Königsberg had become the headquarters and gathering place of all Prussia's dispersed forces had dire consequences. The remnants of the defeated army kept pouring in, the city was overcrowded, and ragged, hollow-eyed soldiers roamed the streets and surrounding villages. All were hungry, only the barest trickle of supplies was getting through, and starvation threatened. As more and more soldiers arrived in the city, more and more civilians left—all those who were not under obligation to stay fled. Kleist had for some time contemplated going to Berlin, where, he thought, it would be easier to get his work published, and now it was clear that he would have to leave Königsberg.

The Elector of Saxony had joined the Rhenish Confederation, and Napoleon rewarded him by making him king. His capital city of Dresden was said to have developed a magnificent social and cultural life. It may surprise us that Kleist should have decided to exploit these advantages for himself and his work; in view of the situation in Prussia, this kingdom by the grace of Napoleon must have been an outrage to his patriotic sentiments. Yet, what with his pleasant memories of Dresden, it was surely preferable to French-occupied Berlin.

He himself admitted to Ulrike later on that he had planned to go to Dresden, "*afin d'y cultiver paisiblement les lettres et les arts.*" In January 1807 he left Königsberg by a route that would have taken him to Dresden—if circumstances had not willed otherwise.

# 15

## AN UNWELCOME DETOUR

KLEIST did not travel alone; he had several companions, two of them discharged officers like himself, the former second lieutenants Carl Franz von Gauvain and Christoph Albert von Ehrenberg. Presenting their discharge papers, the three travelers procured passports in Köslin, had them visaed in Damm and Stettin, where they first encountered French troops, and continued on to Berlin, their first stopping place. Berlin appears to have been a more or less necessary choice, but it was not a fortunate one. Arrived there, the company dispersed. Thinking it advisable to respect the regulations, the former officers, Kleist, Gauvain, and Ehrenberg, presented themselves to the French military government to have their passports countersigned.

But that was not so simple; they were questioned, their discharge papers were scrutinized—hmm, discharged Prussian officers, coming from Königsberg, the Prussian headquarters; wasn't that an odd trip to be taking in the midst of a war? They protested their innocence, cited any number of highly respected persons as references—all very well, but their references were themselves Prussians, so naturally they would back one another . . . In short, they could perfectly well be spies. This was not the first or last time Kleist was suspected of espionage. In the course of his trip to Würzburg in the autumn of 1800, he himself, by the mystifications in his letters, had aroused the suspicion that he was engaged in some sort of industrial espionage on behalf of a Berlin ministry; in 1803, when the army doctor came across him near Boulogne, his wandering about in the midst of the Bonapartist armies mustering for the invasion of England lent plausibility to a far more dangerous presumption; and now, in February 1807, the French military government in Berlin was inclined to believe that this discharged—if he was discharged—Prussian officer must be traveling on a secret mission for the enemy. Each day the three were interrogated, and on the third day their discharge papers were pronounced false. All three were arrested and the following morning transferred to Wusterhausen, where they were shut up in a gruesome underground cell. It was then decided that they were to be sent via Mainz, Strassburg, and Besançon to Joux, a château on the road from Pontarlier to Paris.

Suspicion of espionage was not expressly stated as the reason for their deportation. But this made their situation rather worse than better, for since the authorities never decided whether to regard them as secret agents or as officers, as prisoners of state or prisoners of war, they benefited by none of the advantages ordinarily accorded to one or the other category. True, they were permitted to lodge a protest with General Clarke, the supreme French commander in Berlin. But this, too, did them more harm than good; for, since Clarke was said to be a reasonable, fair-minded man, they kept hoping for a favorable decision and neglected to avail themselves of repeated opportunities for flight; meanwhile, the deportation proceedings took their course.

In one respect, their situation improved; at most of the stopping places on their journey, they were confined not in prisons but in hotel rooms, with guards posted at the door. True, they themselves had to pay for the rooms, or rather, since Kleist had no money, Gauvain and Ehrenberg paid. But physical hardship and lack of funds do not seem to have clouded Kleist's spirit. In a letter to Ulrike, asking her to intercede with General Clarke to obtain his freedom, he told her not to worry and assured her that of the three captives it was he who would suffer least from their misadventures, for, given halfway tolerable living conditions, he could carry out his literary plans as readily in France as anywhere else.

From Alsace on, there were signs of spring; in Besançon, roses were in bloom, but on March 5, 1807, when they reached the Fort de Joux on the north slope of the Jura, there was still three feet of snow on the ground. The old castle, by then maintained only as a prison, stood cold and bare on a cold bare rock, a gloomy, forbidding sight. The sky was overcast and such a storm was raging that, climbing the slope on foot, they were obliged to lean into the wind and fight with all their strength to keep from being blown off the narrow, ice-covered path. On their arrival at the fort, their money—Gauvain's and Ehrenburg's, that is—was taken away. With Kleist serving as interpreter, an officer assured them that they would be well treated during their stay. Then they were led through passage after passage and door after door, each of which was bolted behind them, to their "living quarters," three vaulted dungeons hewn out of the rock and completed with great granite blocks, provided with small, heavily barred windows that admitted but little light and air. Gauvain, as it happened, occupied the very same hole where Toussaint L'Ouverture, the Haitian rebel and liberator, had died after his defeat and capture by Napoleon's General Leclerc, a circumstance which at a later date was to provide Kleist with the inspiration for his short story *The Betrothal in Santo Domingo (Die Verlobung in St. Domingo).*

When the three prisoners were brought their meals, an officer accompanied the orderly and watched them closely; the prison administration was so afraid of "sinister machinations" that, as Kleist whimsically observed, it was a wonder they were allowed knives and forks. So hypersensitive under normal circumstances, Kleist was more equal, physically as well as morally, to the present hardships than were his comrades, who soon fell sick. It was Kleist who appealed to the authorities to provide them with medical care. The commander of the fortress was not a bad man. He interceded with his superior officer, the military governor of Besançon, and obtained certain improvements in the treatment of the prisoners. They were transferred to more inhabitable cells and allowed to take walks on the ramparts. Spring weather had set in and the countryside was taking on a distinctly romantic look. Reasonably at ease in his new quarters, Kleist was now able to work. His spirits rose and he stopped complaining about his situation. His only real trouble was financial—for the status of the prisoners had not been established and they received no remuneration or compensation of any kind. Fortunately, the funds of Kleist's two companions were returned to them, and they helped him out.

Immediately after their arrival, the three had sent a petition to the Minister of War in Paris and a copy to Prince August of Prussia, who was then a prisoner of war. The petition now bore fruit. The ministry ordered their release from the Fort de Joux and their transfer to Châlons-sur-Marne, where, in return for their solemn promise to make no attempt to escape, they were granted full freedom of movement. True, they were obliged to pay for the journey as they had for the journey from Germany; and when in Châlons they reiterated their request for the usual prisoner's pay, it was again received with a helpless shrug—oh, it was not ill will, it was something far worse, namely bureaucracy, that denied them their rights. Their deportation order did not make it clear whether they were prisoners of state or prisoners of war; consequently, they were nothing at all, and could therefore make no claims—a situation as ridiculous as it was maddening.

Kleist did everything humanly possible, wrote again to the Minister of War and to Prince August, and preserved his equanimity through it all. "You have every reason to hope," he wrote to Ulrike, "that these evils will leave me untouched, for I have had ample experience of far greater ones." And indeed, he had the power to endure outward mishaps stoically; money, urgently as he needed it, and even fame, much as he longed for it, were not absolute necessities—this he had realized while still in Königsberg: "For it is not in order to acquire something that we live here below: fame and all the goods of the world turn to dust with our dust."

In the days when Kleist, so well armed against adversity, was strolling through the streets and gardens of Châlons-sur-Marne, a lonely man in a foreign country, his second book appeared in Germany. This was his comedy *Amphitryon*, published at Easter 1807 by Christoph Arnold in Dresden.

Kleist's *Amphitryon* owes a good deal to Molière's, but not its core and essence. The story, treated both as tragedy and as comedy in ancient literature, is briefly as follows: Jupiter falls in love with Alcmene, wife of the Theban general Amphitryon, but she is so virtuous that he is able to approach her only by assuming the form of her husband; on his visits to her he is accompanied by Mercury in the guise of Amphitryon's servant Sosias, who has been married for eleven years to the quarrelsome Charis. While Amphitryon is defeating the Athenians at Pharissa, killing their leader, Labdakus, and sending Sosias to Thebes with Labdakus's jewels as a present for his wife, the deluded Alcmene is lying in Jupiter's arms, enjoying a glorious night of love that makes her feel closer to her husband than ever before. Sosias arrives in Thebes, but Mercury stands at the gate of the palace, refuses to let him in, belabors him with blows, and insists that he, Mercury, is the true Sosias, while Sosias himself is a mere impostor. Uncertain of his own identity, Sosias hurries back to Amphitryon, and the two return to Thebes together. From then on, the story deals with the interaction of the two trios, Jupiter–Alcmene–Amphitryon and Mercury–Charis–Sosias.

This situation, it goes without saying, gives rise to the most fantastic muddles. Not content with having enjoyed Alcmene's love, Jupiter wants her assurance that he is preferred to her husband, whose deified mirror image he is, and that she values his night above all her other nights of love. In order to obtain this admission from Alcmene, he torments the poor woman with all sorts of questions and ambiguous hints, until she is so confused that she could not if her life depended on it say which of the two identical figures standing before her spent the previous night with her, whether it was Jupiter or Amphitryon, who at this point realizes how cruelly he has been deceived, since he was at Pharissa when Alcmene thought she was in his arms. And parallel to this tragic imbroglio, which is parodied as in a distorting mirror, runs a comedy of errors enacted by Mercury, Sosias, and Charis. The satire serves as a kind of commentary on the drama. At the end, the whole tragic-comic entanglement is resolved by Jupiter's promise of mercy.

Goethe observed that the end of this play was weak, Amphitryon's fate cruel and Alcmene's embarrassing. All of which is true, but such objections are far from doing justice to the play as a whole—to the strange tenderness and secret torment of the lusting god or to the brilliant, richly faceted development of the situations, which flow naturally from the passion of an omnipotent god for his creature and from the touching love experience of two human beings, and which never seem contrived or descend to frivolity. The grotesque subplot, the adventure of Mercury, Charis, and Sosias, serves to ennoble the driving passion of Jupiter, Alcmene, and Amphitryon, since the burlesque parallel suggests that what on the "higher" level is represented as sublime and heroic is at the same time part and parcel of everyday human life. True, the resolution of the psychological conflict by Jupiter's explanation and promise of mercy is hardly satisfactory. True, Amphitryon's fate is "cruel" and Alcmene's "embarrassing." But—and this is the crux of the matter—is not the story, as Kleist tells it, true? Where, before Kleist, had this deception, this emotional confusion been treated with greater truth? Where had this theme been treated with equal depth, subtlety, and sureness of touch? That this subject matter touched a profound chord in Kleist can be seen from the letters he wrote during his journey to Würzburg, when his penchant for mystification, not yet transposed into the realm of art, led him to play a game of cat-and-mouse, wounding in the very act of caressing. This was a basic trait of character and, beginning with the Schroffensteins, a permanent source of his artistic inspiration.

The characters in Kleist's *Amphitryon*, both singly and in their interplay, are truly admirable: Jupiter, who, beguiled by desire, tries to cast off his divinity but who, to promote this desire, cannot help letting it shine through now and then; Amphitryon's soldierly straightforwardness, his torments of jealousy, and his desperate fight for his identity; Alcmene, shaken in all her being by love, yet enabled by her purity of heart to preserve her dignity while giving all of herself. And

how these three are parodied in Mercury with his irresistible
effrontery, in the alternately yielding and obstinate, sly and
naïve Sosias, and in the peevish Charis, vulgar to the marrow,
who threatens her bumpkin of a husband with cuckoldry!
Every detail is full of freshness and charm, true to life and
eminently stageworthy. And what splendid language! Each
speaker has his characteristic tone, yet how wonderfully these
tones—crude and elegant, harsh and graceful, rustic and noble
—harmonize to form a dazzlingly original polyphonic unity.
To do justice to the language of this play would require as
many pages as the play itself.

After a swift sequence of tragic and comic episodes, the
play falls abruptly silent, without ceremony or ornament,
with a single final "Oh!" spoken by Alcmene, which, as Jean
Paul shrewdly noted, would mean too much if its meaning
were not so diverse. Her gasp is a question addressed at once to
the unbelievable past and to a future that has become un-
imaginable; for how is a woman who has once been loved by a
god to content herself with the love of a mere man?

It is unlikely that the attractively printed volume reached
Kleist during his stay in Châlons, where it might have cheered
him. For all his stoicism, he could have done with a little
cheer. Sometimes, to be sure, he felt that his long journey had
not taken him to a foreign country, as though his situation had
not changed at all, for he went right on working. But he
was often depressed. The news was discouraging, and he was
beginning to doubt whether this disastrous war between
Prussia and France would ever end in a peace that would
deliver him from captivity. He knew that in such a situation it
was incumbent upon him to forget his personal troubles and
"think only of the world." But this was not easy when he
was surrounded by exiles like himself, all bowed down by the
disgrace of their country and a sense of their own helplessness.
He felt "as alone as in Königsberg," or perhaps more so, for
here there was no one he could make friends with, neither
among the French, whom he had always detested (and now
more than ever, because of the way they had treated him), nor
among these particular Germans.

One evening as he was sitting in the Jard, a little-frequented park, a stranger addressed him in a voice as deep and calm as Pfuel's. Kleist was overwhelmed with melancholy; everything the stranger said to him there in the darkness was vibrant with feeling and recalled the talks Kleist had had long ago with his faraway friend; the recurrent theme was death—life's eternal refrain . . . But this was only a twilight dream; soon he was alone again with his longing to pour out his heart.

He often felt that those at home had forgotten him, but there he was mistaken. The always helpful Marie von Kleist, Ulrike, and even War Minister von Angern made repeated representations to General Clarke, pointing out that there had been no valid reason to deport Kleist and even citing his literary reputation as an argument. In his reply to Ulrike, Clarke called her attention to the fact that her brother was a Prussian officer; that by traveling in civilian dress "to the rear of the French army" he had run the risk of being shot as a spy; and that under the circumstances he had been treated with forbearance. Nevertheless, Clarke went on, he had just petitioned the War Minister to release him. But the spring passed and Kleist was still a prisoner. He suspected Clarke of putting Ulrike off with empty promises. His financial situation was as bleak as ever. For all his complaints, he had not received one centime of pay.

Then in June things began to look up. The Châlons commandant saw the light and arranged for Kleist to receive the customary *traitement* accorded prisoners of war, thirty-seven francs a month. And once again Ulrike, though by then her resources were greatly diminished, came to the rescue with a check. Kleist had still other money owing to him, but somehow it had not arrived, though Rühle, the most reliable of friends, was taking care of the matter.

Though not yet officially discharged from the Prussian army, Rühle had for some time been living as a civilian in Dresden. He was looking for work, writing a book for Cotta, the Tübingen publisher, and, in between, attending to Kleist's affairs. It was almost certainly Rühle who had sold Kleist's *Amphitryon* to Arnold, and undoubtedly he whom Kleist asked to press Arnold for the payment that had been due on publication, some ten weeks before. All Germany was in a turmoil, and we have no way of knowing what had gone wrong. It seems unlikely that Arnold had neglected to pay or that Rühle had delayed sending the money; all we know for sure is that Kleist did not receive it while in Châlons—a niggardly fee at all events, twenty-four louis d'or, not quite five hundred francs, hardly a third of what he would have received under normal conditions. From a letter to Ulrike, we learn that he had two other manuscripts ready, but these were the product of a year's work, which should, he felt, have kept him for two years, yet, as things stood, would scarcely suffice for six months. At about this time, Rühle sold a short story, *The Earthquake in Chile*, which Kleist had written in Königsberg, to Cotta, who published it in the *Morning Journal for the Cultivated Classes (Morgenblatt für gebildete Stände)*.

In view of Kleist's considerable literary output, one thing was clear: when set free, it would be advisable for him to "settle where the book trade is still more or less functioning"—and that meant Dresden. "When set free!" If Clarke's order for his release had arrived just then, at the beginning of June, Ulrike's check and the "travel indemnity" granted to officers would have enabled him to start out. But the order did not come.

But then history intervened. On July 7, 1807, the Peace of Tilsit, a peace as catastrophic as the war it ended, was signed; Prussia was crushed, reduced to half its former area, Westphalia became a French vassal state under Napoleon's youngest brother, Jérôme Bonaparte, King "Immer lustik" ("Always merry"), as he was nicknamed. Only those acquainted with the fierce tenacity of its people could have imagined that Prussia would rise again to become a great power. But this evil, like so many others, had its good side—historically for Prussia, which was forced to take stock of itself, and personally for Kleist, to whom it gave his freedom. The release order, which arrived on July 13, put him on his honor to follow a certain itinerary and to report to General Clarke in Berlin. "What a monstrous thing," he wrote in indignation, "to drive a man from country to country, without stopping to ask where he is to get the money." At first he was not even granted the travel indemnity to which he was entitled. After writing to Rühle, pressing him to send the money due him from Arnold, he more or less resigned himself to waiting for the check to arrive from Dresden, postponing—all the more readily since the excitement had made him ill—his journey for two or three weeks. He wrote Ulrike to this effect the next day, and yet, despite his illness, he was unable to hide his joyful impatience. Marie von Kleist, he wrote, had assured him that, now that the war was over, Queen Luise's honorarium would be resumed and for safety's sake converted into some sort of annuity, which, he said, he would cede to Ulrike so that she, who had been impoverished by his fault, would now be enriched and made independent by his doing. It seems that Ulrike had spent so much money on her brother that she had been obliged to take refuge with wealthy relatives; but with this income, her brother assured her, she would be able to set up a small household of her own; he would move in with her, and they would live together, she would read books and travel on maps as she had done in the old days, while he would write —oh, she must not think of him as the man he had been in Königsberg, then he had been unhappy, but there is "none gentler, none more amiable than your brother when he is happy!"

It was doubtful whether Ulrike would lend ear to this siren's song; he was so unreliable, so unsteady, as he himself was well aware. In a postscript to the same letter, he revised the travel plan he had just outlined. His travel "indemnity" had been granted after all; now he would take what money he had, arrange for the Dresden check to be readdressed to Berlin, and leave Châlons in three, four days, if possible by "courier," that is, in all haste, traveling day and night, so as to reach Berlin in about two weeks. And next day he wrote to Rühle asking him to readdress the check and to find him cheap lodgings, since he was planning to spend only a few days in Berlin and then, without delay, "fly" to Dresden. Apparently, he had quite forgotten the previous day's project of setting up housekeeping with Ulrike.

He arrived in Berlin as planned at the beginning of August,

and it was there that an obscure and none too able painter may have done a miniature of Kleist and another of Ulrike. The portraits show a striking resemblance between brother and sister, though Ulrike, as short and thickset as Kleist, seems ill-tempered and does not, like her brother, force a smile between clenched teeth. The portrait of Kleist shows a broad chest and powerful shoulders, on which the small head sits with Robes-pierrean rigidity; there is a joyful sparkle in his blue eyes; his reddish hair, somewhat darker than when we saw it last, is worn in the "windblown" manner, a wisp or two straggling over his forehead; the slightly bulbous nose has a rustic quality; and a Napoleonic dimple is discernible in the round chin. It is a face charged with energy and—despite the smile—defiance. When this artistically dubious but psychologically revealing portrait was painted, Kleist was not quite thirty.

We cannot be absolutely sure the miniatures were painted in Berlin. It is not even certain whether it was during his stay there or somewhat later that he met with Ulrike. All we really know is that in mid-August he wrote from Berlin to Rühle, whose eyewitness report on the disastrous military events of autumn 1806 had been published by Cotta, advising him to ignore the violent attacks that were being made on the book, announcing his imminent arrival, and bidding him persuade Pfuel to join them.

Kleist then proceeded to Gulben near Cottbus, where Ulrike seems to have been staying with her brother-in-law, Pannwitz, and quite conceivably the miniatures were done in Gulben. In any event, he stopped there for a few days, at the end of which he and Ulrike went on to Wormlage in Lusatia, where they stayed with other relatives. On the way they had a friendly talk, in the course of which she firmly rejected his plan for setting up a household together.

At the end of August 1807, he was in Dresden.

❀❀❀❀❀

# 16

❀❀❀❀❀

## LITERARY LIFE IN DRESDEN

NEITHER before nor after did Kleist embark on his life in any of his numerous places of residence with so much well-founded hope as in Dresden in 1807. The recovery of his freedom was bound to give him new energy and inspiration; the publication of *Amphitryon* and the imminent publication of *The Betrothal in Santo Domingo* brought the young author standing and prestige; *The Broken Jug* was finished, *Penthesilea* and *The Marquise of O.* far advanced, and the *Guiscard* fragment, though he had destroyed the manuscript, was still present in his mind—all masterpieces capable of winning him the fame for which he longed, provided the circumstances were halfway favorable, and it would be hard to conceive of circumstances more favorable than those he now enjoyed in Dresden.

Thanks in part to Rühle, who had taken a post as tutor under Prince Bernhard von Sachsen-Weimar, second son of Duke Karl August von Sachsen-Weimar, Kleist was soon received in the best and most cultivated society. Rühle also managed to find employment for Pfuel—instructing the young prince in the military arts, for which he received an annual stipend of six hundred reichstalers. The three faithful comrades were reunited; Kleist and Pfuel even moved into two adjoining rooms at Rammsche Gasse 123 in the suburb of Pirna. Nothing could have pleased Kleist more. What strength and security he derived from Pfuel's unswerving friendship, from his calm, yet passionate thoughtfulness.

But most important of all for his writing and position in Dresden society was a man he now met for the first time. This was Adam Müller—gifted writer, orator, and philosopher, soon to become a leading light of the romantic school of political economy, who was quick to recognize Kleist's extraordinary abilities. After (thanks to Rühle) reading *The Broken Jug* and *Amphitryon* in manuscript, he had taken them under his wing, recommended both plays to Goethe, and written an enthusiastic, strangely mystical foreword to the Arnold edition of *Amphitryon*. For mysticism, religious and otherwise, was one facet of this complex personality. Born a Protestant, he had turned Catholic in 1805; fiercely opposed to Napoleon, he combined an unusual intellectual liberalism with rigidly conservative traits which had won him the favor of Prince Metternich when Metternich had been Austrian ambassador to the court in Dresden.

This son of a minor Berlin civil servant had a gift for attracting the interest of wealthy and distinguished persons and moved among them with extraordinary self-assurance and grace. For a time he had served as a tutor on the estate of Lord Boguslaus Peter von Haza in Posen, and in 1805, when the family had moved to Dresden for the sake of the children's education, he had come with them. Through his influence on Frau von Haza, the Haza soirees soon became gatherings largely of his friends. Impassioned and often mercilessly critical discussions were held, as we learn from Friedrich von Gentz, the most influential, most highly paid German journalist of the day, whom Adam Müller had won over to Kleist's "immortal genius." *Amphitryon*, said Gentz, was the first German literary work in years that he had read with pure enjoyment, and since he had been in the Austrian service since 1802 and had influential connections in Vienna, his opinion carried a good deal of weight.

Yes, Adam Müller was a many-sided man. He frequented the house of Appellate Judge Christian Gottfried Körner, friend of Schiller and lover of the arts, and was a welcome visitor at the home of Baron Buol-Mühlingen, secretary of the Austrian Legation. At the house of Karl Adolf von Carlowitz, one of the richest men in Saxony, Müller, during the autumn and winter of 1807, delivered a series of lectures based on his book, which had appeared the year before, *On German Science and Literature,* which Goethe had "read, in fact studied, though with mixed feelings," and to which Friedrich Schlegel had devoted a detailed review. In short, when Kleist arrived in Dresden, his admirer, Adam Müller, was a respected writer and a figure well established in social and literary circles.

As one might expect of a man as erratic and many-sided as Müller, he made different impressions on different people. Some spoke of his inborn noblesse and dignity, others of affectation and stilted politesse; Ludwig Tieck thought him "repulsive, self-righteous, pompous, and affected"; according to Varnhagen von Ense, he was complicated but fascinating; Chamisso made fun of the "sedate Monsieur Adam, who, God knows, is not the greatest man in the world"; Clemens Brentano calls him a "most amiable, good-natured man, a better friend than one might have imagined"; and Pfuel had only good to say of him. This man of many faces was thought by some to have had a bad influence on Kleist. In the opinion of certain none-too-discerning Dresden contemporaries, he encouraged Kleist's self-conceit. It is true that he did not always restrain Kleist from acting rashly and may have hurt him in certain instances, and it is equally true that they became violent enemies on several occasions, though here Kleist may have been as much to blame as Müller; but what should be re-membered above all is that, apart from the elder Wieland, Müller was the only contemporary of any standing who fully appreciated Kleist's extraordinary gifts and spared no effort to convince the world of them; and to a man pursued by ill luck, failure, and incomprehension, there could have been no greater kindness. To Kleist's mind, this was undoubtedly an essential point, and it was largely on Müller's account that in 1810, forgetting their old quarrel, Kleist settled in Berlin. On the day before his death, Kleist was to think of Müller with love and esteem.

Adam Müller, as Kleist saw him in Dresden in the early fall of 1807, was slender, graceful in his movements, and something of a dandy. His face bore witness to his keen intelligence but was not exactly pleasant. With his long nose, blue eyes, short ruffled hair, he somewhat resembled his fellow romantic E. T. A. Hoffmann. Kleist, who had not experienced such deep sympathy and understanding since that "proudest moment" of his life, when he had read *Guiscard* to Wieland by the fireside in Ossmannstedt, welcomed Müller's friendship without hesitation and, soon after his arrival in Dresden, found himself in the midst of the city's social life.

In a letter to Ulrike, he described his life as "so rich" that to do justice to it in writing was quite impossible. Müller had taken him to see many of his friends and they made him feel "almost as much at home as he had felt at the Kleists' in Potsdam." He was always welcome at the Hazas'; he was cordially received at the Austrian embassy, and Buol had taken him out to Teplitz to meet Gentz, who had spoken to him of the writer Joseph von Collin, then serving as a secretary at the Austrian court, who through his connections with the Vienna Burgtheater might, Gentz thought, procure for Kleist employment as a director, and would be sure in any case to take an interest in his plays. Kleist's two comedies were read at social gatherings "to repeated applause," and one was selected by Buol for an amateur performance, in which Major von Vieth, a friend of Judge Körner, was to play a leading role.

Years before, Körner had liberated Friedrich Schiller from sterile employment as a dramatist at the Mannheim theater, and they had remained close friends until Schiller's death. Early in 1807, at Müller's suggestion, Körner had recommended Kleist's *Amphitryon*, "that remarkable poetic product," to Göschen, the Leipzig publisher, though without success. His "classical house on Kohlenmarkt," where Kleist was a frequent guest, was a gathering place of the arts, of painters, musicians, and poets. Everything under the sun was discussed, with the one strict exception of politics; there were frequent song recitals and poetry readings followed by discussions. The whole family was devoted to the arts. Dora Stock, Frau Körner's sister, had been a friend of Mozart in her younger days; now, as an elderly spinster, she was known for her ready wit and excellent pastels. Emma Körner, the daughter of the house, a gifted painter of miniatures, was also a trained singer, as was her brother Karl, who some years later, under the name Theodor Körner, was to achieve a kind of immortality as a symbol of romantic youth through his war songs and heroic death. In 1807, aged sixteen, he was already trying his hand at poetry (later, despite a certain animosity toward Kleist, he was to write a play based on *The Betrothal in Santo Domingo*). Lastly, there was Körner's adoptive daughter, Emma Julie Kunze, a girl of twenty, pretty, high-spirited, wealthy, and endowed with a delightful singing voice. It appears that Kleist was anything but indifferent to her.

He also made the acquaintance of several fellow writers. First of all there was Ludwig Tieck, only a few years older than himself and already known as the leader of the new romantic school. An acute observer, he recognized Kleist's dignified pride, found him grave and taciturn, a slow, anxious, conscientious writer, reworking time and time again, never satisfied with what he had done, but at the same time stubbornly unreceptive to the judgment of his fellow writers—a strange impression, for Tieck's influence on Kleist's writing is obvious and not always fortunate. Then there was Rühle's friend Gotthilf Heinrich Schubert, a näive mystic not devoid of scientific knowledge, who with his investigations *Concerning the Night Side of the Natural Sciences*, dealing with visions, mystical sympathies, magnetism, somnambulism, and so forth and so on, stimulated Kleist's interest in mystical phenomena; and Schubert's friend, the physician Karl Friedrich Gottlob Wetzel (long thought to be the author of the brilliant little book *The Vigils of Bonaventura*), who in 1810 was to work with Kleist on the *Berliner Abendblätter;* Friedrich Laun, the translator; Ferdinand Hartmann, a classical painter, who taught at the Dresden Academy of Art. And then there were visitors from abroad, such as the Schlegel brothers and Madame de Staël . . . all in all, an impressive circle, in which the tone was set by romanticism, which was then *the* modern movement and exerted a certain influence on Kleist, though he was not really at home in any literary movement.

According to Friedrich Laun, Kleist once asked a friend to read a passage from his, Kleist's, work aloud to him. Adam Müller, Kleist explained, read it marvelously, but: "In Müller's mouth the basest metal is transformed into pure gold. The weakest, most slipshod passage charms my ear, so it's far worse than if no one had read to me. You, my dear old fellow, on the other hand, read abominably. Your delivery throws a bright light on what has gone wrong, and that is what I need at present."

Even if artistically he was at home neither in classicism nor in romanticism, he welcomed all the help he could get in promoting his works; for he was only too well aware that in order to get on in the world he needed an apparatus which he could not hope to build by himself. He and his comrades were quick to figure out that the publisher of a relatively successful book took in roughly six times as much as the author; this had been the case with Kleist's *Amphitryon* and also with Rühle's eyewitness report, which sold well despite the violent hostility it aroused. Why should they let others reap the benefits of their toil? Kleist, Adam Müller, and their friends were beginning to attract public attention, they were on the threshold of fame. *The Broken Jug* was soon to be produced by Goethe in Weimar, and a number of new works were almost ready for publication. The young men therefore decided to found a publishing house of their own. What made the project doubly attractive was that Rühle had shown unusual business ability in other connections, but had declined Duke Karl August's offer of a responsible position, because he longed to be independent. Rühle was chosen to be the director, while Kleist, Müller, and Pfuel would be the editors. They would need a government "privilege," which cost 1,200 reichstalers but could be resold in case of failure. Thus, there was little risk involved, since they would start on a small scale and, only if luck should decide clearly in their favor, invest all the money they could raise, "on the model of the Fuggers and Medicis."

Pfuel's wealthy brother advanced him his share of the money needed, and Kleist asked Ulrike, who seems to have been rather better off than he had thought only a short while before, to lend him five hundred reichstalers for a year at five percent, if she felt halfway favorable to this promising undertaking.

A letter to Cotta written that same day suggests that the friends were planning from the very start to found a journal. In this letter Kleist asked the publisher to return *The Earthquake in Chile*, explaining that he had now returned from France and wished to dispose of it otherwise. Where could he have placed so short a piece if not in another magazine? And what magazine would he have preferred to Cotta's if not one of his own? But, as usual, Cotta could not accede to his wish, for *The Earthquake in Chile* had already appeared (from September 10 to 15, 1807) in the *Morning Journal for the Cultivated Classes*, under the title *Jeronimo and Josephe: An episode from the history of the earthquake of 1647 in Chile.*

The story is indeed a short one, taking up only a few pages. Full of life, horror, love, and death, of lust and passion, it is the story of a natural catastrophe, over which human beings triumph, only to be destroyed by an orgiastic eruption of darkest evil.

Kleist has woven so tight a mesh, so concentrated his material that its happenings seem to explode like fireworks before the reader's eyes; the whole tale has only three paragraphs, yet despite its breathless pace the author is in full control—for all its wildness, the whole is imbued with an epic serenity. And that is the very essence of Kleist: on the one hand, romantic madness; on the other, the rigid bearing of a Prussian officer—an almost unbearable tension that would have destroyed a man of weaker will. Side by side with deepest despair "in this wretched world," he experienced with equal intensity a delight in this "rich, sweet, colorful life," and with apparent ease forged a harmony of such conflicting sentiments. The reader may feel, to be sure, that so compact a tale makes excessive demands on him; he may even find it difficult to keep the names of the characters straight throughout the story's breathless moments. It is a work that demands concentration because it is a product of concentration and cannot be approached in any other way.

With *The Earthquake in Chile*, Kleist made his first appearance as a storyteller. To the realm of narrative prose he brought something utterly new, as he had to drama. Owing nothing to any storyteller of his day, he had developed a voice that would carry far into the future.

We do not know how *The Earthquake in Chile* was received by the public. The gruesome situation underlying it may, in some quarters, have been taken as an offense against good taste. But the mere fact of its publication in Cotta's prestigious *Morgenblatt* was bound to work in its favor. Moreover, there were many at the time who *wanted* Kleist to be famous, who cosseted his young fame. He was the object of much flattery at the rehearsals for the amateur performance of his comedy at the Austrian embassy. At a banquet given in his honor he was crowned with laurel, "and this by two of the most charming hands in Dresden." Did these hands, as society gossip suggested, belong to Julie Kunze, Körner's adoptive daughter? Rumor had it that Kleist had asked Julie to become his betrothed and to write him letters without the knowledge of her foster parents. When she declined, still according to unsubstantiated rumor, he had—first after three days, then after three weeks, and finally after three months, during which he did not go to see her—repeated his plea, and after the third refusal dropped her. We know that he was given to mystification and secrecy; we know that the aging spinster Dora Stock was not very fond of him and may well have intrigued against him; but the pedantically graduated repetition of his plea to Julie seems compatible neither with his character nor with the circumstances, since he continued to be a frequent guest at the "classical house on Kohlenmarkt."

A young writer can only be pleased at being taken up by gossip; it is a symptom of his rising popularity. Kleist had, indeed, every reason to be content. He was working, and when he looked around he saw that the world was in full bloom, everyone was talking about him, and the prospects for the future were bright. True, Ulrike was taking her time about answering his request for five hundred reichstalers, and when she finally consented, the state publishing "privilege" had been sold to another party. But this proved to be more fortunate than otherwise, for when apprised of the young men's difficulties, Herr von Carlowitz offered them a privilege in Liebstadt, a city where he enjoyed certain hereditary prerogatives. This would allow them to maintain a warehouse in Dresden and presented one great advantage over a state privilege; namely, that it would cost them nothing. And they had yet other grounds for optimism. They had made the acquaintance of the French ambassador to the court in Dresden, Monsieur de Bourgoing, who had written to Paris asking to have the new firm empowered to publish the Code Napoléon, and possibly to act as Dresden distributing agent for all French government publications. True, there was an unpleasant taste about the affair, and it was to be hoped that political inferences would not be drawn—but what good business it would be! Since such an undertaking would call for much more than the two thousand talers the friends had thus far been able to raise, Kleist advised Ulrike to increase her investment, in fact to put in as much as she could lay her hands on and take over his share of the stock, for he found it intolerable that she should content herself with a shabby five percent when the annual profit, conservatively calculated, would come to roughly twenty-two percent. He himself, he said, needed no share in the firm, he could live by his writings, for in the last month, though reserving his manuscripts for the future publishing house, he had earned almost three hundred talers from sales to magazines and theatrical performances, inclusive of the thirty louis d'or the Austrian embassy had procured for him for a performance at the Vienna Burgtheater. Yes, indeed, he was getting along splendidly, and he lacked only one thing for his complete happiness: that Ulrike should change her mind and come to live with him in Dresden, for then she would convince herself at first hand that his proposition was reasonable, and, above all, in view of all the trouble she had had with him, that his present triumph was very real.

All was vell, including the essential, his work. He was devoting as much time as possible to the tragedy begun in Königsberg; at his lodgings on Rammsche Gasse he could sometimes be heard bustling about behind closed doors, and then for a long while all was as still as if no one were living there. Meanwhile, his tragedy was nearing completion. Pfuel, who occupied the adjoining room, relates how one day Kleist stepped through the door, pipe in hand, the tears running down his cheeks in an agony of grief. Pfuel was aghast. "Why, Kleist!" he said. "What's wrong? What has happened?" And Kleist replied: "She's dead." "Dead?! Who, in God's name?" "Penthesilea, of course!" cried Kleist impatiently. Pfuel could not restrain a smile. "And you killed her," he said. Kleist thought it over and nodded. "I suppose so," he said. Then he, too, smiled and gradually calmed down. This was Pfuel's version of the scene. Kleist's is somewhat different. In a letter to Marie von Kleist, he announced the completion of *Penthesilea* with the following sentence: "She really devoured him out of love," and went on to tell how, pipe in hand, he went to Pfuel's room and informed him of Penthesilea's death. Two great tears had welled up in Pfuel's eyes. "You know his antique countenance. As he read the last scenes, death could be seen on his face. That made him so dear to me, so human."

The play, Kleist thought, was calculated to appeal to Pfuel's "warlike nature"; it was less suited to women, and for that matter, few men would like it. The play had been read twice at social gatherings and tears had flowed, "insofar as horror, which was inevitable, allowed." He thought a production unlikely and even undesirable as long as actors were trained for nothing but the sentimental trash of Kotzebue and Iffland, and as long as the audience was full of women, who falsified the whole character of drama with their moralistic prudery. Never would Greek tragedy have developed if *they* had been admitted to the audience; they should be kept out of the theater, or else a separate theater should be built for them. What surprising words to hear on Kleist's lips! Had he not just said that most men would relish this play no more than the women? Wasn't he well aware that there are just as many prudes and cranks among men as among women? As a young man, a product of the Enlightenment, he himself had preached a withering brand of morality, and now, as a mature young writer, he had been known to say that beauty cares nothing for any conventions whatsoever. Why then—since such a man could not possibly have believed that one sex provided a better theater audience than the other—why then this animosity toward women? The note of dissatisfaction with which he speaks of the reception of *Penthesilea* at public readings provides an explanation: women, especially, no doubt, Dora Stock and the other ladies of the art-loving Körner household, had reacted unfavorably; his instinct told him that attacks on his work were to be expected from this quarter, a first barely perceptible threat to the beginnings of his fame. Small wonder that his fears should have made him just a little petulant. As a poet and dramatist, he knew he was in the right, knew himself to be one with *Penthesilea,* and said as much in his next letter to Marie von Kleist: "It is true that my innermost being is in this play, and this you have seen with true clairvoyance—all the suffering and at the same time all the radiance of my soul."

Fortunately, he was leading too full a life to be seriously upset by petty annoyances; on the whole, his star was rising, the spotlight of fame had touched him—one more step and he would be at the center of it, visible to all eyes. "One of the foremost among living writers," wrote Cotta's *Morgenblatt*— what would they say when he had developed his full capacities? Of course there were obstacles to be overcome, some indeed which beset him at every turn. His physical condition was poor, as he informed his old friend Adolphine von Werdeck. His intervals of good health were short, his nervous system was shattered. But more than from any physical ills, his condition seems to have derived from his psychic makeup, from his constant struggle to hold a balance between depression and euphoria, to oppose every drive with a contrary drive—a battle of opposites that he carried over into his dramatic work.

No sooner had *Penthesilea* seen the light of day than a counterfigure, *Käthchen of Heilbronn (Das Käthchen von Heilbronn),* made her appearance. Kleist was later to call her "an excellent invention"; but in the superficial sense of the word, he was no more an inventor than most great writers. Under other names, the Käthchen theme was as old as the hills; it had been dealt with over and over again, by the Indian Kalidasa,

by Boccaccio, in countless folktales and fables, and more recently in Bürger's ballad *Count Walter*, which even in certain details anticipates Kleist's version. A body of social and
literary gossip grew up around the genesis of Kleist's *Käthchen
of Heilbronn.* One story is that Kleist wrote it to show
Körner's adoptive daughter, Julie Kunze, the true nature of
maidenly love; according to another, he had been inspired
by a "cartoon" that had fallen into his hands somewhere in
Swabia; we also hear that Schubert, in his lectures *Concerning
the Night Side of the Natural Sciences,* had referred to the
sleepwalking daughter of a Heilbronn town councilor, and
that this accounts both for Käthchen's somnambulism and for
the choice of Heilbronn as the locale. Kleist himself tells us
that certain of the play's weaknesses stem from his effort to
make it stageworthy, and it is also certain that outside in-
fluences, especially Tieck's, were at work. Later on, to be sure,
he made changes, polished and cut, so that when Tieck saw
the 1810 edition, he deplored the omission of a scene in which
Käthchen, strolling about on the top of a cliff, hears the call of
water sprites and wants to fling herself into the lake below;
a line from this lost scene had stuck in his memory: "And
there beneath the stone the sound wells up again . . ."

Regardless of the play's genesis, the material, the story of a
love bond rooted in a dream dreamed by both lovers, fell in
with Kleist's increasing penchant for mysticism and spiritual-
ism. His reading may well have played a part, but his mystical
bent was innate and so pronounced that he himself sometimes
joked about it. Pfuel tells of a visit to a female somnambulist
in Dresden, who, so it was claimed, could, without looking,
identify any metal she was touched with. Pfuel filled his
pockets with all sorts of metal objects and took the fascinated
Kleist to see her; though they prodded her with one object after
another, she only sat there with closed eyes, concentrating
and obstinately silent. Suddenly Kleist broke the silence and
tension by saying: "Look, touch her with a hard taler, she'll
know what it is." That is the typical, crudely realistic, down-
to-earth humor with which he tempered his own flights of
exaltation, the specifically Prussian wit that gives to *The*

*Broken Jug* its hearty, pithy quality, to *Amphitryon* its appeasing smile, and sometimes contributes a breath of reconciliation even to his tragedies.

In the fall and winter of the same year, Kleist and Adam Müller seem to have had their first falling out. Its cause was not literary but quite personal and intimate; to wit, Müller's affair with Frau Sophie von Haza, the wife of his former employer, at whose house Kleist was a frequent guest.

Frau von Haza, the daughter of a Polish colonel, was a woman of thirty-two. The mother of four children, she was comely and softly feminine, with a full face, a round forehead, a straight, shapely nose, slightly pouting lips, and an expression that did not seem quite trustworthy. There may have been some substance behind the report drawn up some years later by a Vienna police informer, calling her something of a gossip and troublemaker, who always said what her interlocutor wanted to hear, and then got him to do whatever she wanted. Undoubtedly, her feminine charms made a powerful impression on the opposite sex—Kleist, too, had a weakness for her, dedicated a jestingly amorous poem to her, let her look at his (unfortunately lost) journal, gave her copies of his manuscripts, and preserved his affection for her even at the most difficult times.

In the autumn of 1807 her heart veered to Adam Müller; up till then he had been her protégé, now she became the witness of his increasing success; it was *his* friends who made her salon the meeting place of Dresden's Catholicizing romantics; she fell in love with him and he with her. Rumor had it that he had abducted her "in due and proper form"; in any event, the affair created a scandal. Yet, as late as the end of November, with divorce proceedings already underway, her husband urged reconciliation; but carried away by her passion, she would not hear of it. Only a few months had passed since the unsuspecting von Haza, at Müller's request, had recommended one of Müller's manuscripts to Goethe; now he was deserted, left alone with his four children—a desperate situation, which aroused Kleist's sympathy. He took Herr von Haza's part, and his attempts to patch up the broken marriage resulted in arguments and scenes between him and Müller. But Müller was in earnest about his love and determined to marry Sophie. When Kleist saw that his efforts were in vain, he resigned himself to the inevitable. He went so far as to help the lovers to straighten out their affairs and legalize their situation.

At all events, the quarrel between Kleist and Müller was neither long-lived nor very serious, for their publishing plans meant too much to both of them. Rühle (who was on the point of becoming a major and a chamberlain at the court of Sachsen-Weimar) had just received three hundred talers for a new printing of his controversial book. If they had published it themselves, the amount would have been two thousand. Three works by Kleist were ready for the printer, *The Broken Jug, Penthesilea,* and *The Marquise of O.* What profits they would bring in! The Hardenberg family offered them the complete works of Novalis, who had died in 1801, demanding not a penny in return, but only their undertaking to bring out a splendid edition. There was talk of their being declared an "association of scholars" and granted a publishing privilege free of charge. Of course, the four already-established Dresden publishers protested, but the government wished to stimulate this branch of industry through increased competition. Every detail had been worked out; even the name, the Phoenix Publishing House, had been chosen. They were ready to start at a moment's notice, but since their privilege had not yet come through, they decided to embark on a venture that required no privilege; to wit, a literary monthly, which they named *Phöbus.*

Their calculation was simple and seemed reasonable enough. Operating costs for the whole first year would come to 2,500 talers. Pfuel would contribute 900, Rühle 700, and Kleist the 500 promised by Ulrike—for a total of 2,100 talers; the rest would be covered by receipts from subscriptions, the price of which was set at ten talers a year. True, Kleist's professed belief that *Phöbus* would face no competition to speak of was hardly realistic, since there were several similar publications in existence, the Vienna *Prometheus,* the Heidelberg *Tröst-Einsamkeit,* edited by Arnim and Brentano, Wieland's *Teutsche*

*Merkur,* and still others. He counted on fifty subscribers in Dresden and was convinced that if they acquired just one subscriber in every other German city, their worries would be over. Schiller's *Horen,* in its time, had had a circulation of three thousand. Had the prospects then been more favorable than now for *Phöbus?* Wasn't Kleist's name on everyone's lips; wasn't he, in the opinion of all the cognoscenti, a genius? Didn't his fellow editor, Adam Müller, whom August Wilhelm Schlegel called "a divine man of unfathomable learning," have a resounding name? An abundance of material from their own hands was in readiness, and they had important connections. Subscription lists would be on display at the leading foreign embassies in Dresden; copies of the first issue, printed on fine vellum, would be sent to all the courts of Europe. He never doubted for a moment that the great literary celebrities would lend their support—Goethe, who was planning a production of *The Broken Jug* for the following year; Wieland, who was so devoted to him; Jean Paul, who thought the world of his work; romantics such as La Motte-Fouqué and the Dane Adam Oehlenschläger; such prominent figures as Johannes von Müller, the Swiss historian, and the archaeologist Karl August Böttiger. No, there would be no lack of fascinating contributions, if only because *Phöbus* would be offering a fee of thirty talers a printed sheet, which of course would be suitably increased in the case of the most prominent authors.

In their effort to secure the support of leading writers, the editors spared no pains. Kleist's appeal to Wieland has been preserved. Part personal and part business letter, it evokes the days when Kleist read *Guiscard* to Wieland in Ossmannstedt, asks Wieland to recommend the new magazine and requests an occasional contribution, informs Wieland that Kleist has "coughed up" another tragedy, and with flattering tact takes account of the fact that even in his own magazine Wieland made very sparing use of his own name. The task of writing to Goethe and Gentz seems to have fallen to Müller; in any case, similar letters, some signed by one, some by the other, went out to a good many prominent persons. The editors felt certain that their "journal for the arts" would soon become a rallying point for the best literature of the day, thanks to the editorial principle forced on them by the diversity of their own writing; namely, to commit themselves to no special trend, but to take quality alone as their criterion.

A sales network was built up, with exclusive rights assigned to the most highly regarded booksellers: Bertuch in Weimar, Dieterich in Göttingen, Cotta in Tübingen, Breitkopf & Härtel in Leipzig, Perthes in Hamburg, the Realschul-Buchhandlung in Berlin, the Industrie-Kontor in Vienna. The editors wrote, printed, and mailed out an announcement which clearly defined their aims and program, and which must have created quite a stir: "We can conceive of no more honorable place for our works than side by side with others of equal distinction and rigor; opinions and works can perfectly well conflict without annulling one another. But since we ourselves are armed, we shall suffer no unarmed or lightly armed antagonist to confront us in the arena we are hereby opening."

Clearly, they were not inhibited by false modesty; in their hubris, they failed to see that such fulsome claims laid them open to the attacks of the envious. In all innocence they thought they were saying no more than the truth, and with that truth they addressed themselves to an easily ruffled public and to their real or supposed friends. Kleist himself sent copies of the announcement to Herr von Auerswald, Herr von Altenstein, and Ulrike, and asked Ulrike to bring it to the attention of their relatives and of his old teacher Martini, since there must in Frankfurt be readers' clubs and hence potential subscribers. Ulrike, at the time, had not written for three months and had not yet sent the promised five hundred talers. Though she sent the money in response to a reminder from Kleist, her silence makes it quite clear that his activities inspired little confidence or sympathy in the family.

But what did that matter! All Dresden was waiting eagerly for the new magazine; even the preparations were a social event. Herr Eichler, the Austrian police commissioner in nearby Teplitz, kept a friendly eye on their undertaking and sent a pompous report to the authorities in Vienna, declaring that the "forthcoming publication," which the editors wished to present to the emperor as "the born and natural sovereign of all the Germans," had as its aim "a salutary union between the south and the north of Germany, at least in respect of art."

In short, everything was coming along splendidly. Soon after the middle of January 1808, the first number appeared, fifty-six pages attractively printed in quarto, with, as headpiece, a drawing in the classical manner by Ferdinand Hartmann: Phoebus driving his chariot toward the viewer in the rays of the sun rising over Dresden. The chief contribution was "An Organic Fragment from the Tragedy *Penthesilea*," which Kleist offered to Goethe "on the 'knees of my heart.'"

◊┼◊┼◊┼◊┼◊

# 17

◊┼◊┼◊┼◊┼◊

# PHÖBUS, A JOURNAL FOR THE ARTS

L ET us take a closer look at the play that Kleist offered Goethe "on the 'knees of my heart.' "

What was it that so fascinated Kleist in the late Greek legend of the bloody battle between Achilles and Penthesilea, Queen of the Amazons? He felt no need—a unique instance among all the great dramas of world literature—of so much as a semblance of plot, let alone a genuine dramatic conflict. He was content with the fight as such, with its barbaric bludgeoning, gouging, rending, and dragging back and forth. In his conception, both contestants were in equal measure victor and vanquished, equal in stature and status, both overwhelmed by the same wild passion for and against each other, an extreme passion which, unfulfilled, would give no peace and, fulfilled, would pull all other life down to death with it. Thus, it ultimately made no difference who defeated whom, whether Penthesilea slaughtered Achilles or Achilles Penthesilea, since victory was just as annihilating as defeat. And it is fully in keeping with the inexorable logic of this conception that love and hate lead equally to death, to the murder of Achilles in a drunken fit of blood lust and, when Penthesilea awakens from her drunkenness, to her suicide, for which, quite logically, she needs no weapon, but only insight, a coming to consciousness —in other words, it is a psychogenic suicide.

Only a writer as keenly aware as Kleist of the destructive ambivalence of life drive and death wish could have fashioned this gigantomachy of the passions into a powerful and readily intelligible drama.

An archaic drama, as it were: two primordial forces recognize each other, clash, wrestle to the point of unconsciousness, mutter dream phrases, reemerge from the night. Through it all, they are surrounded by impotent helpers, onlookers and speakers, who, like the chorus in the Greek theater, bear witness, praise, or deplore the action of the protagonists. These figures represent human reason, which watches the frenzied action, sometimes applauding, often protesting, but never capable of decisive intervention. And suddenly one understands: what happens here in the cosmos of poetry is at the same time taking place in the microcosm of the human personality, not only Kleist's, but the human personality in general, the struggle of the atavistic bipolar powers *within us*. What at first sight seemed no more than a poetic treatment of an ambivalent legend becomes, on closer scrutiny, a psychological portrait of the poet—and of all men.

Kleist, a psychological visionary of the first rank, possessed knowledge which his contemporaries had no suspicion of and which, when it was brought to their attention in *Penthesilea*, they did not understand. He had insights which today are the concern of depth psychology and which have perhaps been expressed most uncannily by Rilke in his *Duino Elegies*. In a very strange way, Kleist had followed Rousseau "back to nature" and with clairvoyant eye looked into the darkness of the human soul. But the people of his time did not understand him.

*Penthesilea* is formally quite perfect; small effort is needed to discover its rigor, purity, and relentless drive. Consider the directness with which this work presents itself to the mind of the audience: a brief salutation, and there we are on the fields of Troy, looking on as the armies of the Greeks and Amazons slash and claw each other like two enraged wolves. "By Jupiter! they know not why!" One cannot conceive of a quicker introduction; six lines and the problem is formulated, not a word or second wasted on atmospherics. The mood and atmosphere are *in* the actions and reactions of the figures, which convert what is ordinarily regarded as "exposition" into amazement, incomprehension, anger, horror, determination. Every word evokes a

reality and presence, compels a necessary association. Never a
pause: when the action seems to rest, it is discernibly ferment-
ing within, the viewer's foreboding is aroused—and rightly so,
for the whirl and rush of the events that will emerge from this
false stillness will be stormier than ever. There is no change of
scene, in a manner of speaking no scenery; the only visual
change is choreographic—the movements of persons swept this
way and that by the hurricane of battle. And in this drama
(though in it the world comes to an end), no more time elapses
than is registered by the viewer's timepiece.

Once the destinies of the protagonists are consummated, only
nine lines are spoken before the curtain falls, and in those lines
the movement of the whole is completed as simply, with as little ornament, as in the first six lines. No greater economy can
be imagined: every word, every movement has its exact dynamic or suggestive function. In this play Kleist realized the
dream which had almost cost him his life years before, when he
was struggling with his *Guiscard*—the dream of forging Greek
drama and Shakespearean drama, myth and psychology, the
static and the dynamic into a unity.

This fusion of the archaic Greek and modern worlds is the
basic idea that gives *Penthesilea* its special character. What was
originally the function of the Greek chorus is distributed among
individuals, but this does not empower them to intervene effectively in the action of the two protagonists. For each is the first
of his camp: Achilles is the strongest and fiercest among the
Greek heroes; Penthesilea is Queen of the Amazons. The illustrious Achilles would no more dream of bowing to the decisions of the Greek council of chiefs than would Penthesilea of
giving heed to the pleas of the high priestess. True, Penthesilea
shows a certain sisterly submission to her "soul sister," Prothoë,
but only after Prothoë has forfeited her life by serving Penthesilea's will. In short, the two protagonists know only one
law, their passion, which drives them into each other's arms in
such a frenzy of desire and blood lust that they are utterly
blind to the destinies of others.

But these others are human beings with individual impulses
and opinions, leading lives of their own side by side with the

fury of the protagonists. While on the one hand the passive element in this complex of forces is endowed with activity and personality, on the other hand the active element is humanized in spite of its frenzied instinctual blindness. Though of heroic stature, Penthesilea and Achilles are human beings and arouse sympathy by their humanity. As we have seen, they represent equal energies, yet in ways that are both touching and horrible, they are man and woman, horrible because of their frantic passion for each other, while Penthesilea is touching in the irresistibly poignant charm of her virginity and Achilles by virtue of a certain awkward good nature and credulity which, by giving rise to misunderstanding, disarm him and deliver him up to the misguided passion of his beloved. In their desire, they are both too passionate and too pure, they cannot live together and so they encompass each other's death. Out of this view of the contending forces rise the many lifelike and the two grandiose figures of *Penthesilea*, a work unique of its kind in the dramatic literature of Germany.

The form and language of a literary work cannot be separated, they are two aspects of the same thing. Kleist's language in *Penthesilea* shows supreme mastery. Grandiose but not highflown, it is all passion, rhythm, movement; it is rigorous in its richness, wise in its naïveté, powerful but never uncontrolled. Considered as music (and Kleist liked to relate literature to music), it is richly orchestrated, with trumpet blasts and drum rolls, yet pure and clear in its solo parts; taken as painting, it dazzles and overwhelms us with its precision of line and wealth of color.

Kleist now offered a long excerpt of this work to Goethe "on the 'knees of my heart.'" In an accompanying letter he wrote that *Penthesilea* had no more been written for the stage than *The Broken Jug*, which, he surmised, Goethe was producing only in order to encourage him; the situation of the German theater, with regard both to performance and to audience, was so discouraging to an author that, though very much a creature of the moment, he felt obliged in this respect to put his hope in the future.

Though only too well justified, these remarks were hardly

tactful. After all, Goethe had indicated by his readiness to produce *The Broken Jug* that he regarded the Weimar theater to
some extent as an experimental stage for rising young drama-
tists—a fact which Kleist here failed to acknowledge. In the
same letter, moreover, Kleist asks Goethe rather importunately
for a contribution to *Phöbus*, or at least for an immediate
explanation, "by return mail if possible," of his refusal. Despite
repeated requests, Goethe had already shown his reluctance to
commit himself, and now Kleist, in his impatience, was trying
to force his hand. Goethe may well have sensed that Kleist's
"on the 'knees of my heart' "—which Kleist himself had put in
quotes—and similar expressions of esteem, were no more than
polite phrases, behind which almost anything can be hidden.
And indeed, as we learn from Pfuel, Kleist's attitude toward
Goethe was ambivalent; sincere admiration was mingled with
almost fanatical hatred, which he did not keep to himself but
expressed openly in the cry: "I'll tear the wreath off his head."
Goethe, for his part, was undoubtedly influenced by his distaste
on the one hand for so-called "characteristic art" and the "new
technicians," and on the other hand for Berlin, Prussia, and the
political liberation movement that had its home there.

He replied that he would have to get used to Penthesilea, that
he had not been able to make friends with her, she came of "too
wondrous a race." And he went on: "Permit me to say that it
dismays and alarms me to see young men of intelligence and
talent waiting for a theater that is yet to come . . . Standing
before the simplest wooden platform, I would say to any true
dramatic genius: hic Rhodus, hic salta!"

One can hardly find fault with Goethe for countering what
he must have regarded as the extravagance of Kleist's artistic
ideal with the realism and moderation dictated by his own
character and experience. Moreover, there is nothing disparaging in his remarks about the play; in saying that he would have
to get used to Penthesilea and that he has not been able to make
friends with her, he is merely stating a personal reaction; and
in saying that she comes of "too wondrous a race," he is expressing not a value judgment but a neutral observation.

Still, there is something chilling about this neutrality, this refusal to commit himself with regard to a work such as *Penthesilea*. Admitted that the storm-and-stress aspect of the work—an attitude and style which he had overcome in himself —was bound to repel him; admitted that the conception of antiquity here revealed (insofar as one can speak of a conception of antiquity in Kleist) was a slap in the face to his own, one would nevertheless have expected him to acknowledge the grandeur of Kleist's achievement, even if he criticized it in the same breath or hedged his appreciation round with reservations. But instead he maintained the cool, amiable serenity of the master. His reply, in short, was not insulting, only very, very disappointing. Kleist had nothing more powerful or more personal than *Penthesilea* to offer; in a letter to Wieland, he wrote that with *Penthesilea* he had fulfilled the promise given with the *Guiscard* fragment. If *Penthesilea* could not win him Goethe's favor, nothing could, and this meant the loss of an invaluable supporter in Kleist's struggle for fame. Goethe's indifference was a cruel blow to his self-confidence, all the more ominous because the blow fell at a time when readings from *Penthesilea* were being unfavorably received in the Dresden salons.

By and large, *Penthesilea* met with a negative reception. While Goethe reacted with Olympian serenity to the heroine's "too wondrous race," lesser minds were put off by her monstrousness. She shared the fate of so many original creations. The play was widely acknowledged to be a work of talent or even of genius, but that made it all the more unacceptable. To this attitude Kleist responded with an epigram. "By God," he wrote, "I only made the verses. Believe me, I took the world as it is." Like many an artist before him, Kleist had horrified his fellow men by seeing and saying what they, too, knew but were profoundly unwilling to recognize; the "public" does not love the truth.

Who could have been expected to love *Penthesilea?* Müller, for one, loved it, and some of his friends censured him for this, implying that he praised the play against his better judgment. Even Gentz, who was well aware of Kleist's genius, detested *Penthesilea*. Müller defended it emphatically, pointing to a future that would transcend the cant and hypocrisy of his contemporaries: "We, however, hope for a time when suffering and the most tragic emotions find man armed as he should be, when sensitive souls feel the most crushing destiny to be understandable and no longer a paradox. In *Penthesilea* Kleist, fighting the battle of the future, has won this victory of the human soul over colossal, heartrending misery." Gentz persisted in his rejection; he thought *Penthesilea* "forever detestable," though this did not diminish Kleist's greatness in his eyes. Müller's perceptive lines accentuate the avant-garde character of the play; slowly or quickly, according to their abilities, people would get used to it. Such was the case, among others, with Varnhagen von Ense, who a year later sent some excerpts to Rahel Levin with the comment: "A masterpiece, to which I was formerly . . . quite blind." And that was true. Though he had "felt sorry" for Kleist, he had been blind to the merits of his drama, and as for the "knights of *Phöbus*," he hadn't a kind word to say for them. We hear of no one who had. Brentano ridiculed them, the press attacked them mercilessly, the Berlin *Spenersche Zeitung* published a contemptuous warning against the new journal, and when someone suggested to Goethe that he commission Müller to edit his works, he replied that Müller would need all his energies "to feed the steeds of the sun."

Kleist and Müller were determined to fight the hostile current; in February the book edition of *Penthesilea* went to press and the second number of *Phöbus* published the unabridged *Marquise of O.*, the effect of which on an already hostile public should not have been hard to foresee.

As we have seen, *The Marquise of O.* harks back to an anecdote told by Montaigne in his essay on drunkenness. Kleist had been fascinated by the story ever since he first read it, probably in 1805 in Königsberg. He changed the setting from France to Italy, the time from past to present, and the milieu from the rural bourgeoisie to the military aristocracy. With these changes, the story became a challenge to the moral sensibilities of Kleist's day. For an incident which would be regarded as perfectly natural and therefore acceptable as long as it was relegated to the rustic past could not but be found offensive when placed in contemporary high society. A widowed lady of spotless reputation puts a notice in the papers to the effect that she is with child—she has no idea how it happened—and asks the guilty party to present himself with a view to marriage! Yes, on the face of it, a scandalous idea. But in Kleist's story it is precisely the heroine's moral purity and fortitude, and the guilty "hero's" honest determination to repair the wrong he has done in the confusion of a day of battle, which in the end triumph over all difficulties, misapprehensions, and prejudices, and compel everyone to forgive everyone else—a forgiveness which does not call the moral code into question but places the pure and loving heart above it.

The excessive character of Kleist's *Marquise of O.* lies less in the story taken from Montaigne (which in Montaigne seems rather mild and good-natured) than in Kleist's way of treating it, above all in the violent reactions of the characters, which he describes with appalling precision. His predilection for extreme states borders on exhibitionism and sometimes oversteps the limits of good taste. Excessive is the tearful, abject misery of the marquise before she brings herself to feel justified in her innocence; excessive is the wrongheaded violence of her father, who disowns her and comes close to shooting her as she lies prostrate on the ground; and most excessive of all is the contrite father's *lust* for the affection of the daughter to whom he has been so cruelly unjust. More lying than sitting on his lap, she leans her neck back and closes her eyes, while he, like a lover, "his great eyes full of glistening tears, pressed long, passionate, avid kisses on her lips . . . he bent her over, as if she were his first love, positioned her lips, and kissed her."

It must be admitted that, precisely because the image is so apt, this "positioned her lips" seems shocking; it verges on obscenity and makes the fatherly emotion seem dubious, almost prurient. But what if this were true in a sense? This excess of affection is undeniably the counterpart of the preceding excess of rage and disappointment; one gives the other its depth, and the two, taken together, breaking with all convention, point to the perilous depths underlying all human emotion. And the same contrast, the same contradiction in the human character —a contradiction which must somehow be resolved—is once again expressed poetically at the end of the story in the heroine's confession to the man who, representing himself as her protector, took advantage of the faint into which she had fallen, and who succeeds only by long trials in transforming her loathing into love. He could not, she says, have appeared to her as the devil when she learned what he had done if he had not struck her as an angel at their first meeting.

Angel and devil in one, we are reminded of Dmitri Karamazov; but the earnestness with which the man thus characterized transforms his inner conflict into harmony is Prussian, and one might also consider Prussian the disciplined manner in which—not excluding the passages in which *tact* is forgotten— the story is told. Much is excessive in this story, but even the excessive is kept under control; it stays within the limits of the picture, never blurs the outlines, never overflows the frame; excessive content is expressed in terms of form and action, character and movement.

It is characteristic of this story, and of Kleist's fiction in general, that, emanating as it does from an essentially dramatic cast of mind, it knows no pauses, no descriptions; landscape is present only insofar as the development requires. *The Marquise of O.* has no "Italian" atmosphere; the atmosphere is merely that of a passionate world, just as the characters, though supposedly Italian or Russian, have in reality no other home than humanity. This might be a fault if their way of acting and suffering raised the question of their nationality, but this is no more the case than in *Penthesilea*. Sharply delineated, clear at all times, the characters struggle—each according to his temperament and powers—to fulfill their destiny, which is endangered by the incursion of the demonic. Nothing more is involved. Thus *The Marquise of O.* is a highly moral tale; it might indeed be termed harshly Prussian, both in its love of truth and in the succinct hardness of its style, which is absolutely free of editorializing.

The language is equally lofty and rigorous. As one might expect in narrative, it is rather more subdued than that of Kleist the dramatist, but it is just as relentlessly dynamic. Observing the method set forth in his Königsberg essay *On the Gradual Formation of Ideas in Speech*, Kleist produces, before the eyes of the reader, the images, impulses, conflicts that a more static art displays ready-made; in other words, his language is a language in process of formation, which from step to step overtakes the elements to be narrated, apprehends them, condenses them, and joins them together, a procedure which, until the reader gets used to it, gives him some difficulty in following the story. Meaning no disparagement, Tieck called Kleist a mannerist, and—even if we go beyond the romantic understanding of the word—he was right. Undoubtedly, there is artifice in the language of Kleist the storyteller. One need only contrast it with the simplicity and directness of his epistolary style. Something more than communication is aimed at in the language of his stories. One might say that this language is *willed;* in any event, it is not nature—though it reflects a kind of nature, a Prussian nature, comprising strong doses of ambition, striving, and self-control.

This language, it must be admitted, is not ingratiating, and to the first readers of *The Marquise of O.*, it sounded shrill. The public rejected *The Marquise* with indignation, as they had *Penthesilea*. But while in the case of *Penthesilea* the dominant emotion had been a more or less acceptable dread of the abyss, and horror at such a glorification of mad passion (a few superior minds may even have thought of Tieck's early prophecy: "And once again a poet will appear . . . to loosen the tongues of horror and wild desire"), here, in the case of *The Marquise of O.*, it was nothing more than the most common prudishness which, instead of falling into a faint as it were, cackled and spluttered with rage; the philistines of convention are less scandalized by monsters than by the plain unvarnished truth. This story was shameless, indecent, the salons were horrified. How were respectable citizens to admit that what offended them most deeply was in essence something strictly moral? Where would such literature lead? Adam Müller informed Gentz that not Kleist but he, Müller, had been responsible for printing the story and that the public, especially the ladies, were "most displeased" with both of them. And he continued with forthright dignity: "This novella, equally magnificent in art, manner, and style, cannot be written off as easily as my writings . . . If a work is truly divine, it is doomed to float around for thirty years or more in the earth's atmosphere before even one other person appreciates it; this is the lesson of history, of the Bible, and will also prove true of the works disseminated in *Phöbus*." "Disseminated?" In a manner of speaking. Not all the distributing agencies were functioning as they should. The second issue was coming off the press before the first had even been announced in Vienna; from the Industrie-Kontor, which represented them there, the editors could obtain no explanation, and Kleist was obliged to ask Joseph von Collin to look into the matter.

But how did he react to the glaring failure of the works from which he had expected so much—popularity, money, fame? We have no exact information, but we can imagine. Some months later, Karl August Böttiger, himself a contributor to *Phöbus* and Dresden representative for Wieland's *Merkur*, referred in a letter to the unspeakable conceit of "these gentlemen who like Ossian's ghosts walk in clouds of vapor." In such remarks the venom of a slighted literary mediocrity is discernible, but they doubtless contained a grain of truth.

Thrown back on himself, Kleist had become a harder man. How else was he to prevent the ill will he met with on all sides from impairing his self-esteem and interfering with his work?

On March 2, 1808, *The Broken Jug* was performed in Weimar. To speak of a failure would be understatement. The evening was a disaster.

Goethe, who had had misgivings from the start because of the "stationary nature of a trial," had done his best in the rehearsals, but had been unable to remedy the hideous "dragging and drawling" of the actor playing the part of Adam, the village judge. The intolerable slowness of his diction so blurred the psychological development of the play as to make it seem nonexistent—especially to an audience accustomed to the masks and statuelike figures of the classical theater, to whom it did not so much as occur that there was something more than declamation in this Adam's "dragging and drawling," and that the key to the plot was to be sought in his speeches. What was needed was a great character actor and an audience trained and disposed to discern the glittering malice, the keen psychological insight in these leisurely scenes; in short, a theater quite different, both in its performers and in its audience, from this little court theater in Weimar.

Here an audience closed in its smugness was confronted with the meaningless grimacing of an inferior actor. His manner of speaking was unnecessarily stilted, he dragged and drawled and went on and on. Oh well, the audience may have thought, at least the evening had begun with a pretty little opera, and the intolerable play was broken up into three acts to let the spectators relax a while in the foyer. Goethe, as director, had felt obliged to make these concessions to his public; he had meant well, no doubt, but the unwarranted breaks had contributed to the slowness of the performance and totally obscured the form of the play. What was left? The action was submerged by the actor's intolerable droning, the subtly insidious tension was destroyed, the atmosphere which should have been at once comic and menacing was dissipated. What remained was talk and more talk, entangled in its own snare, turning round and round, leading nowhere. No wonder the audience was restless.

And their restlessness mounted. Suddenly a long, piercing whistle was heard; Duke Karl August leaned over the balustrade and shouted: "Who is the insolent boor who dares to whistle in the presence of my spouse? Hussars, arrest the man!" The offender, a petty civil servant, tried to slip away, but was caught and dragged to the guardhouse, where he was held for three days. After this incident, the coughing, throat clearing, and stamping of feet swelled to a mighty din. By the beginning of the third act, the noise was so loud that not a word spoken by the actors could be understood. They gesticulated and moved their lips as in a dumb show, until at last, to everyone's relief, the curtain fell.

The Weimar court theater had never known so resounding a debacle. High and low were agreed in their anger and contempt. Goethe was reported to have said the next day of the obstreperous member of the audience who had been thrown into jail for whistling: "The fellow was not so wrong, I'd have joined him if propriety and my position had permitted." It did not occur to Goethe that he himself might have been partly to blame for the catastrophe; far from it, he stressed the trouble he had taken with the rehearsals of "*The Water Jug*" and said: "I have every right to find fault with Kleist, because I loved him and exalted him." What he meant by "loving" and "exalting," it is hard to say. He also said that the subject of the comedy was as "witty and humorous" as the comedy itself was inept. This opinion was shared by many others, including Karl August, who wrote in a letter to Goethe: "In the Kleist of *The Broken Pot*, I see a kind of Lavaterian otherworldliness, he shows some talent and a good deal of wit and intelligence in amusing himself, but lacks the faintest notion of how others may feel"—a statement which narrowly misses the truth, since it recognizes the "detachment," the self-sufficiency of the play, but takes this rather as a vice of the author than as a virtue of the work. For great art is a world apart and has no regard for the public, though this is one of those unpalatable facts that the public is reluctant to acknowledge. This reaction, of course, was unknown to Kleist. But a long account of the Weimar scandal soon appeared in the *Journal for the Fashionable World* and this Kleist was doomed to read. The writer deplores the play's long-windedness and its shortage of action, and suggests that it might have been a success if it had been compressed into one act.

Even before the appearance of this review, Kleist realized that the reactions to *The Broken Jug* as performed in Weimar had been catastrophic. "An atrocious comedy," "an indelibly disagreeable impression," "boring, in bad taste"—Kleist cannot have seen these words (from a letter by Fräulein Henriette von Knebel to her brother Karl Ludwig); even without them, he was well aware that the public had responded to his work with a unanimous, shrill "No!" But Kleist was not a man to take defeat lying down. His answer was an equally resolute: "We shall see!"

The third, March issue of *Phöbus* was revised; the projected publication of the *Guiscard* fragment was postponed and an excerpt from *The Broken Jug* put in its place with the explanatory notice: "Since this little comedy, written some years ago, has just foundered on the stage at Weimar, our readers may welcome the opportunity to see for themselves, as it were, why this should have happened. We are publishing it here as a novelty of the day." Thus he appealed to the readers of *Phöbus* to act as arbiters in a case which had been decided against him, but in which he nevertheless felt that right was on his side.

Of course, right was on his side, and still is. With the possible exception of Lessing's *Minna von Barnhelm* (and perhaps of Grillparzer's *Weh dem, der lügt*), it is the most powerful and enduring comedy in the German language.

The setting is a village in Holland. Adam, the village judge, lusts for the pretty and buxom Eve Rull. He manages to convince her that her sweetheart, Ruprecht, who has been called before the recruiting commission in Utrecht, is not, as he has been officially informed, being assigned to the provincial militia, but will be put on board a ship bound for Batavia and almost certain death—unless he, Adam, provides her with a forged medical certificate authenticated with the official seal. Ostensibly to complete this certificate, he enters her room in the middle of the night, deposits his wig on top of a jug on the windowsill as though getting ready to write, and is about to assault her when Ruprecht, sensing that something is amiss, creeps in from the garden and sets up a hellish din outside the bolted door. Escaping through the window, Adam grabs his wig at the last moment and in so doing knocks the jug off the sill. Ruprecht, in a jealous rage, forces the door, rushes to the window, still clutching the doorknob that he has wrenched off, and with it belabors the head of the fugitive, who has his foot caught in the latticework. Adam falls to the ground, hurls a handful of dirt in the eyes of his enemy to keep from being recognized, and limps away in the darkness. Aroused by the noise, Eve's mother appears, sees her beloved jug in shards, sees the infuriated

Ruprecht, and inevitably takes him for the culprit—a mistake which her sobbing daughter cannot correct, since for Ruprecht's sake and her own she cannot tell her mother that another visitor has been there before him. Next morning the guilty judge in a sorry state—sprained ankle, bumps all over his naked skull (for his wig has been ruined)—has to sit in judgment on the complaint brought by the indignant Frau Marthe Rull, inconsolable over the loss of her jug. His situation seems desperate since the girl knows the truth, and to make matters worse, his superior, Justice Walter, a man known for his unflinching rectitude, has come to the village on a tour of inspection and is present in the courtroom. Even so, one cannot help feeling that thanks to his uninhibited rascality and the inexhaustible stream of lies and distortions he pours forth, he would come through unscathed, if he did not, in Licht, his clerk, find an adversary as wily as himself, whose suspicions have been aroused by the most tenacious of motives, namely, ambition, for he longs to take Adam's place as judge.

In the short preface to *The Broken Jug*, the Le Veau print (which had hung in Zschokke's room in Bern and which provided the inspiration for the play) is described, and a special point is made of the clerk's distrustful glance at the shady judge, "comparable to the glance which on a similar occasion Creon cast at Oedipus, when he began to suspect who had killed Laius." This comparison is no accident, for there is a patent kinship between the dramatic conception of Sophocles' tragedy of Oedipus and that of Kleist's comedy of Adam. When the curtain rises a few minutes before the opening of the trial, the crucial event has already occurred, and everything that takes place on the stage has but one purpose: to disentangle the crime step by step from a complex skein of motives, interests, and deceptions, and bring the guilty party to just punishment.

And what a tangle of motives we have here: Judge Adam's determination to foist the blame for his offense on someone else; Eve's fears for Ruprecht, whom she believes to be in danger; Ruprecht's jealousy, Licht's ambition; Frau Marthe's anger and distress over her broken jug, which, though without actual bearing on the case, has set it in motion and will lead to the ultimate disclosures. A witches' Sabbath of all too human drives and foibles, which could easily—a mere twist would suffice—turn from comedy to tragedy.

The same principle lies at the base of the modern crime novel and, on a higher level, of such masterworks as *The Brothers Karamazov*. In every case, the author is at pains, so far as his talents permit, to lay bare the hidden guilt, the tangled motivations of the human soul, by examining, dissecting, and finally resolving a mystery. To suppose that he gave the name Adam to his tragicomic hero because no better name occurred to him would be to underestimate Kleist. No, the judge is so named because he is the old Adam, a slave to the flesh, crafty, deceitful, and yet deserving of pity in the trouble he has brought on himself; one hardly knows whether to laugh or cry at the sight of him wriggling and gasping for breath as he tries to escape from the net of truth. He is a wretched, disgraceful sort of man, more and more so as his situation becomes more hopeless, and just that is what makes him so utterly human, an extreme case and yet an exemplar. It seems likely that the audience in Weimar were so incensed because they dimly sensed just this, for otherwise it would be hard to account, not for the failure of *The Broken Jug*, but for the immoderate reactions it aroused. Why speak of an "atrocious" comedy, of an "indelibly disagreeable impression," unless it touched a sensitive nerve? It might have been found long-winded, here and there a coarse expression might have given offense, a certain smug malice might have warranted a degree of annoyance—but to have provoked the *rage* it did, the play must have cut deeper.

Was it the explosive hilarity with which a shameful story is told that so enraged the audience? There is more to this hilarity than meets the eye; it is anything but simple. The ambience is that of the common people, for all the characters, old and young, good and bad, are of that class, and the one exception, the only member of the "educated" classes, is Justice Walter, the inspector, a wise, fair-minded gentleman with a deep sympathy and understanding for the common people, wherein he resembles the author, though without his good-humored chuckle. Fontane speaks somewhere of a "winning familiarity with the common people" as an endearing trait of the Prussian nobleman. And in *The Broken Jug* Kleist shows just such familiarity with his characters. He knows these people through and through and looks upon them with a benevolent eye; he sees their wickedness, their touching naïveté, their peasant slyness, their blatant rascality, their distrust of others and incredible know-it-allness, their obstinacy and incorrigible superstition; all things considered, and the world being what it is, he approves of these people, but his approval does not impair the sharpness of his vision. He never idealizes his characters, and just this shows the authenticity of his goodwill. Between the characters and their creator there is a "natural" harmony, which turns wit into humor and lends the humor its incomparable spontaneity and candor, its rough-hewn friendliness and love of life. This is a kind of humor that acknowledges the existence of villainy and transforms it by enchantment into something almost idyllic, though the humor itself is not without malice. On the contrary, this bucolic merriment goes hand in hand with an impish *Schadenfreude*. The author amuses himself inventing more and more hilarious mixtures of active peasant cunning and of passive helplessness, and richly varied comic situations are heaped up in an orgiastic crescendo. His gleeful pleasure in teasing, tormenting, mystifying can fairly be termed satanic or sadistic and reminds us not a little of Kleist the wicked betrothed writing letters to his fiancée in the course of his journey to Würzburg in 1800. This humor is Janus-headed, its benevolence cannot be counted on; there is kindness in its malice, refinement in its simplicity, love in its cruelty. And in all its combinations it is at every moment natural.

All this need not necessarily have made the play unpopular, for most of us take a secret delight in the humiliation of our fellow men. What so infuriated the Weimar audience must have been the complacency with which he played his game of cat-and-mouse, the obvious self-satisfaction of his deviltry, in other words, its perfect naturalness, with which they had no more desire to identify than with its victim. It would be no exaggeration to say that it was always the same quality in Kleist that so antagonized his contemporaries: excessive truthfulness, the effect of which, in this case, was exacerbated rather than attenuated by the chuckle.

"The truth," said Goethe, "is a torch, but a monstrous one; that is why we all blink and try to pass it by, for fear of getting burned." But this truth was a difficult one to pass by, for it was many-layered, embodied in a human portrait whose validity could not be doubted. Adam, the village judge, is a character who bears comparison with Molière's Tartuffe and may even surpass him in a way, for his exuberant vitality makes him not so much an object lesson as a living, flesh-and-blood man. And this overflowing vitality distinguishes all the characters, even the housemaids, whose domestic activities give them opportunities for true-to-life comedy, though they are almost mute. Eve's gentle yet vigorous womanhood; Ruprecht's naïve, now good-natured, now angry submissiveness; the sobbing, brokenhearted fervor with which Frau Marthe Rull displays the broken jug and bewails her irretrievable loss: "Here on this hole, where now there is nothing, the entire Netherlands was handed over to Philip of Spain"; Tümpel, Ruprecht's peasant father, with his old man's moderation, wisdom, and authority; the wide-eyed lust for grim detail with which Frau Brigitte, the neighbor woman, a chance witness, describes the wrongdoer's flight through the night, his bald head gleaming like phosphorescent wood on the path through the linden trees, his hasty limp—which attributes made it only too clear that he could be none other than the devil himself; the wily singleness of purpose and never-failing amusement with which Licht the clerk manages to steer the proceedings on the right course; and Justice Walter's dignified sternness and humanity—all this is so wonderfully true to life; indeed, there is so much life that the "trial form," criticized by Goethe, can hardly be called "stationary," and in any event there can be no question of dryness. All this play needs to make it thoroughly lively and entertaining is an adequate performance.

In form, *The Broken Jug* adheres to the Sophoclean model, but not slavishly. Its psychological acuteness makes it more modern, but without impairing its self-contained perfection. As for the language, it sounds as pithy and vigorous as if it were first spoken yesterday. Apparently, the public of Kleist's day—despite the romantic predilection for folk songs and folktales—had not yet developed an ear for the pithiness of his language; they seem to have been shocked by its candid plainspokenness, which was indeed a far cry from the watery jargon of the salons. Yes, that was the long and the short of it: in this play the common people were not seen through romantic eyes, they did not speak a romantic language, they spoke plainly, called a spade a spade, and cared nothing for the proprieties.

*The Broken Jug* had no better luck with the readers of *Phöbus* than with the Weimar audience; publishing it was a grave blunder and only added to the widespread abhorrence that was felt for it. The utterances of the ladies of the Körner household, for example, suggest not individual distaste but the irritation of a whole class, the frequenters of the literary salons —these are summary condemnations made with the assurance of persons knowing that their opinions enjoy wide support. On April 11, 1808, Dora Stock wrote to Professor Weber in Frankfurt: "His talent is unmistakable, but he lets himself be misled by the heroes of the new school, and I am afraid that Müller has a bad influence on him. His *Penthesilea* is a monstrosity to which I could not listen without horror. His *Broken Jug* is a rogues' play that lasts too long and verges constantly on indecency. As for his story *The Marquise of O.*, no woman can read it without blushing. Why this tone? All in all, I am afraid *Phöbus* will not live more than a year. Even now, it is neither awaited with pleasure nor read with interest. And yet these gentlemen aspire to stand in the forefront of literature and to destroy everything around them."

And on April 15, Emma Körner, the judge's daughter, wrote to the same Professor Weber: "Though Kleist is anything but conceited, he undoubtedly needs a severe critic to direct his extraordinary talent to other subjects than those he selects for his writings. He likes to struggle with his subject matter, but it's a pity if he wastes his strength. Perhaps Müller doesn't find enough fault with him, perhaps he thinks everything he does is perfect, and this can only harm Kleist." One might almost be touched by the naïveté and impertinence of this critic, so sure that she is better able than Kleist to direct his "extraordinary talent"—one might be touched or amused if such statements did not reflect the arrogance of a whole class of critical dilettantes, who so often, and in Kleist's case with disastrous effect, drown the voices of our greatest authors with their cackling.

But how did all this affect Kleist, who could not have seen these letters but was well aware of the kind of opinions expressed in them? Sympathy cannot be forced, and there can be little doubt that lack of sympathy was at the root of his difficulty. In such a situation, bitter as it may be, the best policy is to do nothing. But since his sudden decision to publish his "failed" play, the review in the *Journal for the Fashionable World* and other details of the Weimar fiasco had come to his attention, and suddenly he realized—or so he thought—who was to blame for his disappointment: Goethe, whom he had approached "on the 'knees of my heart,' " who had not found a single good word to say of *Penthesilea*, who with his disgraceful production and arbitrary dismemberment of *The Broken Jug* had brought him an unparalleled defeat, from which he might never recover.

He was not entirely wrong in supposing that the great man in Weimar, with his faint and hesitant praise and his high-handed methods as a director, had injured and dishonored him. Yes, dishonored—Kleist remained a Prussian officer and a nobleman, he regarded the matter as an affair of honor and resolved to act accordingly. So at least it was said, and evidently it came to Goethe's ears that Kleist, whom he had "loved and exalted" and whose interests he had taken so much trouble to promote, wanted to challenge him to a duel—"a grave aberration of nature, justifiable only by illness or excessive nervous irritability" —in any case an absurdity, both grotesque and tragic, and not wholly attributable to the "grave hypochondria" which, according to Goethe, was destroying Kleist both as a man and as a writer.

Does it not seem more likely that Kleist's absurdly pedantic touchiness sprang from a despairing intimation of ultimate failure, from the devastating insight that he had put into the mouth of Penthesilea: "The deciding die is cast; it has come to rest /

And I must own—own that I've lost"? Here was this man in Weimar, the nation's leading literary light, from whose forehead he had wished to tear the wreath, but who had instead struck him a shameful, irremediable blow. What could have been more natural for his extreme and overwrought mind than to conclude that they must confront each other, sword or pistol in hand? Since he had been offended, was it not his duty to challenge the offender? Be that as it may, no such duel came to pass, his friends seem to have talked him out of it; the quarrel hung fire, poisoned the atmosphere, and prejudiced Goethe irrevocably against Kleist.

Achim von Arnim tells us that the Weimar affair left Kleist with a lasting bitterness, which he never overcame. A more reasonable man would have let the matter rest, but that he was unable to do; sooner or later he would have to get it out of his system, and in the end he did so in a manner verging on literary suicide.

The reception of the first three issues of *Phöbus* was disheartening—an enormous effort gone up in smoke; the initial favor of the public squandered, indeed, converted into antagonism, exasperation, and indifference; irreparable loss of prestige, especially after the failure of the Weimar production had opened people's eyes to the fact that Goethe's support, which (according to Varnhagen von Ense) "had been thundered into people's ears with vast cannonades," did not amount to much. It was obvious that what Kleist still had to offer was not calculated to save a situation that was as hopeless economically as otherwise. There were too few subscribers and little hope of new ones; the editors were reluctant to write off their investment and drop the whole venture—which, apart from other objections, would have created something of a scandal. All they could do was tighten their belts and look around for another publisher. To give themselves a breathing spell, they decided to skip the April number and compensate the readers with a double issue in May.

This issue, like those preceding it, carried a good deal of

Kleist: the *Guiscard* fragment, which came to over five hundred lines, the first act of *Käthchen of Heilbronn,* and twenty-four epigrams. The epigrams, at least, promised to arouse public interest—but, in the present case, was this desirable? For, on the one hand, they threw a bright light on Kleist's falling-out with the deified Goethe and, on the other, they scoffed at the carping attitude of the critics and public toward Kleist's work—both subjects concerning which a more circumspect writer would have kept silent.

He made fun of Goethe. The aging poet, he said, was dismembering the beam of light he had cast in his youth. This was not witty. He ridiculed Goethe's antipathy for dogs and wrote that in the event of a production of *Penthesilea* in Weimar their howling would probably have to be set to music. That *was* witty, but also catastrophic, for a malicious reader could be expected to know that there was little fear of such a production. And the readers, who were expected to enjoy these little pinpricks, were themselves ridiculed in a letter by a fictitious reader of *The Marquise of O.,* declaring her faint to have been a shameless pose—wasn't it obvious that she had just closed her eyes while being raped?

How could a readership treated with such contempt be expected to appreciate the serious content of these malicious epigrams? In response to those who find fault with Sophocles for the monstrousness of his subject matter, Kleist observes that the true poet loves to coax flowers of beauty from beds of decay—a truth no doubt, but one which in this context was bound to seem presumptuously *pro domo,* since in the preceding epigram Kleist had anticipated the indignation of the public which, just as in *Penthesilea* it had noticed only madness, would in *Guiscard* see nothing but plague sores. All this was extremely insulting, and when in passing he enjoins his readers to have *faith* in the author, in order that he might thrive and fulfill all their wishes, one is reminded of the king of Prussia who cried out while flogging his subjects: "Scoundrels, I want you to love me!"

It is true that the benevolence indispensable to the public reception of a work of art was then in short supply; but it is also true that what little may still have remained was destroyed by Kleist himself with his epigrams. They were indeed an act of self-destruction, an abreacting, which found its fullest enjoyment in the harm it was bound to inflict on the enjoyer. The most hateful publisher could hardly have devised a more insidious means of prejudicing the public against the *Guiscard* fragment. Yet it is one of the world's greatest literary fragments and might even then have been accorded the recognition it deserves, had the atmosphere been less poisoned.

More powerfully perhaps than the opening of any other of Kleist's tragedies, the *Fragment from the Tragedy of Robert Guiscard, Duke of Normandy* presents a picture of grandeur and purity, of sublime perfection. Thus, when it breaks off, one cannot help wondering whether the beginning may not be too grandiose to permit of being sustained at the same level, much less raised to a higher one. For the presentation of action and character in these few pages is so dense, clear, and controlled that one is left with a well-nigh miraculous impression of dark splendor.

Through Guiscard's camp outside Constantinople, which he must conquer in order to fulfill his dream—a Norman kingdom of Greece—the plague stalks like a ghost, breathing its poisoned breath into the people's faces from swollen lips. Terrible is the groaning, panting, gasping agony, ending in madness and death, while the vultures wait impatiently. A delegation of the sufferers, led by a stalwart old soldier, approaches the general's tent, which suddenly seems to conceal an evil secret. To get rid of the intruders, first the duke's daughter, a figure of noble womanhood, emerges, then his son and his nephew, both princes, rivals for Guiscard's crown. To curry favor with the men, one of the princes reveals the secret of the tent; Guiscard has taken sick during the night, he is burning with the heat of Etna, thirsty enough to drink up the Dardanelles; he too, perhaps, is a victim of the plague. At this point Guiscard steps out of the tent, an imposing figure, sternly benevolent, serene in his majesty. He laughs at the thought that he, *he* should be sick, stricken with the plague, and yet he cannot fully dispel the suspicion, he has to sit down, and while his wife, who has appeared with him, reels in a sudden faint and is quickly removed from the sight of the delegation, the aged spokesman states the army's demands: withdrawal, return to Italy: "Oh, lead us back, back to our home country."

Here the text breaks off, and we have no indication that Kleist ever took it up again. Which suggests that it could have been carried no further. Early in our century, it was produced just as it stands, with but one change—not until the very end does Guiscard feel the need of sitting down. Due to this change —so a discerning witness tells us—the monumental fragment made the impression of a self-contained tragedy. This is quite possible, for a mere reading leaves one with an unforgettable impression; one seems to recall an imposing sculpture, a block of marble, from which emerge muscular limbs, sinewy torsos, heroic masks, half-finished figures frozen in the process of coming into being, and yet, as though whole, forcing the mystery of their lives upon the beholder. But if such magic can emanate from an unfinished work, may we not conclude that this work did not *want* or need to be completed? It is severe and grandiose, more classical than any of Kleist's other works, deeply moving without so much as a tremor of sentimentality, pure splendor without ornament. Perhaps we could more easily dispense with any other of Kleist's works than with this unfinishable one, which shows what immoderate demands he made on himself. Upon the forehead of this magnificent fragment might be inscribed the words of *Penthesilea:*

> *The most that human power can accomplish,*
> *That have I done—attempted the impossible—*
> *Staked all I had upon a single throw.*

Of course, one work should not be exalted to high heaven at the expense of another, for every work of art establishes its own standards; the excellence of one work cannot detract from that of any other. Of this truth the double issue of *Phöbus* offers a convincing example—though from the standpoint of editorial policy this may have been unwise. Along with the powerful *Guiscard* fragment, this issue carried the first act of *Käthchen of Heilbronn*. One might suppose that this mere beginning of a play would look pale in the shadow of the great unfinished work. This is not at all the case. The incisiveness of the figures that inhabit the first act, the freshness of the dramatic action, the power and sureness of the language are not in the least impaired by the proximity of the *Guiscard* fragment. *Käthchen* is simply something different, to be judged as such. And in publishing these two very different kinds of beauty side by side, Kleist cannot have meant them to compete with each other; he thought of them as equals.

But compared with each other or not—what the two plays had to offer, the romantic charm of Vehmic horror and lilac fragrance in the one act of *Käthchen*, the classical rigor and the power of *Guiscard*—both works were self-contained and self-sufficient, addressed to no one in particular, and for that reason limited in their appeal. The epigrams, on the other hand, were addressed directly to a specific public, which they mocked and reproved for its complacency. Naturally, it was they that decided the public reaction to the issue, which was ruinous: Here we've spent our good money on a journal that scolds us and pokes fun at us. We won't stand for it, least of all from a writer who doesn't even spare the greatest of all poets his venomous mockery, to whom, as we've suspected all along, "nothing is sacred." After the bloodthirstiness of *Penthesilea*, the obnoxiousness of *The Marquise of O.*, the boorish indecency of *The Broken Jug*, comes this piece of impertinence. No more of this, if you please. Enough is enough. The general mood was summed up in a letter to Goethe, describing the April–May number of *Phöbus* as "a prodigy of pretentiousness and bad taste." And one can almost admire the moderation with which Goethe replied: "I broke with the Dresdeners at once. For though I hold Adam Müller in high esteem, and though von Kleist is no common talent, I recognized only too soon that their *Phöbus* would turn into a kind of *phébus* [bombast]."

The situation of *Phöbus* had become hopeless; Rühle offered the journal to Cotta, Kleist offered it to Göschen, under conditions which—the editors would contribute free of charge—

amounted almost to a gift; but no one wanted *Phöbus* or Kleist's work even as a gift—a glaring but by no means unique or even unusual example of a noble undertaking succumbing to the narrow-mindedness and insensitivity of the world. Yet, with difficulty, the editors kept it afloat and published a June issue, so completing their ruin in the eyes of the public; for Kleist was not a man to draw sensible conclusions from bad experience.

If their new gaffe had been only an offense against reason, tact, and good taste! But it was more. Among the epigrams published in the June issue of *Phöbus*, there was one bearing the title "The Precocious Genius." It runs as follows:

> *Now, that I call an early-ripened talent! At his*
> *Parents' wedding he sang the epithalamium.*

This barb, as everyone knew at the time, was directed against Goethe, who had married Christiane Vulpius in 1806, seventeen years after the birth of their son. But only the stuffiest of moralists had taken umbrage, and here was Kleist making common cause with them. Kleist siding with the wretched philistines, in whose eyes his own writing was pure filth! Could he fail to see that he was slapping himself in the face, degrading and besmirching himself? If at least this unfortunate gibe had been written in the first flush of anger—but more than three months had elapsed since the Weimar fiasco! Even those who loved and admired him must have had difficulty in finding excuses for this. At best, one might argue that such long-lived fury showed how deeply he had been hurt by the Weimar debacle, and that he must have known how dearly his ill-advised action would cost him. Indeed, the price he paid was far more than he could afford, and in this, after all, there is a kind of noblesse.

To the remaining nineteen epigrams in the June number of *Phöbus*, no great objection could be raised; one, advising the critics to learn the art of reading before setting out to judge that of writing, shows a certain asperity but is hardly insulting, and the rest were general and rather mild in character. The public had all the more reason to concentrate its attention on the one defaming Goethe. The most liberal readers could not help agreeing with the most hidebound that no one should say such things, let alone print them, and that to do so was tactless to the point of boorishness, an act of impiety which thoroughly and definitively discredited its author. Oh, not that one hadn't known all along what to think of him, but now he had gone out of his way to prove that he stopped at nothing and that nothing was sacred to him.

Of course, if anyone had wanted to play the devil's advocate he might have referred, in the same issue, to the beginning of Kleist's great novella *Michael Kohlhaas* and pointed out that its author clearly did hold some things sacred, that he was obviously obsessed with the ideals of justice and truth—an obsession growing out of careful thought but ultimately resolved to go to any length, to sacrifice reason, practical advantage, and life itself to advance these ideals and set an enduring example to mankind.

The section printed in *Phöbus* tells the following story. In the course of a journey, the horse dealer Michael Kohlhaas is stopped at the castle of Tronkenburg, on the border between Brandenburg and Saxony, where he is asked to pay an obviously unjustified fee. Leaving two horses as a pledge in the care of Herse, his servant, who also stays behind, he continues on to Dresden, where he obtains an official declaration that no payment beyond the usual toll is due. He then returns to the castle, where he finds his horses in a pitiful condition and learns that Herse has been beaten and driven away "for misconduct."

Abandoning the useless horses, he returns home, questions the severely beaten Herse, and after carefully weighing the facts concludes that a glaring injustice has been done, which he is determined to remedy. But because of the Junker von Tronka's high connections, Kohlhaas, try as he will, can accomplish nothing by legal means; quite the contrary, his efforts, what with a concatenation of disastrous circumstances, lead to the death of his beloved wife. In the end, he liquidates all his property and sets out with a band of servants to obtain with fire and sword the justice that has been denied him.

Here, then, we have a sense of justice which ultimately, in spite of every scruple, drives a man to the realization that, since the world does not respect his "inalienable" rights, he himself must vindicate them, by violence if need be, and so preserve his own dignity and that of his fellow men. This hypertrophied sense of justice is the theme of *Michael Kohlhaas*. With meticulous, almost pedantic care, it is illumined from all sides, studied in all its preoccupations and self-doubts, and finally presented as a kind of moral obligation to engage in violence. The manner of telling is impressive; the narrative rushes like a wild mountain torrent, twists and turns, forces its way between boulders, then, liberated, pours into the open —and so Kohlhaas's ideal of justice seeks its way through obstacles, through ever new disappointments, insults, and calamities, and finally, freed from all restraint, breaks through to decision and irrevocable action. Even when dealing with the human mind, the writing works with sensuous images, never loses itself in speculation, never becomes breathless or hysterical. Despite the headlong pace, the noble language is controlled, concrete, and clear and makes for an atmosphere of thoughtful moderation, a quality of epic objectivity.

*Michael Kohlhaas* is a daring tale built on a daring thesis; namely, that under certain circumstances right, if taken seriously, must necessarily turn into wrong. The story undoubtedly shocked its first readers precisely because the protagonist overshoots the mark by taking his ideal of justice so seriously as to value it above life itself. The readers of *Phöbus* might at least have argued in this way; they might have questioned the ethical validity of such an extreme attitude but never its basically ethical character. Indeed, anyone really wishing to do Kleist justice would have been obliged to conclude that in the light of such ethical fanaticism the affront to Goethe—distasteful as it was—carried no weight. On the one pan of the scales a lasting exemplary virtue, on the other a momentary failing. And to see this would have required no great penetration, only some small love of the truth.

The fury with which Kleist was attacked on this occasion seems almost inconceivable. Fraülein Henriette von Knebel wrote to her brother Karl Ludwig: "Herewith the Princess sends you another *Phöbus*. What outrageous sacrilege to give this name to a mud puddle, though on it, too, no doubt the sun shines. One really ought not to set aside a louis d'or for such shameless beggary." The shrillness of tone, disconcerting in a lady ordinarily so well spoken, seems disproportionate, to put it mildly, and it seems safe to assume that it was precisely the "cultural elite" who felt injured, in the person of Goethe, the living embodiment of the cultural ethic by which they lived.

As for Goethe, his sense of humor failed him when aspersions were cast on his private life; Herder's remark about Goethe's play *The Natural Daughter*—"I prefer your natural son!"— had put an end to a lifelong friendship. Goethe never gave utterance to the resentment that Kleist's insolence must have aroused in him, but just that may account for its longevity.

Never again did he show the least sign of goodwill toward Kleist (which the production of *The Broken Jug* undoubtedly was). To our knowledge, he never uttered a single word in acknowledgment of the younger man's genius (of which he was assuredly well aware), and he was far from chary of words to his detriment.

He asked a friend, whom he knew to be "well disposed" toward Kleist, to read *Käthchen of Heilbronn;* only when he had heard his friend's opinion would he think it over and decide whether he himself could bear to read it—for in reading *Penthesilea* he had really suffered too much. But when his secretary handed him the book, observing that they might want to produce it, Goethe was said to have flung it into the fire and cried out: "I will not produce that, not even if half Weimar demands it!"

His critical observations reveal a venomous sharp-sightedness, and yet a curious blindness to the essential. Of *Penthesilea* he said: "In some passages the tragedy borders on high comedy; for example, where the Amazon appears on stage with one breast and assures the audience that all her emotions have fled into that second, still-remaining half." What a vicious formulation—and how false! No Kleistian character ever "assures" the audience of anything whatsoever, since each one of them is utterly obsessed with himself or his opposite; in the whole of Kleist's dramatic work there is not a single address to the public.

Of *Michael Kohlhaas*, Goethe was quoted as saying: "It is nicely told and cleverly constructed . . . but, on the other hand, it takes a great spirit of contradiction to generalize on a single instance with such consistent and radical hypochondria; there are unbeautiful, terrifying things in nature, with which literature, however skillfully it may treat them, ought neither to concern nor to reconcile itself." But is it not precisely the function of literary symbols to "generalize," that is, to give universal validity to single instances of this kind? And would it not be a regrettable restriction on art to forbid it to deal with such "terrifying" cases? And ought we not to wish that Kleist's "spirit of contradiction" and "hypochondria," in other words, his fanatical and unswerving passion for justice, were far more widespread than they are? And is it conceivable that Goethe, the wisest of men, didn't know all this?

No, all he lacked was goodwill toward Kleist, toward the man and his work. Of course, there was a grain of truth in what he said, but that makes things worse rather than better. This author, he was to say later, had always filled him with "horror and revulsion, as if a body which nature had intended to be beautiful were afflicted with an incurable disease"; there was "something barbaric, misshapen" about him. He was "a Nordic phantom of acrimony and hypochondria"; and as late as 1826, when Tieck published his edition of Kleist, Goethe spoke of "Kleistian mischief and sick spooks."

It is futile to argue which of the two, Kleist or Goethe, was more to blame for their quarrel. But one thing is certain: it played a decisive role in Kleist's life. How much importance was attached to it by his family may be judged from the fact that after Heinrich's death the very mention of Goethe's name was taboo in the Kleist family circle.

Kleist's situation at this time was critical. *Phöbus* was in serious trouble and the printing of *Penthesilea*, begun in February and now well advanced, had to be suspended for lack of funds. Kleist was obliged to cede the work to Cotta on terms none too favorable to himself: the publisher would take over the printing costs and himself fix the amount of Kleist's fee, which would not fall due till Easter 1809. At the same time, he tried to interest Cotta in a yearbook, for each number of which he undertook to provide a play illustrated by Hartmann, starting with *Käthchen of Heilbronn* or another one, as yet unfinished, and further asked him to publish in his *Morning Journal for the Cultivated Classes* a review, to be written either by Friedrich Schlegel or by Friedrich Gottlob, of the first five issues of *Phöbus* and an advance notice of the sixth, which was to carry contributions by Friedrich Schlegel and by Madame de Staël. The proposed notice also stated that the journal's difficulties had been overcome as a result of the promised collaboration of these and other well-known authors.

This optimism was not entirely unfounded. True, the editors of *Phöbus* were not exactly popular with the Dresden publishers, who suspected them of planning various kinds of disloyal competition. But apparently Georg Moritz Walther, who had recently taken over his father's firm, Walther's Court Publishing House, did not share the animosity of his colleagues. After negotiations, presumably conducted for *Phöbus* by Adam Müller, Walther declared his willingness to try to save the journal. We are not fully informed about the agreement, but we do know that it was a short-term one, and there is reason to suspect that the knights of *Phöbus* were still secretly hoping for some sort of participation on the part of Cotta. In any case, the July issue was published by Walther, and in October an agreement was signed, by which he accepted responsibility for the journal until at least the end of the year. But nothing much came of the loudly trumpeted collaboration of well-known authors; under the title *La Fête de la victoire ou le retour des Grecs*, Madame de Staël contributed a French translation of Schiller's *Das Siegesfest*, but neither Schlegel nor Tieck contributed anything at all, and it must have been clear to anyone familiar with the situation that *Phöbus* was not long for this world.

Kleist, too, cut down drastically on his contributions, perhaps by his own decision and perhaps at the more or less explicit demand of the new publisher, who may have been frightened by the poor reception given to Kleist's previous contributions. In the next six issues, he published two further acts of *Käthchen*, a few topical poems written long before, and an insignificant idyll.

He cannot have been happy over this relative withdrawal from the journal, which was to have brought him fame. Yet, when Cotta expressed an interest in the yearbook, Kleist replied with a prodigious show of composure: "If I can *write*, that is, if with every work I produce I can earn barely as much as I need to write another, then my demands on this life will be satisfied." And in the same letter, written at the end of July 1808, he thanks Cotta for sending him a total of 353 reichstalers to cover the printing costs for *Penthesilea* and the author's fee. "I feel certain," he wrote, "that under the present circumstances there can be no other motive for this purchase than the goodwill which forbids you to let a writer, whom these times cannot sustain, go under."

Though Cotta's "goodwill" was to prove more than questionable, on one point Kleist was undoubtedly right: he *was* a writer "whom the times could not sustain."

◊┼◊┼◊┼◊┼◊

# 18

## KLEIST FLINGS HIMSELF
## INTO POLITICS

KLEIST was doggedly at work. As long as he worked, he could hold out. He completed *Käthchen of Heilbronn*, and began an acting version; he went on with *Michael Kohlhaas* and started work on a new play which he had already asked Cotta to announce as "forthcoming." This feverish activity, a postponement of inevitable collapse, was a gift of the times which "could not sustain" him and which suddenly offered him a refuge, a prospect of influencing his fellow men by other than literary means, a way out of timelessness and into the present, to which, as he had written in a letter to Goethe, he would so gladly have belonged. Now suddenly it became not only his good fortune but his duty as well to participate in the life of his place and time, to subordinate his individual concerns to those of his country, for the fate of Germany and of freedom itself was at stake.

The political situation, which was brewing up so promisingly, had its focal point in Spain. In May, Napoleon had forced the Bourbon dynasty to abdicate and had set his brother Joseph on the Spanish throne; but the new monarchy and the French military occupation met with unexpectedly stubborn resistance, which led Talleyrand to cry out prophetically: "*C'est le commencement de la fin.*" Enslaved Germany rubbed the sleep from its eyes. The German people had looked on as powerful Prussian fortresses surrendered with hardly a fight, and now an unknown Spaniard, one José de Palafox y Melzi, and his guerrilleros were holding Saragossa month after month against the French. In July 1808, at the capitulation of Bailén, twenty thousand French soldiers were taken prisoner; England saw that its hour had come. In August, Wellesley, the future Duke of Wellington, struck, and although he is said to have slept through the battle under the table, dead drunk, he inflicted a critical defeat on the French near Torres Vedras in Estremadura.

The Spanish example aroused a storm of warlike enthusiasm in enslaved Europe. Best prepared for a war of liberation was Prussia, where, after the Peace of Tilsit in 1807, Baron vom und zum Stein, invested with almost unlimited powers, had initiated and in part carried out far-reaching social, political, and military reforms, so preparing the country both physically and psychologically for a general resurgence. Seized with the fever of the day, the then more powerful Austria rearmed energetically and quite openly. Napoleon tried to counter these menacing developments by diplomatic means, convening the Diet of Princes at Erfurt in October (on which occasion he granted Goethe an audience) and reinforcing his alliance with Russia; but diplomacy proved insufficient and he soon saw himself obliged to take more drastic measures.

The writers, not least those of North Germany, poured oil on the flames. August Wilhelm Schlegel called for a vigorous patriotic literature in keeping with the times; Friedrich Schlegel wrote patriotic songs. Adam Müller turned from aesthetics to political science; his lectures on political economy, delivered at the house of Prince Bernhard of Sachsen-Weimar in Dresden, were attended by the entire diplomatic corps, with the exception of the French ambassador. Under such conditions, Kleist was not one to hang back.

His hatred of the French was not new. Since 1802, when the machinations of that "damned consul" had frustrated Kleist's plans to settle in Switzerland, much had happened to increase his loathing: Ulm, Augsburg, the piratical Peace of Pressburg, the division of Germany into two hostile camps by the founding of the Confederation of the Rhine, the final abolition of the Holy Roman Empire, the invasion of Prussia, the battles of Jena and Auerstedt, his own arrest and deportation, the emasculation and partition of Prussia, the coronation of Jérôme Bonaparte in Westphalia—one act of violence and treachery after another had taught him to regard this tyrant as the evil spirit of the age. At his very first encounter with the French, those "apes of reason," in 1801, he had begun to dislike heartily their mercurial wit, which struck him as frivolous, their hedonism, which struck him as immoral, their bureaucracy, of which he was to feel the full force five years later, during his illegal imprisonment at Châlons-sur-Marne. And on top of all that, serving such a master! Did they not deserve to be destroyed?

True, Kleist had been opportunistic: he had settled in Dresden although Saxony was dishonored by its membership in the Confederation of the Rhine and could almost be regarded as enemy territory; as co-director of the Phoenix Publishing House, he had planned to print the Code Napoléon and other French government publications; he had accepted the patronage of Monsieur de Bourgoing, the French ambassador. But all this had been done under pressure of seemingly unalterable political circumstances; if something could be done to change these circumstances, to overthrow the French power, then he was all for it, he would do his duty. Even if the attempt should fail and all should be lost. What mattered to him was not victory or defeat, but the battle itself. He was now resolved to do battle with the weapon he was best able to handle, his pen—with that weapon he would fight for the cause, for honor, freedom, and fatherland!

But he does not seem to have fought exclusively with his pen; he appears to have been involved with the Prussian Free Corps. At least the future General von Hüser, who along with Gneisenau, Lützow, Arndt, and others collected arms and stored them in rural hiding places, tells us that he rode many times to the Saxon border, where he met "Heinrich von Kleist, the well-known author, who lived in Dresden and shared our convictions," and gave him "papers"—the content of which is unknown to us.

We know little of Kleist's activities during the autumn and winter of 1808. From his none-too-informative correspondence we glean the following. In August, he informed his sister Ulrike that because the booksellers were hopelessly in arrears he would be unable to make the interest payments that had come due on her loan of five hundred talers. At the end of September, he asked her to visit him in Dresden on urgent business, since he himself was prevented from traveling by a tooth abscess, and she complied. Early in October, he completed the acting version of *Käthchen*, sent a copy to Joseph von Collin in Vienna, and another apparently to Berlin. In November, he reported to Ulrike that *Phöbus* had now been definitely taken over by Walther, who had assumed responsibility for all expenses, and that he, Kleist, was obliged, in the interest of the "amiable and excellent" Frau von Haza, to go to Lewitz in Posen, where apparently he had undertaken to see her ex-husband or her parents and straighten out certain difficulties in connection with her property. In December he thanked Collin for making certain cuts in *Käthchen*, informed him that the Berlin theater which was producing it was also making cuts, and at the same time asked him to collect and send his fee; on the first day of the year 1809, he gave Collin his new play *The Battle of Teutoburg Forest*, expressing the wish that because of its better chances of success it might, if possible, be produced before *Käthchen*.

Meanwhile, his good friend and collaborator Karl August Böttiger, the Dresden representative of Wieland's *Merkur*, had written secretly to Cotta, warning him against taking over *Phöbus*, as he seems to have considered doing, arguing that the boundless conceit of the editors, added to their total ignorance of all matters "concerning the great public of prospective buyers," had alienated everyone, with the result that some two thousand talers had been lost on the first five issues. And he concluded his friendly advice with the words: "Destroy this letter." Soon Böttiger was able to thank Cotta for having so graciously accepted his warning, which he assured him had been "well meant."

Probably Cotta needed no warning; the tactless behavior of *Phöbus* had undoubtedly been brought to his attention; Goethe was thought to have brought his influence with him to bear against Kleist, and we know for certain that, when Varnhagen von Ense visited him in November, Cotta spoke of his "dissatisfaction" with *Penthesilea* and said he had decided not to advertise it, for then no one would ask for it. And that is just what happened; at the beginning of our own century, some of the seven hundred and fifty copies comprising the first edition could still be purchased at the original catalogue price. Such was the conduct of the man whom Kleist, in July 1808, assured of his "sincere and undying devotion" for his willingness to publish *Penthesilea*. In writing this, Kleist intended no irony; he had no suspicion of what was being done behind his back to him and his work; his eyes were on the struggle and promise of the future, for which he was resolved to forge weapons, to pen resounding battle cries that would fire the irresolute with enthusiasm for the war that had become necessary.

This was the purpose of *The Battle of Teutoburg Forest*, which, as Körner reported to his son in December 1808, had been read at a number of gatherings but could not be printed, because, "strange as it may seem," it had a bearing on the present situation: "I do not like a writer to base his work on the real world; for it is precisely to escape depressing realities that we take flight into the realm of fantasy." This, undoubtedly, was one view of art; as long as Kleist had shared it (to some extent, that is, for he had always had a certain kind of "reality" in view), he had won little public favor, but now he was far beyond it. Flight into fantasy? By no means! In *The Battle of Teutoburg Forest*, fantasy was to be a whip to deter Kleist's fellow Germans from flight.

It is a propaganda play, pure and simple, and makes no attempt to be anything else. It is this singleness of purpose that gives it the brutal power which has kept it alive and young for more than a century and a half. Not for one moment does it distract us with beauty; not for one moment does the dialogue stray from this thesis: Germany must be free in order to be united, united in order to be free, and if any man has persistence, guile, courage, and fanaticism enough to undertake and perform this great task, let him be Germany's master! This man is Hermann (Arminius) the Cheruscan, a man of the world, affable in his conversations with Varus, the Roman general and governor, friendly but close-mouthed in his dealings with the kings of other German tribes, indulgent even toward those who were allied with the enemy (provided they showed their goodwill when the time was ripe), respectful to Marbodius, King of the Suebi, whom Roman diplomacy played off against him as a rival for leadership and to whom he entrusts his sons as hostages in pledge of his loyalty; a softspoken, circumspect, tireless intriguer, charming in his guile, a fox—but as fierce as a famished wildcat once his patient intrigues have borne fruit, springing at the enemy, ruthlessly destroying everything that stands in the way of his country's freedom.

The code is easily deciphered. Rome is Napoleon, Hermann and Marbodius are Prussia and Austria (or the other way around); the malcontents, the neutral German states, allied with Rome, are the princes of the Confederation of the Rhine. Rome/France has still other vassals—the women, who allow themselves to be beguiled by Gallic charm; in the play, one of these is Hermann's wife, Thusnelda, but gently, though not without cruelty, her husband instructs her, and she becomes the most bloodthirsty hater of all. And Germania's worst enemies are the "good" French, whose personal rectitude helps to maintain the general injustice.

> *You know what's right, accursed scoundrel,*
> *And yet, unwronged, you've come to Germany*
> *To oppress us.*
> *Take a club of double weight*
> *And strike him dead!*

In all this a politically and morally complicated picture is clarified, and the way out of an intolerable situation expounded by dramatic means, defended in debate against every possible objection, and proclaimed as the ethical imperative of the hour. The didactic qualities of this play are exemplary: the lucidity with which tangled situations are made clear without being oversimplified; the dramatic mastery with which the underlying conflicts are laid bare, intertwined, raised to the highest pitch, and at last cathartically resolved; the primordial passion, whose spell it is hard to resist even when it turns to berserk frenzy; and above all, the extraordinary character portrayal, which gives substance to those figures that are barely sketched, and truth and nobility to the protagonists: Thusnelda, commonplace, easily flattered, but terrible in the wrath of her offended vanity and honor; and above all Hermann, who shrewdly conceals so much behind his affable front—heroic ladykiller and grand seigneur, wise even under the most gruesome circumstances, a leader in the best sense of the word.

*The Battle of Teutoburg Forest* is a fully successful venture; if we nevertheless cannot give it our undivided love, it is because Kleist did not put his whole heart into it. Here he was obliged to defer his absolute strivings, for a propaganda play must argue a very definite and limited point and address itself to a very specific public. One might even go so far as to say that the more perfect such a play is of its kind, the further removed it is from "pure" literature. Asking for no remuneration, Kleist recommended it to the Vienna Burgtheater with the words: "It is my gift to the German people."

*The Battle of Teutoburg Forest* seems to have been favorably received from the start; otherwise, considering the public's recent unpleasant experience with its author, it would hardly have been "read at a number of gatherings." What with the urgency of Germany's plight, all had apparently been forgiven and forgotten. After having been virtually ostracized, Kleist had slipped back into public favor through the back door, so to speak. He soon had good reason for confidence in his popular appeal, especially since, far from contenting himself with *The Battle of Teutoburg Forest*, he had resolved to write only works that "are central to the times." What the times needed was clear: the situation was becoming more and more desperate; in January 1809, Napoleon mustered the Army of the Confederation of the Rhine for an invasion of Austria; it was essential to fire the nation with enthusiasm for the impending war. The fury Kleist set out to instill in the Germans was in his blood; and in the war songs and poems he wrote at this time, as well as in his play, he expressed it with virtuosity, pulling out all the stops. His tone could be solemn, imploring, or comic; he could make himself sound like a street-corner orator or a ballad singer.

In the most important of these pieces, *Germania to Her Children (Germania an ihre Kinder)*, the summons, with its merciless imagery suggesting the dark splendor of Gryphius, is answered in words of strident rejoicing, a kind of barbaric hunting call:

> *Let their whited skeletons*
> *Cover field and city square.*
> *Those that fox and vulture spurn,*
> *Let them be the fishes' share.*
> *Dam the rivers with their bodies,*
> *Let their flesh divert the Rhine,*
> *Send it round the whole Palatinate,*
> *There to be the borderline.*
>
> CHORUS
> *Hunt the wolf with dog and gun,*
> *Come and join us everyone.*
> *Shoot him dead and watch him die,*
> *No judge on earth will ask you why.*

By contrast, we find a tone of thoughtful, dignified exhortation in the poem *To Archduke Karl (An den Erzherzog Karl)*.

> *The German does not ask for victory,*
> *As he stands helpless over the abyss,*
> *But only that the torch of battle shine bright,*
> *Worthy of the corpse being carried to the grave.*

And then, in *War Song of the Germans (Kriegslied der Deutschen)*, the merry hurdy-gurdy tune:

> *Shaggy bear and panther beast*
> *Haven't roamed our woods for ages.*
> *At the very most we see them*
> *Penned in wire cages.*

. . . . . .

*Snakes we never see at all*
*And with otters it's the same.*
*Vanished is the dragon host,*
*Seven-headed, spewing flame.*

*Only Frenchmen still abide*
*In our German sphere.*
*Brothers, take a mighty club,*
*Drive them out of here.*

No less than *The Battle of Teutoburg Forest*, these poems bear witness not only to Kleist's virtuosity but also to his conviction that "a man must throw his whole weight, be it much, be it little, into the scales of the times"; they are a first fulfillment of his wish that he had "a voice of brass with which to harangue the German nation from the highest peak of the Harz." Nothing in them reveals his dangerous weakness at the time, his precarious mental state and dwindling self-confidence. One day, according to a story that comes to us at third hand, Rühle found Kleist lying unconscious after taking a massive dose of opium; but apart from this intimation of an unsuccessful attempt at suicide, nothing suggests that either he or his friends were aware of his alarming state of mind. His despair hid behind (and possibly stimulated) his martial enthusiasm, and may in part have been submerged by his daily cares, by his eternal money troubles (although Aunt Massow's death held out the prospect of a small inheritance—a drop in the bucket), by professional problems and private quarrels.

These last had largely to do with Adam Müller. The resentment he felt toward Müller has never been fully explained, but we do know that disagreements in connection with *Phöbus* had something to do with it. The twelfth and last issue, due in December 1808, had finally appeared in February 1809. The editors were trying to persuade Walther to keep it going for another year. Müller, who represented *Phöbus* in the negotiations, seems to have relinquished a claim of 136 reichstalers without obtaining Kleist's consent. We cannot be certain whether or not this claim had to do with the booksellers' arrears Kleist had mentioned to Ulrike; in any event, Kleist felt wronged or at least offended by Müller's high-handedness and wrote him that if Walther undertook to publish *Phöbus* for another year he, Kleist, would either resign or look for a co-editor to replace Hofrat Müller. (For Müller in the meantime, probably in recognition of his lectures at the house of Prince Bernhard, had been made a privy councilor of the Duchy of Sachsen-Weimar. It seemed as though everyone in Kleist's circle was winning titles, posts, honors—everyone except Kleist himself.)

The letter also makes it clear that apart from Müller's high-handedness, other matters "that have no place in this letter" had marred their friendship. As so often in Kleist's biography, our only indication of what these matters may have been is rumor. Rumor had it that the two friends quarreled over Sophie von Haza, who, after obtaining her divorce in 1808, had become Müller's wife. While walking with a certain lady on the Brühl Terrace, Kleist allegedly cried out: "I must have Müller's wife; if he refuses to step aside, he must die!" The lady, it seems, was much taken aback, for Kleist's interest in Frau Müller came as a complete surprise to her. Later in the day, the story goes on, Kleist met Müller on the Elbe Bridge and threatened to throw him into the river.

Kleist's relations with women (with the sole exception of Wilhelmine von Zenge) are so shrouded in mystery that it is not even possible to determine whether he actually slept with any of them; there is some reason to doubt it. Possibly he was physically or psychologically incapable of a "normal" sex life and expended his libido on his work. Still, the rumor about Kleist and Sophie von Haza may not have been entirely unfounded. There are numerous indications of his feeling for her: he stood by her during the divorce proceedings; he gave her (as one of her daughters by her first marriage told Tieck) a copy, or possibly the original, of the lost *Story of My Soul (Geschichte meiner Seele)*, which was said to have been a unique record of his inner life; she was permitted to read his (likewise lost) journal, and he wrote her a most affectionate letter on the day before his death. Of course, all this does not prove that he loved her, but it does leave open the possibility of a fit of jealousy during one of his manic periods.

The quarrel with Müller, in any event, was not long-lived, though for a time it was so violent that Müller challenged Kleist to a duel—which fortunately never came to pass. We also hear that Kleist, usually enthusiastic about his friend's skillful elocution, took to ridiculing his nasal voice and, when Tieck asked him why he had been absent from Müller's reading of *Käthchen*, cried out in indignation: "Can you expect me to sit there and listen while that fellow massacres my writing!" Yet, in January 1809, Kleist wrote to his patron, the finance minister Baron zum Altenstein, warmly recommending Müller for a post in Berlin. At the beginning of 1810, Kleist went to Berlin, chiefly, as he himself said, because Müller was there. And indeed what contemporary was better able to understand Kleist, the man as well as his work, than the friend who said that Kleist loved death as the spice of an insipid life?

On April 6, 1809, Archduke Karl, the Austrian Minister of War, issued a proclamation saying: "The cause of Germany is our cause," and three days later Austria declared war on France. Karl invaded Bavaria, uprisings fomented by Austria broke out in the Tyrol, some of which under such leaders as Andreas Hofer were temporarily successful. In Dresden, as Kleist heard, Bernadotte urged the king, with the "most monstrous threats," to leave his residence, and the king and queen drove away in tears. Whereupon Bernadotte destroyed all the cannon and ammunition wagons he could not take away with him, and marched out of Dresden at the head of the Saxon army. On the 16th, Archduke Karl occupied Munich, but on the 22nd and 23rd Napoleon stopped his advance in a series of bloody engagements, the last being the battle of Regensburg, and compelled him to retreat with heavy losses. In Prussia, meanwhile, all was quickly made ready for war; impatiently, Dörnberg, Schill, and Duke Wilhelm of Brunswick advanced with their Free Corps, in the hope of carrying all North Germany along with them.

Kleist's friends were dispersed by the whirl of events: Varnhagen von Ense joined the Austrian army; Rühle, as an officer in the army of Sachsen-Weimar, was with Prince Bernhard on Bernadotte's staff; Gentz went to Vienna; Adam Müller had remained in Dresden for personal reasons but was soon to apply for a government post in Berlin. And Kleist? As far as we know, he showed no eagerness to join the army; he did not think of himself as a soldier, and hoped for the present to stay where he was and go on working. He made up his mind to leave only when the course of events made it seem urgent. Then he procured a passport for Austria. It was made out for two persons: himself and Friedrich Christoph Dahlmann.

This Dahlmann, born in Weimar in 1785 (which made him seven years younger than Kleist), had come to Dresden early in 1809 in the hope of giving lectures there. Later he wrote histories of Denmark and of the English and French revolutions, and was highly esteemed as a scholar and a man of integrity. In 1837, with the Grimm brothers, Gervinus, and others, he belonged to the famous "Göttingen seven" (who were banished for their condemnation of the King of Hanover's anti-liberal coup de force) and in 1848 participated in the efforts of the Frankfurt parliament to frame a German constitution. In 1809 he was an idealistic young man, wondering "what to do with himself in this Napoleonic world." His lecture projects had fallen through and he was leading a lonely and aimless life in the Dresden suburb of Pirna. One evening, his friend the painter Ferdinand Hartmann introduced him to Kleist. When Karl August Böttiger (who had written so "solicitously" to Cotta on the subject of *Phöbus*) arrived and started to monopolize Hartmann with his chatter, Dahlmann asked Kleist to accompany him to a nearby tavern. There they struck up a lively conversation, quickly discovered a mutual sympathy, and decided to set out on foot together for Austria, where they would try to find a way of making themselves useful.

On April 29, Kleist set out from Dresden with his new friend, leaving nothing behind except a few debts with the merchant Salomon Ascher, which he asked Ulrike to pay out of his share of Aunt Massow's legacy.

The two friends, tied together like a married couple by their "double passport," had toyed with the thought of traveling with Baron Buol of the Austrian embassy, but Buol had left Dresden before them. Nor did they find him at Teplitz, so they continued alone, heading for Vienna via Prague. Kleist's power-

ful personality made a deep impression on young Dahlmann and
their journey was favored by a warm and spirited comradeship.
Often Dahlmann was asked to read aloud, as Hartmann the
painter had done before him. (Hartmann had told Dahlmann of
Kleist's reason for employing him as a reader: "You read so
abominably, dear Hartmann, that if my writings still appeal to
me when read by you, they must be good.") Or else Kleist
read to Dahlmann. Occasionally, when Kleist felt critical of
his own work, he would begin to stutter; but sometimes he read
in a tone of hard passion which remained forever engraved in
the memory of his listener, as for example when he declaimed
these lines of the Chorus of Bards from *The Battle of Teutoburg Forest:* "For many years we've practiced / Forgiveness as
the gods have taught us. / But now the yoke has grown too
heavy / And demands to be thrown off." And then they discussed what had been read, and argued about it; for, despite his
great admiration, Dahlmann found things to criticize in Kleist's
work. He disliked Kleist's mystical bent and his "tiresome Berlin habit" of resorting to ugliness as well as tricks and manner-
isms for the sake of effect, a tendency which in his opinion was
quite incompatible with the elevated tenor of the works. But
Kleist, who was of course far more experienced than his young
companion, knew how much calculation is implicit in art, and
also knew that a writer must reconcile himself to the specific
demands of his art, however repellent. Thus, he never gave in,
never accepted any other criticism than his own, but clung to
his opinion "with the stubborn rigidity that was his basic nature." But this rigidity did not impair Dahlmann's affection,
which stayed with him for life. Later on, after he had become
a professor in Kiel, he heard that Kleist was having a bad time
of it in Berlin and wrote him a letter (which unfortunately
never reached him), suggesting that they pool their resources
and live together. And long after Kleist's death he wrote: "His
death made a hole in my life that has never been filled"—and
yet they had spent only a few months together.

In Prague, they at last caught up with Baron Buol, who introduced them to Count Kolowrat-Liebsteinsky, then city-
captain and later governor and minister. The connection with

him was expected to open up all sorts of possibilities, but for
the present nothing came of it, unless, as has been supposed,
the friends' hurried departure from Prague was the result of
some agreement between Kleist and Kolowrat, of which Dahlmann learned nothing. In any case, they had hardly arrived in
Prague when they were on the road again, though we do not
know exactly when they left or what their new destination
was. It was probably Vienna, but on May 13 Napoleon made his
entry into the Austrian capital and the friends had to relinquish
any thought of going there.

They plodded on side by side, often keeping silent for hours.
Then suddenly one of them would open his mouth and pursue
a thought which the other had been thinking in silence—so
intimate had they become, so much of one mind, especially
where the one overriding question was concerned: the fate of
Germany in this war. Kleist, with his firm belief that ideas were
formed in the process of speaking, may have used these conversations to clarify certain concepts which he committed to
writing either during their journey or immediately afterward.
Yes, Kleist and Dahlmann understood each other perfectly.
When they stopped to rest, they devoted themselves with equal
enthusiasm to the game of Kriegsspiel, a kind of strategic chess,
invented by Pfuel for training purposes and played on a map
with movable markers representing the troops of two opposing
armies. They devoted considerable time to it, convinced of its
educational value despite the contrary opinion of Prussian Lieutenant Colonel von dem Knesebeck, whom they chanced to
meet at an inn in Znaim.

Karl Friedrich von dem Knesebeck, later field marshal, a
personal friend of Friedrich Wilhelm III and IV, and inciden-
tally the second husband of Kleist's old friend Adolphine von
Werdeck, had been commissioned to represent Prussia in secret
negotiations with Austria aimed at an alliance between the two
countries. Since his Austrian interlocutor was Archduke Karl,
Knesebeck had chosen to establish himself and his retinue in
Znaim, which was not far from Austrian headquarters. He
knew Kleist well from Berlin; Kleist's passion for Pfuel's Kriegsspiel provoked first his ridicule, then his anger. Sheer nonsense,

he said, having no bearing whatever on military theory. This touched a sore spot in Kleist, who defended the game, adducing more and more arguments in its favor, becoming colder and stiffer as Knesebeck's fury increased. In the end, Knesebeck shouted: "The devil take them!" and rushed out of the room.

Another strange incident was soon to follow. Dahlmann had bought himself a brace of pistols. Kleist loaded them in spite of his friend's warnings, then forgot about them and left them in the dining hall. The next morning a young officer belonging to Knesebeck's staff picked one of them up; it went off and the bullet almost grazed Dahlmann's temple. "Thank God you're not hit!" cried the horrified officer. "But damnation, *I* am!" Knesebeck roared, holding the shoulder where the bullet had lodged.

The friends went on to Stockerau. On the morning of May 22, they were sitting immersed in their game of Kriegsspiel, when the landlord rushed in and cried out: "Gentlemen! How can you sit there playing games! Haven't you heard? The battle has started." There was no holding Kleist. He jumped up and marched straight to the Bisamberg, a hill overlooking the Danube. From there, through his field glasses, he saw the massed advance of the French divisions and saw a number of villages taken and retaken in the course of furious engagements. At noon the Austrians counterattacked and in the afternoon both armies withdrew. This was the battle of Aspern and Essling, the only serious defeat suffered by Napoleon in this war. Full of enthusiasm, Kleist returned to Stockerau, wrote a report on what he had seen, and sent it via Count Kolowrat to Knesebeck, whose wounded shoulder had obliged him to leave Znaim for Prague.

The world was beautiful. Kleist's shining hope, the one thing that had made his life worth living, was about to be fulfilled. He felt the need of watching the war more closely, of seeing everything with his own eyes. Unable to sit still, he persuaded the landlord to harness his carriage and drive Dahlmann and himself to the battlefield at Aspern. There, in the midst of sickening devastation, they saw a peasant collecting bullets. Kleist went over and questioned him about the battle. Had the

French built a bridge, or was this arm of the Danube shallow enough to ford? The peasant looked at him distrustfully. What peculiar German the man spoke! His suspicions aroused by Kleist's Prussian accent, the peasant slipped away and reported the two friends to the nearest Austrian guard post. Suddenly they saw soldiers coming, more and more of them, converging from all sides, and a moment later they understood what the soldiers were shouting to one another: "French spies! Spies!" The friends were surrounded, some officers appeared. Dahlmann thought he would faint when Kleist, asked for identification, reached into his pocket, pulled out some poems, and handed them to the officers. The fighting men went purple with rage: poems as identification papers! And to make matters worse, war poems. The gall of this civilian, meddling with their serious trade. And when at last the Austrian officers read his name, they vented their contempt for Prussia and the once-warlike Prussians. And wasn't Kleist himself ashamed to bear the name of his kinsman, General von Kleist, who had surrendered Magdeburg? But, on the other hand, was he telling the truth? Was that really his name? Who were they anyway, and what were they doing here on the battlefield?

The soldiers dragged them away to the village of Aspern. There, in a half-demolished apothecary shop, they were questioned and their answers taken down. So they had come from Stockerau, had they? In their landlord's carriage? Exactly, and the man was waiting to drive them back. Splendid! But what had become of this mysterious landlord with his carriage? He was nowhere to be seen, for, on observing his guests' difficulties, he had driven away as fast as he could, for fear his team would be requisitioned. And so, since everything they had said was untrue, they were sent on to headquarters at Neustadl, where Baron von Hiller, who was in charge, listened to their story with a smile. A bit rash of them, he said, roaming around on a fresh battlefield, but no harm done. He nodded with friendly condescension, and they were discharged.

For Kleist it was an unpleasant little adventure, the fourth time—after Würzburg, Boulogne, and Berlin—he had got himself suspected of espionage. Could this be an evil omen? Both men felt humiliated and discouraged. Utterly exhausted, they had a good hour's hike ahead of them until at last they found shelter at the village of Kagran.

But the adventure was soon forgotten amid the rejoicing over the great victory of Aspern and Essling. Their feeling of triumph was further nourished by the uprisings in northern Germany, by the success of the Duke of Braunschweig-Öl's "Black Band" and of Major von Schill's campaign. On May 31, when the friends arrived in Prague, they could not yet know that Schill had fallen that same day while defending Stralsund, or that the Archduke Karl was lying idle by the Danube, apparently failing to notice that Napoleon was busily mustering reinforcements with which to avenge the defeat of Aspern and Essling.

In Prague the friends took up lodgings in a house that is still standing today, at Brückengasse 39, across from the Café Steinitz; they had only a few steps to go to Karmelitergasse, where they took their noonday meal, or to the Karlsbrücke, with its turreted gates and statues of saints. On one side of the bridge, looking upstream, they could see the Hradčany; on the other, the gray houses of the old city rising from the water and the swiftly flowing river with its verdant islands. A good place in which to live a quiet life, secretly forging weapons for the German war of liberation.

Kleist worked with renewed enthusiasm, producing fine, well-polished essays on patriotic subjects, which were read aloud to Count Kolowrat and his friends, who applauded them and supported Kleist and Dahlmann in their decision to make such material available to a larger public by founding a weekly magazine. The name *Germania* was decided on, a publisher was mobilized, and an application for a license submitted to the Ministry of the Interior through Burgrave von Wallis. Kleist personally asked Friedrich Schlegel, then secretary at the imperial chancellery and consequently stationed at the Archduke Karl's headquarters, to use his influence at the ministry and to contribute to the magazine. Contributions, it was decided, would be paid for and would appear unsigned (except when the author expressly wished to be named) so as to enable German writers in countries that were still officially neutral to work for the great cause.

At this point in his career, Kleist cared nothing for fame and was interested solely in the cause. He was a fanatic, but there was wit in his fanaticism, and that is rare, for as a rule fanatical outpourings are as monotonous as the barking of angry dogs. The essays Kleist wrote for the projected *Germania* are brilliant and varied, providing solid logical underpinning for the ideas expounded poetically in *The Battle of Teutoburg Forest*. The need for German unity in this war; the need to subordinate all considerations of local or personal power and advantage. The need to sacrifice moral scruples to the sacred ideal of freedom; disparagement of every inclination to "play it safe" in this bitter battle, which had better end in death and destruction than remain unfought; the need to hate the enemy with all one's heart and soul, to take every opportunity to injure and if possible destroy him—these are the themes by which not only Kleist the patriot but, with slight changes of emphasis, Kleist the artist can be identified, and it is the common root of his political and artistic passion that gives these short pieces their power and authenticity.

It also gives them their amazing formal virtuosity, their self-assured humor, their perfect diction. They are masterpieces of pamphleteering, hard as steel and free from bombast; their trenchant wit is good-humored, one might almost say genial, their dogmatism spiced with surprises. Whatever his subject, he casts it in highly original and appropriate form: as philippic or exhortation, as fable, satire, didactic dialogue, or pseudo-scientific treatise; he plays with different styles, but never for their own sakes, never to flatter his artistic vanity; the substance of even the most entertaining pieces is deeply serious, discernibly and demonstrably based on his own experience, as, for example, in the short essay *What Is Important in This War?* (*Was gilt es in diesem Kriege?*): "Is it the fame of a young and energetic prince, who has dreamed of laurels in the fragrance of a soft summer night?" These few words were the first announcement of the play that was to be the crown of Kleist's lifework.

For the present, he belonged to the moment with all the exultation, all the passionate hope and expectation of a proud and untamed heart. But anxiety was never far off. He saw clearly that the Austrian preparations, paralyzed by considerations of domestic policy, always lagged behind the course of events, for much as the Austrian leaders feared Napoleon, they feared revolution and democracy more. Drastic action must be taken at once—such was Kleist's demand. The Emperor Francis must issue a proclamation calling for a people's war, or, as we would say today, for total war. All males over sixteen years of age and under sixty must be called to arms; any German captured while fighting on the enemy side must be tried by court-martial; and when the war was over, a Diet should be summoned to draft a suitable constitution. Kleist titled this essay *On the Salvation of Austria (Über die Rettung von Österreich)*, which must have sounded almost blasphemous after the victory of May 21–22 but was far from exaggeratedly pessimistic. On July 5 a battle was joined at Wagram, which, after initial Austrian success, brought a crushing defeat and led, before a week had passed, to the armistice of Znaim, after which no saving military action was possible.

Wagram came as a terrible blow. As he wrote to Ulrike, Kleist was stunned—not so much by the events, which could more or less have been foreseen, as by being condemned to survive them. Apart from his shattered hopes, hadn't "the whole business of writing" become pointless, since the topical character of his recent work doomed it to failure, while the untimeliness of his earlier work deprived it of all interest? A hopeless dilemma; he could not help seeing that along with the Austria and Germany of his dreams he, too, had been destroyed at Wagram—intellectually, emotionally, and materially. All was over. There was no more future, not a glimmer of hope. "How shall I ever pull myself together? I cannot say."

# 19

# THE PRINCE OF HOMBURG

LEIST's collapse in Prague is shrouded in even deeper darkness than the similar episodes in his past—in Thun, in Paris, and in Mainz.

According to one report, he was cared for at the monastery of the Knights Hospitalers; but Dahlmann, who was in Prague with him the whole time, makes no mention of any hospitalization, and Kleist's name does not appear in the hospital records.

A rumor that he was dead made its way to North Germany; Müller heard it in Berlin, and Wilhelm Grimm wrote about it to his brother Jakob.

Friedrich Laun tells us in his memoirs that Kleist had hatched a plan to do away with Napoleon. Apparently, Kleist had asked Hartmann to procure a certain quantity of arsenic for him; Hartmann had replied that Kleist was not the man for such a task, but Kleist had only repeated his request. It seems that Hartmann actually procured the poison, but then handed it over to a Dresden apothecary. If there was any truth in the story, the absurd idea that an outsider could poison the closely guarded emperor must have been a mere pretext—possibly to cover up an attempt at suicide.

Fifty years later, in a letter to Emil Kuh, Friedrich von Raumer quoted Chancellor von Hardenberg as saying: "Don't waste any more time on the poor fellow! Kleist, you know, once spent several months in the district insane asylum at Bayreuth." If true, this story might throw some light on Kleist's disappearance. But, in point of fact, painstaking research has provided no other indication that Kleist ever spent any time in a mental institution.

Be that as it may, Kleist disappeared from mid-July to the end of October 1809. We have no news of him whatever for this period, and for the next three months only the vaguest information. The door was wide open to rumor; there was talk of illness, insanity, attempts to assassinate Napoleon, death, and suicide. All we know for sure is that he must have been having a very bad time of it.

The defeat had come as a cruel blow to him, but still worse was the ease with which the vanquished seemed to be accepting their lot. When it became known that the peace terms would not be too hard, that what the Little Corporal had really set his mind on was marrying into the house of Habsburg, the mood suddenly changed. Gloom gave way to optimism, hostility to friendship, hate to love. Napoleon, soon to be the Austrian emperor's son-in-law, suddenly became an object of adulation, the people prayed for him in church, his green frock coat became the height of fashion overnight. One of Kleist's most powerful patrons, Count von Wallis, Burgrave of Bohemia, was among the first in Prague to sport the splendid new garment.

The people had such a shamefully short memory—that was what shocked Kleist most deeply, that and the realization that the "people" are not by any means recruited exclusively from the lower classes. Yet no bitterness is discernible in his writing. His disappointment did not mar his spirit, and when in his despair he grasped at the one thing he had left, his work, a luminous, flowering world full of dreamlike beauty came into being.

He had begun, even before the disaster of Wagram, to think about his new play—*The Prince of Homburg* (*Prinz Friedrich von Homburg*); the previously cited allusion to it in his essay *What Is Important in This War?* shows that it had already taken on definite form in his mind.

It has been claimed that Kleist attended an art exhibition in Berlin in 1800 and there saw a picture by the Brunswick painter Kretschmar, showing the Prince of Homburg and the Great Elector together. We know for sure that he later read Frederick the Great's *Memoirs of the House of Brandenburg*, in which it is related how in 1675, at the battle of Fehrbellin, Homburg attacked the Swedes in direct disobedience of orders, so obliging the Elector to support him as the only means of saving his own troops from destruction. After the victory, the Elector forgave the prince for the folly that had endangered the very survival of the state, saying: "Under a strict interpretation of military law, you should have been put to death, but it would be displeasing to God were I to stain my laurels with the blood of a prince who has been one of the foremost instruments of my victory."

And something of the sort had happened in the course of one of Frederick's own campaigns. In 1758, at Zorndorf, where Frederick had defeated the Russians, General Seydlitz had disobeyed a strict order. Called to account, he said: "After the battle, my head is at the king's disposal; during the battle, I claim the right to use it in the king's service." The Fehrbellin incident, however, is a fable, which Frederick, who visited the battlefield in his days as crown prince, had culled from the mouths of the local population and gladly written down. The historical truth is somewhat less romantic. Homburg had not disobeyed orders, he had merely been dissatisfied with his share of the spoils, and to calm him down the Grand Elector had promised him "extraordinary delectations" for the future; moreover, this Homburg was not a prince but a landgrave, the "landgrave with the silver leg," a hardened old soldier in his forties, twice married and the father of a large brood.

The historical reality—assuming it was known to Kleist—was useless for dramatic purposes, whereas the popular legend taken down by Frederick the Great was inspiring and not without a certain bearing on the present situation, since Frederick William III condemned the bold independence of the Free Corps commanders as indiscipline; and Kleist, as we know, was close to the Free Corps movement. In the dramatist's mind the story took the following form. The young hero is given to sleepwalking. Only half awake when orders are issued, he barely listens. Later, on the battlefield, he disregards the order not to move from his position until notified, attacks and defeats the enemy. But military law is severe, and he is sentenced to death for his disobedience. At the sight of the grave that has been dug for him, he is seized with panic fear, and has no other desire than to *live*. But then, faced with an ultimate choice, he brings himself to choose death, if it can be avoided only by a dubious manipulation of the law. Here we have a typically Kleistian theme, which in its elaboration was to be intertwined with dreams of love and country and of Prussian military prowess, of alarums and excursions, Blücherian daring and brilliant leadership—a patriotic play, capable of becoming an enormous success in this (as he later wrote to Fouqué) "somewhat barren, but for that very reason, if I may say so, alluring field."

When one thinks of *The Prince of Homburg*, what comes first to mind is not the plot and not the central problem, but the accessories, the atmosphere, the musical, dream quality. Kleist himself, in his first reference to it, speaks only of the young hero's dreaming in the "fragrance of a soft summer night." And indeed, little or nothing would be gained, and the reader would be brought no closer to the essence of the play, were we to attempt a detailed treatment of the dramatic structure or the moral conflict. The heart of the work is in the atmosphere, the dreamer's smile, the memories of a lost childhood, the prince's integrity, the pious harmony created by the strange consonance of the opening and closing scenes, the unique correspondence between beginning and end. The German theater knows no more beautiful, more moving hymn to love of country than this play. One might compare it with Schiller's *Wilhelm Tell*, which is also celebrated—and rightly so—for its poignant picture of a country and its people, and yet it does not bear comparison with *The Prince of Homburg*, because it *declaims*, with ringing words to be sure, a love of country which here as though by enchantment informs every single word.

And yet, with all its lyrical qualities, *Homburg* is a drama, a stageworthy, well-constructed play. It starts with a scene that establishes the hero's sleepwalking (here again, somnambulism is the opening theme) and moves along at a sprightly pace. A joke is made of the prince's idiosyncrasy, "a mental aberration,"

as one of the officers calls it, but from out of his dream the
sleepwalker discloses his secret love for the Elector's niece, and
thus, as though in passing, the first knot of the conflict is tied.
Here lyricism and drama are one, just as in previous plays the
static and the dynamic, myth and psychology were one. With
every scene, almost with every word, the plot moves toward
its ultimate goal. Nearly everything that happens comes from
within the characters and next to nothing from outside, but this
does not impair the forward movement and certainly does not
produce the effect of dramatized psychology. Nevertheless, the
action is psychologically accurate, true to life, and in the highest degree original. In this play, the characters are seen from
within: the prince with his intermingled love, dreams, and
youthful heroism, trembling before the yawning emptiness of
the grave, and at the end ennobled by the reborn courage which
enables him to hallow justice by surrendering to the harshness
of the law; Colonel Kottwitz, the rough but sensitive old soldier, who boldly speaks his mind, even in the presence of the
highest authority; Princess Natalie, a great lady despite her
youth, innocent, sympathetic to the weakness of the beloved
Homburg, proud of his brave readiness to sacrifice himself, so
moved that she puts her love into words, and calls out to him
as though sending a message to the other world: "I like you!"
—as simple and honest and warmhearted as a young lady of the
Prussian country nobility;* and the Elector, that eminently
mature ruler, utterly devoid of egoism, with his wisdom, his
firmness tempered by gentleness, and his pardoning gesture,
tinged ever so slightly with cruelty.

These are the characters who create the action, who weave
it into a conflict that threatens disaster, and finally resolve it in
a spirit of conciliation which seems to whisper soothingly to
the frightened audience: "Take heart. It's only a play." Thus,
in the last scene the Prince of Homburg receives what in the
first he only dreamed of, receives it as in a dream: "Oh, tell me,
is it a dream?" Kottwitz replies: "A dream, what else?"

* The German "*Du gefällst mir*" does indeed mean "I like you," but
in this context implies admiration or approval: "I like you and approve
of you," "You are a man after my own heart."—Trans.

In this dream the wildness, the excessiveness we find in Kleist's other work are toned down and transformed into something benign—Kohlhaas's fanatical, self-destructive passion for justice into the Elector's *idea* of justice as pillar and prop of the state; the orgiastic blood lust of the heroes of *Penthesilea* into Kottwitz's rugged and Homburg's romantic soldierliness; Penthesilea's erotic raving and Käthchen's masochistic submissiveness into Natalie's charming forthrightness: "I like you"; the sadism of *The Broken Jug* and *Amphitryon* into the Elector's fatherly instruction, his character-building game of pronouncing the death sentence when he has secretly decided from the start to pardon; the sensual Karamazovism of *The Marquise of O.* into the modest dignity of a Prussian lady; the patriotic frenzy and guile of *The Battle of Teutoburg Forest* into a patriotism that has no need to gesticulate.

In the language of *The Prince of Homburg* there is a mature naturalness, a graceful innocence that never strikes a false note; it has no need to hammer its point home, no need of pathos to move us or of dialectic to convince us. Despite a certain old-fashioned fairy-tale quality, it is fresh and strong, a strangely irresistible mixture of the pithy and the delicate, and all in all a product of somnambulistic, musical harmony.

What, one is inclined to wonder—what, in view of Kleist's deep distress, was the source of this harmony? "I have closed my accounts with the world," says the Prince of Homburg. And the man who wrote this play was finished when he wrote it, no further hope or fear disturbed his peace of mind. This was a peace which the poet, if not the man, could welcome in the words of Homburg: "O immortality, now you are wholly mine!" In this peace celebration, which was an anticipated leave-taking, everything he loved, everything that had put its imprint on him reappears: Prussia, Brandenburg, its staunch, truehearted people, as unchanging as the gold ground of old paintings, which gives the figures of heroes and rulers their full depth and form, the bond of unservile reciprocity between masters and servants, and the clumsy rectitude that made him smile. For that he was able to do—smile. Can any other serious German play smile as winningly as *The Prince of Homburg?*

And what bonhomie there is in this humor, even when it
touches on last things! In the prince's speech, for example, when
someone along the way to his supposed execution hands him a
carnation: "Oh, thank you. I shall put it in water when I get
home." The man who could utter these words had done with
his sorrows, had merged them with a serene joy, had somehow
created a unity of here and hereafter. After that, nothing remained to be done. *The Prince of Homburg* was Kleist's death
song; its harmony is the harmony of death, its appeasement
that of a man weary of torment, who lays himself to rest with
a happy sigh.

But Kleist the fallible man had not yet reached the same
point as the poet; ample trouble and suffering still lay ahead of
him, and the serene evening sun that illumined his life as an
artist shed few of its rays on his daily existence.

True, we know next to nothing of his life at this time. We
do know that on October 30 he and Dahlmann applied to the
provincial government in Prague for passports to Dresden, and
that Kleist turned up in Frankfurt shortly before the end of
November. While there, he met Luise von Zenge, the "golden
sister," for the last time. He recited one of his poems to her and
when she could not identify the author, he lamented: "O Lord,
what do I write poems for!" He had come on Ulrike's account,
or more precisely because he needed money. But Ulrike was
off on one of her innumerable trips, this time to Pomerania.
Though unable to consult her, he nevertheless applied to the
merchant Johann Samuel Wöllmitz, who made him a loan of
five hundred talers, secured by Kleist's share of the house on
Nonnenwinkel. At the same time, Kleist left instructions that
all income from the house and his share in a possible sale should
automatically be made over to Ulrike as part payment of his
debt to her—a gesture which did not entirely make amends for
his highhanded and probably illegal borrowing against jointly
held property. He had behaved in very much the same way in
connection with Aunt Massow's estate. Though strictly speaking not entitled to dispose of his share, he had nevertheless sent
for portions of it, first from Dresden, and later from Prague,
which he would otherwise have been unable to leave.

Alas, creative genius is "priceless" in both senses of the word, and there was no end to his poverty. Ulrike, who was not wealthy, kept having to help him out, with no other return than empty promises of repayment. Her friendly feelings toward him were seeping away; she had no appreciation of his greatness as an artist and was gradually coming to share the family's conviction, which brother-in-law Pannwitz had once put into words: "If only he had a grain of sense, he'd have made his fortune long ago with his genius." She failed to understand that *not* having a grain of sense was an integral part of his genius, and her annoyance was increased by Kleist's failure to discuss financial matters with her. On the present occasion he again neglected to do so, and merely wrote that the reasons for what he had done had no place in a letter and that he was returning to Austrian territory.

Did he actually return? We do not know. The surviving letters show only that at the beginning of January 1810 he was— for what purpose, it is impossible to ascertain—in Frankfurt on the Main, from where he sent Cotta a manuscript of *Käthchen* with a request that the fee be sent as soon as possible, and that at the end of the same month he stopped for a short time in Gotha, where he seems to have made some sort of financial deal with his old friend Hartmann von Schlotheim. From there he wrote to Collin, asking about the destinies of *The Battle of Teutoburg Forest* and *Käthchen*. Had the latter been produced? As it happened, *Käthchen* was performed (without noteworthy success) on the evenings of the 17th, 18th, and 19th, in connection with the Vienna Nuptial Festivities—in honor of Napoleon, so to speak.

On February 4, 1810, Kleist returned to Berlin for the last time and for good.

# 20

# LITERARY BERLIN IN 1810

O N Kleist's return to Berlin, his situation was similar to what it had been on his arrival in Dresden two and a half years before. Apart from minor pieces, he had to his credit several important works that had not yet been published in book form: plays—*Käthchen of Heilbronn, The Battle of Teutoburg Forest, The Prince of Homburg*—as well as stories—*The Earthquake in Chile, The Marquise of O.,* a good part of *Michael Kohlhaas,* and probably a certain amount of preparatory work for *The Betrothal in Santo Domingo.* He had his entrées everywhere, both in literary circles and in high society, and he was as desperately poor as he had been in Dresden. There was only one important change: his life drive had been dangerously sapped, though his Prussian self-discipline hid this weakness from others and perhaps even from himself. Yet he was in apparent good health, a thickset young man of thirty-two, with a small round head, short hair that had darkened from chestnut to almost black, and expressive blue eyes, which, though habitually thoughtful and grave, could take on a mischievous twinkle.

Adam Müller was in Berlin, where he had arrived in 1809, hoping, according to his detractors, "to smuggle himself into the university that had just been founded"; he apparently had some sort of connection with various government departments and at the time of Kleist's arrival was giving a course of lectures on Frederick the Great. The two friends had quarreled seriously; Müller had gone so far as to challenge Kleist to a duel, but now Kleist, who could not help loving the man who understood his work so well, turned up at Müller's quarters as friendly and smiling as if nothing had happened. Delighted at the renewal of their friendship, Müller spoke of Kleist to his friends as of one "who had mystically risen from the dead."

Müller introduced Kleist to Clemens Brentano and Achim von Arnim, the leaders of the romantic movement, who had also come to Berlin in 1809; while visiting them, Kleist probably met Joseph von Eichendorff, who was there for a short stay. What is certain is that Kleist took his noonday walk almost daily with Brentano and Arnim, and settled in their neighborhood, at Mauerstrasse 53, in the house of Quartermaster Müller, while they lived at Mauerstrasse 34 with Privy Postal Councilor Pistor, an intelligent, cultivated man who installed a bowling alley in his garden, which became a meeting place for his lodgers and their friends. Though Kleist spent a good deal of his time with Brentano and Arnim, we have no indication that they found him unduly depressed. Brentano described him as "uneven in his moods, good as gold, poor and staunch," while Arnim thought him the most outspoken person he had met in a long time, "almost to the point of cynicism"; and there is no doubt that with his dry wit and radical love of the truth Kleist must sometimes have made a cynical impression. Arnim, himself a Prussian nobleman, a Protestant and a North German through and through, was well equipped to understand Kleist; he characterized him aptly as "strange and slightly unbalanced," the sort of personality that almost always develops "when talent works its way out of the old Prussian mold."

Through his friendship with Brentano, Arnim, and Müller, Kleist met the leading Berlin publishers, first of all Johann Daniel Sander, "good fat Sander, who goes crazy once every year," as Brentano said of him. At Sander's home, men and women of wit and talent gathered in an atmosphere of perfect informality; one of his regular guests was Charlotte von Kalb, celebrated for her romantic affairs with Schiller and Jean Paul. She is known to have read and admired *The Schroffenstein Family* and possibly other works of Kleist's.

With the wealthy Georg Andreas Reimer, owner of the

Realschul-Buchhandlung (founded in 1750 but so named only in 1809), Kleist had a point of political contact even before they actually met, for both had been connected with the Prussian Free Corps movement. From time to time, Ernst Moritz Arndt, who had been banished from Germany and was supposedly living in Sweden, would visit Reimer in disguise and under a false name; he, too, had belonged to the Free Corps movement. During the *Germania* period, Kleist had written an article justifying the apocalyptic prophecies of Arndt's *Spirit of the Times* against the critics who thought them "exaggerated," and it seems more than likely that Kleist met his fellow patriot now in 1810.

He was already acquainted with Julius Eduard Hitzig (or, more properly, Itzig), whom he had met at the house of Ezechiel Benjamin Cohen in 1804–5, in the days when the poets of the Northern Star Association, Varnhagen, Ludwig Robert, and Chamisso, were preparing their *Green Almanach of the Muses*. Hitzig, the son of a well-to-do Jewish family in Potsdam, had then been a jurist and associate judge, but was already passionately interested in literature; since then, he had worked with Reimer to learn the publishing trade, and in 1808 had set up his own publishing house. On friendly terms with Zacharias Werner, with Brentano, whose fellow student he had been, and with Müller, whose lectures *On the Idea of Beauty* he had published the previous year, this able and enterprising man was at the very center of the literary scene. In later years he became the successful publisher of Fouqué and of his wife, "Serena." With all his other qualities, he was a staunch friend in time of need; during the Wars of Liberation, for example, he stood by Chamisso, who, because of his French extraction, had become the butt of the most virulent slanders and suspicions.

Kleist was connected with the nobility by family and other ties. In 1805, while preparing for his official functions in Königsberg, he had worked in the office of Baron von Stein zum Altenstein, then a privy finance councilor and now Finance Minister. Altenstein's mother had been staying with him since the death of his wife, and his sister was in charge of his household. The two ladies and the baron, who had always taken an interest in Kleist, would ask him for news of Ulrike: "What is your sister doing? Why doesn't she come here?" "I haven't been as successful as you," Kleist would reply. "I can't afford to keep my sister with me as you do."

Friedrich August von Stägemann, in Kleist's Königsberg period a finance councilor and now a privy councilor of state, was deeply interested in literature and even tried his hand at poems glorifying Prussia. His daughter, Frau von Olfers, remembered in later years how at the house of her parents Kleist had read both *Penthesilea* and *The Prince of Homburg* aloud, with his at first stuttering but then fluent and passionate delivery.

Prince Anton Heinrich von Radziwill, married to Princess Luise of Prussia, governor first of the Grand Duchy of Posen, later of the Grand Duchy of Hessen, lived in the building on Wilhelmstrasse that housed the chancellery until the collapse of the Third Reich. An excellent cellist, he made a name for himself as a composer with his musical adaptation of Goethe's *Faust;* the plays and concerts at his palace were attended by almost the entire court—a fact which on several occasions proved useful to Kleist.

But even more important for Kleist than these friendships and social connections were the women to whom Müller introduced him: Sophie Sander, Henriette Vogel, and Rahel Levin, each a typical representative of the "interesting women" cultivated by the Berlin romantics.

Sophie Sander, wife of the "good fat [publisher] who goes crazy once every year," was the cynosure of the Sander circle. Aged twenty-three, liberal-minded, and pretty, she had been the mistress—as was generally known and as Varnhagen tells us—first of Müller, then of his friend Theremin, the court preacher, both of whom had left Henriette Vogel for her.

Having lost two lovers to her younger and prettier rival, Henriette, wife of the good-natured accountant Louis Vogel, was all the more zealous in pursuit of Kleist. At first, however, he was not attracted, possibly because (as Pfuel once remarked) she bore "the sign of falsehood on her forehead." Moreover, at the age of thirty-three (thirty by some accounts), she was anything but pretty: long, pointed nose; large, dark, somewhat insolent eyes under heavy brows; wide mouth rising at the corners; abundant brown hair hanging down over her forehead; rouged, lightly pockmarked cheeks, sallow skin, full, heavy breasts—small wonder that Kleist found her appearance almost frightening.

But she had her qualities; an excellent housekeeper, she devoted her mornings to domestic tasks; she dressed with care and good taste, and those who met her at social gatherings were impressed by her wit and her boundless thirst for knowledge. She was eager to learn cabinetmaking and fencing, and wanted Kleist to instruct her in military tactics; though she did not write for publication, the little of her writing that has been preserved shows decided talent, and her gift for singing, especially religious music, and accompanying herself on the piano, was widely admired. It was probably music which gradually brought him close to this highly emotional woman. At all events, he became a regular visitor at her house on Behrenstrasse, in whose "green room" such tragic decisions were to be made, and it was not long before Brentano joked that Kleist had put on "Adam Müller's worn-out love-slippers."

But the house he frequented most sedulously at first was that of Rahel Levin (who was later to marry Varnhagen von Ense) on Jägerstrasse. He had probably met her during his earlier stay in Berlin. She was now thirty-seven, a handsome woman of irritatingly mercurial charm; her character was full of contradictions and she did not find herself easy to get along with. Although she was a celebrity in literary circles and corresponded with counts and princes, she suffered from being a Jewess; men found her attractive but "somehow" lacking in true womanly grace. She was original, but because she was bent on being so, she tended to exaggerate her true perceptions in expressing them. She was intelligent and witty and, as a rule, radiated simple good nature. At other times, she would betray a touchingly naïve preoccupation with the impression she was making or would seem to be suffering from her own selfishness. Kleist, she remembered regretfully, thought her looks more "droll" than touching. "He must be afflicted with some sort of cataract," she said, "for he doesn't *see* me quite right." Still, she held him in high esteem and may have been slightly in love with him. But in May 1810 she wrote to her friend Alexander von Marwitz that much as she was taken with Kleist, and though undoubtedly he liked her, "not a single ray of tenderness, of reassurance, comes to me from his eyes." But she was not disappointed, for her instinct told her that this was an honorable and important man. "I like him and I like what he does. He is true and sees true." That is strongly felt and strongly spoken, and shows that Rahel was worthy to enjoy Kleist's confidence, if not his love, on this last leg of his journey.

His love belonged to another—to his cousin by marriage, Marie von Kleist, née Gualtieri, whose brother had at one time wanted to take Kleist with him to Madrid. They had seen a good deal of each other in those days; she had taken a kind of maternal interest in the young man's intellectual development and had procured him Queen Luise's "honorarium," which may, as some presumed, have come out of her own pocket. When he now reappeared, they greeted each other with the most natural affection. Though the nature of their relations has never been fully elucidated, we know that he became more intimate with her than he had ever been with any other woman. This is not without psychological interest, for she was almost fifty, a good fifteen years older than he, and in a way his feeling for her suggests the enthusiasm of very young men for mature women. It had in it a streak of infantilism, of psychosexual immaturity that seems strange in a man of thirty-three. Since Marie and Heinrich von Kleist destroyed almost all the documents bearing on their relationship, we have no detailed knowledge of it; but the openness with which she spoke of it to her son after Heinrich's death suggests that sexuality was as absent from this greatest love of his life as it had been from all his previous loves, and that it consisted exclusively in a spiritual harmony.

Their spiritual harmony must have been almost complete. According to Princess Radziwill, Marie von Kleist was so "Kleistian" in her likes and dislikes that in her eyes a person could only be divine or diabolical. Kleist was divine, not only a genius, not only an admirable man, but the *most* admirable, *most* poetic person she had ever known, and as she wrote to her son, it was his honesty, his integrity that had instilled in her such an insuperable "horror of all dissembling, all boasting, all affectation." Just as he took first place in her heart, so did she in his; they seemed destined for each other. Marie could have been free, since she was unhappily married (and was to obtain a divorce two years later), while Kleist had no ties that would have prevented him from giving himself wholly to his love. There was nothing to threaten it—nothing, that is, but Kleist's gnawing desire to die; of this he made no secret, but on the contrary suggested on several occasions that they die together. In this "proposal" Marie was no more interested than were the others to whom he had made it in the past. Possibly she was at fault for failing to take the dangerous obsession, which had been with him since childhood, seriously enough.

Yet he seemed so full of life and creative energy that she could hardly have suspected the intensity of his death wish, and he gave her only the most superficial account of other relationships which may have increased his danger, just as to others he revealed so little of his intimacy with Marie that not even the literary and social gossips, always so keen of hearing, got wind of it. Of course, he had good reason for his caution, but here, too, one cannot help discerning the same touch of infantilism as in his love for a woman sixteen years older than himself. At first, to be sure, there was little to keep secret; things dragged on from month to month, and when they finally erupted, it was with a devastating suddenness.

At first, the danger was imperceptible; Kleist was in good spirits, and made use of an opportunity that must have been procured for him by Marie von Kleist, who, it will be remembered, was on intimate terms with Queen Luise. Kleist had written and several times reworked a poem in the queen's honor, and now, on March 10, her birthday, he recited it in the presence of the whole court. The queen was moved to tears, and despite a certain animosity on the king's part he felt assured of her favor. Since, moreover, *The Prince of Homburg* was to be performed before long, first at the home of Prince Radziwill and then at Iffland's Nationaltheater, after which it would be printed and dedicated to her, he was convinced that she would do something for him; already he was dreaming of a post at court. The outlook was indeed promising. *Käthchen*, in Collin's adaptation, was produced in Vienna, with Christiane Dorothea Pedrillo, a popular favorite and Gentz's mistress, in the leading role. The public reception was cool and the press extremely critical, but merely to have had the play produced was an achievement, a first step, that would no doubt lead to others. (As indeed it did. *Käthchen* was performed that December in Graz, and in the autumn of the following year in Bamberg, at the instigation of the musical director, E. T. A. Hoffmann, who himself designed the sets.)

Under such favorable auspices, Kleist thought the time had come to remedy his soured relations with Ulrike. He wrote to her, suggesting that she interrupt her present stay at the Stojentins in Pomerania and visit him for a month or two in Berlin. Not that she should live with him; the lodgings of his friend Gleissenberg, who had gone away for three months, were at her disposal. She would have ample opportunity to call on the Altenstein ladies, who were constantly asking after her, and she would be able to help him by speaking to them of certain things that he himself could not very well mention to the minister. But that was not his reason for wanting her to come —oh, she must not misunderstand him!—it was solely to give her pleasure, and how happy he would be "to kiss your hand and account to you for a thousand things concerning which I must now ask you to keep silent." A rather timid, almost humble letter, which apparently brought no response. As far as we know, he wrote to her only twice after that and saw her only once—a disastrous meeting of only a few hours, which may have undermined his already shaken morale.

In general, his hopes had a way of not coming true, of being transformed into disappointments. Cotta expressed his regret that he would not be able to publish *Käthchen* "in the course of the year"—which amounted to a rejection. This and the publisher's refusal, under all manner of pretexts, to pay Kleist various sums owing to him made Kleist's financial situation desperate. Moreover, *The Prince of Homburg* had infuriated a number of prominent persons in the army and at court; notably, the queen's brother. What aroused their indignation was the hero's terror at the sight of the grave that had been dug for him, for such weakness is unthinkable in a German officer. This reaction, of course, made it impossible to perform the play at Prince Radziwill's, much less at the Nationaltheater. Next, the Dohna–Altenstein cabinet fell, so depriving Kleist of his most influential patron, and Hardenberg became chancellor. And finally, the death of Queen Luise on July 19 deprived Kleist not only of the royal favor but also of his small honorarium. The calamities came thick and fast.

Kleist might well have despaired if he had not had other irons in the fire. *Käthchen* was in the hands of Iffland, director of the Nationaltheater, and influential friends of Kleist were bringing their influence to bear, though as a rule Iffland had little use for rising talents, but preferred to fill his house with the help of the usual bourgeois tearjerkers or thrillers, many of them from his own pen. In the end, he returned *Käthchen*, declaring that the play was unsuited to his repertory, and when it was brought to him a second time, presumably in Collin's adaptation, he remarked that despite all its good qualities, it could not possibly hold the stage without being rewritten from beginning to end.

We can sympathize with Kleist's indignation, for it was quite disgraceful that Prussia's leading theater should find room for every kind of trash, but not for his work. The reason for Iffland's rejection may not have been transmitted to him faithfully, but in any case Kleist gave vent to his anger—as he had once done with Goethe—by a vicious thrust at an aspect of Iffland's private life; namely, his homosexuality. "*Käthchen of Heilbronn*," he wrote in a letter to Iffland, "has been returned to me with your comment that you did not like it. What a pity . . . that it's a girl; if it had been a boy, Your Excellency would probably have liked it better."

After that, Prussia's leading theater was closed to Kleist for good. Iffland wrote a dignified reply, denying that he had said he did not like the play; "that would have been base, and though basely dealt with, I shall not respond in kind." But Kleist was convinced that he had been wonderfully clever and repeated his little quip to everyone he met; the affair became so widely known that it even found its way into the Hamburg *Northern Miscellany*.

As we see, Kleist was not one to learn from experience. Adam Müller was a man of a very different stamp. Whereas Hardenberg's accession to power had come as a hard blow to Kleist, Müller immediately thought of an amusing way of turning it to his advantage. Karl August Baron von Hardenberg was an experienced statesman, who had already proved himself in a number of important diplomatic missions and government posts. When he became chancellor, now invested with almost unlimited powers, Hardenberg immediately made contact with Baron von Stein, whom the king, under pressure from Napoleon, had banished, and arranged to carry on with Stein's reforms, while at the same time scrupulously maintaining an appearance of friendliness to the French, suppressing all demonstrations of sentiment hostile to Napoleon and all news items that might be displeasing to Davout, the French commandant in North Germany, making every effort to raise the exorbitant "contributions" demanded by France, and pretending to carry submissiveness so far as to welcome an alliance. The purpose behind all this, however, was to strike out against Napoleon as soon as the time was ripe, and in the meantime secretly to stir up the anti-French sentiment of the people whenever possible and quietly build up an army despite the impoverishment of the country—a two-faced program, which could hardly enjoy great popularity, for one thing because it called for an almost unbearable tax burden and for another because it was bound to incur the opposition of the conservative nobility, who regarded Napoleon as a bulwark against the revolutionary currents of the day.

Adam Müller now offered to put out two newspapers at once, one supporting the government and the other the opposition, so as to treat the political events of the day from contrary points of view. This, he maintained, would enable the government to keep public opinion under control and at all times

manipulate it at will. Müller's brainstorm may have been inspired by a similar idea put forward in one of Kleist's *Germania*
articles, the satirical *Manual of French Journalism* (*Lehrbuch
der französischen Journalistik*). Müller's offer was not accepted, but it won him Hardenberg's favor, and the chancellor
later rewarded him with a solatium, while Kleist, as usual, came
off empty-handed.

Kleist had meanwhile arranged with Reimer for publication
of a book of short stories, to be titled *Moral Tales* (*Moralische
Erzählungen*) and to include *The Marquise of O.*, *The Earthquake in Chile*, and *Michael Kohlhaas*, on which last he was
still working while the book was being set in type. He had obtained an advance of thirty talers and was to receive another
twenty on publication, for a grand total of fifty talers. Unfortunately, he was obliged to lay more stress on quick payment
than on the amount of his fee, but as always he insisted on clear,
attractive print. In August, he undertook with his usual disarming candor to content himself with eighty or even sixty talers,
provided the book should appear in time for the Autumn Fair.
In the end, he received fifty and in all likelihood was quite
content.

Concerning Kleist's social life at this time, an odd anecdote
was later told by War Councilor Ernst Friedrich Peguilhen, a
self-important little man who was on friendly terms with the
Vogel family and who was to play a strange role in Kleist's life.

According to Peguilhen, a wealthy patron of the arts once
invited Kleist to dinner and placed him at table next to the
beautiful Henriette Hendel-Schütz, a well-known actress married to a professor of philosophy at the University of Jena.
Invoking the close ties between the theater and literature, and
the easy morals of stage folk, she beset him with her amorous
attentions. Kleist answered her in monosyllables and concentrated on his food. But after a while, unable to bear the siege
any longer, he jumped up and, hiding his fiery face in a hand-
kerchief, "rushed," still trembling with indignation, to Peguilhen. Why Kleist should have "rushed" to Peguilhen of all people it is hard to say, since he hardly knew him and could not
even spell his name correctly. But the fact is that Berlin gossip

numbered the famous actress among Kleist's loves, and after
Kleist's death Judge Körner wrote his son Theodor a letter for
no other reason than to tell him that Kleist had not loved la
Hendel but another woman. Still, neither this gossip nor the
fact that Frau Hendel-Schütz was known to take an interest
in Kleist's work sufficed to lend plausibility to Peguilhen's
anecdote.

We know for sure, however, that in the autumn of 1810
Kleist revisited the spot on the shore of the Wannsee where
nine years before he had discussed with friends the most reliable
way of committing suicide and which a year later was to become the scene of his death. On this second visit, he met with
Fouqué, to whom he had sent a message by way of Rahel's
brother Ludwig Robert, suggesting that, since they had both
made something of themselves as writers, they should clasp
hands "in token of friendship and joyous association." This
Baron Friedrich de La Motte-Fouqué, whom Kleist had first
met in 1794 in Frankfurt on the Main, was a fortunate man—
handsome, charming, cultivated, and wealthy. He lived with
his beloved wife, who under the name of Serena had achieved
considerable success with the reading public, on her estate,
Nennhausen, near Rathenow, and was himself a popular author,
whose poetry, in the astute judgment of August Wilhelm
Schlegel, suffered only from the fact that "no real misfortune
has ever befallen him." He accepted Kleist's proposal "with
great joy" and they met on the shore of the Wannsee. There
they celebrated their brotherhood as poets, which Kleist had
initiated "with his amiable proposal." Later they exchanged
letters, books, and invitations, and in the professional collaboration that soon developed, not the slightest quarrel ever marred
their friendship. The excellent Fouqué was to remain faithful
to this bond of brotherhood for years after Kleist's death.

Rahel's recollection of an evening at Madame Sander's salon
may give an idea of Kleist's life at that time. A niece of Baron
von Stein, the wife of General von Helwig, had wished to make
Rahel's acquaintance, but since Rahel had been introduced under her recently adopted name, Robert, Frau Helwig had not
recognized her and Rahel had been "obliged" to spend "the

whole evening speaking only [!] with Heinrich Kleist and Adam Müller." Arnim and Brentano, both elegantly clad in black, had totally monopolized the interesting and distinguished lady and had allowed no one else to approach her; "Kleist and I, he in his street-battered boots, sat in a corner quietly laughing and amusing ourselves."

For Kleist the most memorable and enjoyable event of that autumn was the publication of his two books. The story volume was at the printer's, and as we have seen, he was gradually completing *Kohlhaas*, which was being set in type, paragraph by paragraph, as it came from Kleist's desk; concurrently, he made a number of changes in the text of *Käthchen* in response to criticism from Reimer. We have already reported briefly on these two works, but there is something more to be said, for *Kohlhaas*, apart from being the pièce de résistance of the story volume, is Kleist's longest and perhaps most important story, while *Käthchen* is his most popular play.

The material for *Kohlhaas*, originally brought to his attention by Pfuel, then further investigated on his own, had occupied Kleist for years. As we have seen, the beginning had been published in *Phöbus* in 1808. This first part, roughly a third of the whole, carries the story up to the storming of the Tronkenburg. It tells how Kohlhaas, with his exacting sense of justice, suffers graver and graver wrongs. Unable to live in a world governed by injustice, he comes little by little to the conclusion that his only hope of justice is to take up arms against those who have wronged him. But, by taking justice into his own hands, he transforms right into wrong, virtue into vice.

The more opposition Kohlhaas encounters in his violent pursuit of justice, the more ruthless he becomes, but the opposition increases with his savagery—a fatal chain of cause and effect, which exacerbate each other, until what began as a quest for justice develops into a sinister threat to all law and authority, a sort of civil war, and one man's misfortune becomes a public catastrophe. Kohlhaas cannot pick and choose; to build up his band, he is obliged to recruit the worst sort of predatory ruffians. After defeating the troops that have been sent out against him, he sets fire to every village and town in which he thinks the Baron von Tronka may be hiding. Since Kohlhaas is a subject of Brandenburg and his depredations have taken place on Saxon territory, they threaten to provoke a conflict between two states.

To avoid this, the Saxon court, through the intercession of Martin Luther, offers the horse dealer safe conduct to Dresden and a fair trial, on condition that he dissolve his band. But in Dresden he suffers further injustice, though at every step his persecutors invoke legal forms. First his freedom of movement is restricted, then he is imprisoned, and finally, by the use of legislative skulduggery, he is condemned to a shameful death. At this point the Brandenburg authorities step in and send a sharply worded note demanding the extradition of their subject to Berlin. There he is given a really fair trial, in which he is declared in the right against Tronka but in the wrong toward Saxony. Accordingly, his claim for damages is met, and "on the Monday after Palm Sunday," he is publicly beheaded for breach of the peace. A grieving populace attends the execution, which the Duke of Brandenburg transforms into a posthumous triumph of justice by knighting the beheaded Kohlhaas's sons.

On the plane of ideas, *Kohlhaas* is a story with a happy ending: Kohlhaas pays with his life for his crimes, but the justice for which he has committed them triumphs; moreover, he pays willingly, without a whimper, which makes him a hero. But in the German mind he has also become something more than a hero; namely, a household word, comparable to Don Quixote, Don Juan, or Tartuffe. When we see an incorrigibly fanatical defender of justice, his name comes to mind, and we say: "Why, the man is a regular Kohlhaas." He owes this rare popularity to the extraordinary intensity, denseness, and clarity of Kleist's writing, and in particular to Kleist's faculty, heightened by his experience as a playwright, for developing a character with logic and consistency.

The development of Kohlhaas's character might be called perfect were it not for the last fifth of the story, which strikes us as an irritating appendage. Kohlhaas has in his possession a prophecy, the content of which the Elector of Saxony is determined to discover, because it concerns the future of his house; in this he fails, and is tormented by dark fears and forebodings forever after—his punishment for not keeping faith with the horse dealer.

Why did Kleist introduce this seemingly extraneous complication? Probably, as some critics have suggested, for political reasons. Apparently, he could not resist the temptation to strike a blow at contemporary Saxony for its treasonable submissiveness to Napoleon. In any event, the episode has no place in the narrative and denatures the character of Kohlhaas by making him pursue his vengeance with niggling rancor at a time when the dauntless warrior has at last made his peace with the world. But even if we find it psychologically justifiable (a distinct possibility), it is artistically disturbing, because the hard logic of the plot is diluted by this excursion into the irrational: fortuitous meetings; obscure relationships; mysterious similarities in name and appearance between Elisabeth the old gypsy fortune-teller and Kohlhaas's dead wife, Lisbeth; dark allusions to ghosts and to reunions in a happy afterlife—in short, an elaborate mystical apparatus that is decidedly out of place in a story told with such magnificent sobriety.

Yet this somewhat unfortunate episode has never detracted from the standing of *Michael Kohlhaas*. It does not even seem to shake the reader's faith in the credibility of the story as a whole, its worthiness to bear the subtitle "From an old chronicle." In spite of its anachronisms, even historians have regarded *Kohlhaas* as a faithful account of historical events—a view rendered plausible by the actual historical core of the story, by the historical dating of the execution on the "Monday after Palm Sunday," the archaic wording of the so-called Kohlhaas Manifestos (a pure invention of Kleist's), and finally by the actual existence of a village named Kohlhasenbrück (Kohlhas Bridge) near Potsdam. At any rate, this widespread belief in the historic veracity of the story is almost as characteristic as the fact that the name Kohlhaas has become proverbial; it is symptomatic of the story's concentrated reality content. *Kohlhaas* can equally well be regarded as a character study or as a tale relating the adventures of an idea; for Kohlhaas is the embodiment of an idea, and his tragic obstinacy springs from the idea's homelessness in this life. He comes to grief, because the idea of justice cannot triumph in this world without exacting human victims.

Ideas are treated so concretely in *Kohlhaas* that they become one with their embodiments; one cannot speak of a symbiosis, for here we have unity, not only in the person of the hero, but in the story as a whole, in the characters, even the minor ones, in every detail of the action, in the tone and rhythm of the narration, and not least, in the wealth of images sometimes bordering on the grotesque—for example, the picture of Kohlhaas's horses craning their long necks above the pigsty in which they have been lodged in the Tronkenburg, so that they look "like geese." And the more abstract parts of the story operate in the same way; in Kohlhaas's "Manifestos," for instance, the language becomes wilder and wilder until in the end he is referring to himself as "Vicar of the Archangel Michael" and speaking of "our provisional world government," so reflecting an exaltation that increases with every successful raid or engagement. And the same unity between idea and embodiment appears in the style, which is by turns hot and cold, stormy and thoughtful, passionate and objective.

In *Kohlhaas*, as in most of his work, Kleist wrote what he had to write and concerned himself very little with public favor. But as the high-sounding title—*Käthchen of Heilbronn, or The Ordeal by Fire: A great historical chivalry play*—shows, the play published at the same time was a deliberate attempt to exploit the contemporary taste for street ballads and medieval claptrap. The story is briefly as follows: Käthchen is the daughter of a Heilbronn armorer. One day, on entering her father's forge, she sees a knight—Friedrich Wetter, Count vom Strahl—and collapses at his feet as though thunderstruck. When he leaves, she jumps out of the window. Her injury keeps her at home for some weeks, but no sooner recovered than, drawn by some magical force, she starts in pursuit of him and follows his trail unerringly in a somnambulistic trance. The count asks her what she wants. "Oh, your lordship," she answers with a blush. "You know what I want." But, though by no means blind to her charms, vom Strahl wants nothing to do with her because a fortune-teller, who appeared to him during a siege of fever, had prophesied that he would marry an emperor's daughter. First gently, then not so gently, he tries to shake Käthchen off, and finally succeeds by means of rather drastic threats.

Now, vom Strahl is involved in a quarrel with Lady Kunigunde of Thurneck, a beautiful but wicked woman of imperial blood, who puts forward all manner of spurious claims in an attempt to rob him of Stauffen, his estate, and incites one warlike admirer after another against him. By a strange turn of fate, she falls into vom Strahl's hands and he carries her off to his castle, where she succeeds in transforming his hate into love, and of his own free will he writes a deed of gift, making her a betrothal present of Stauffen. He escorts her home to Thurneck, and no sooner have they arrived than her former chief protector, feeling betrayed by her, decides to seize the castle by ruse. By one more miraculous turn of fate, Käthchen (who was on the point of entering a convent) gets word of vom Strahl's danger. She hastens to Thurneck, bursts in, and loudly demands a hearing. Strahl is about to flog her for her pains, but then at last he understands why she has come. The attack is repulsed, but the castle is set on fire. In the presence of Strahl, Kunigunde, who has hidden the deed of gift behind a picture, sends Käthchen to get it. In this, Käthchen is successful, and just as the castle collapses with a crash behind her, she appears in a gateway that has remained standing, followed and protected by a cherub (who is visible to the audience).

This cherub is the supernatural link between Käthchen and Strahl; he has figured prominently in the count's vision and at the exact same time in the dream that has imposed this humiliating pursuit upon Käthchen. Now, in a somnambulistic half-sleep under the elderberry bush, she relates her dream. She has come through the ordeal by fire unscathed, but this is not the end of her troubles. It remains for her to expose Kunigunde, who is in reality a ghastly old hag, her beauty a product of cosmetics, padding, false hair, and false teeth; in short, an illusion that seems scarcely less supernatural than the cherub.

In the meantime, armorer Friedeborn has brought an action

against the count for abducting and bewitching his daughter, first before the Vehmic court, then before the emperor, who discovers, while looking into certain aspects of the case, that Käthchen is in reality his illegitimate daughter. He makes her Princess of Swabia, and still in danger of being poisoned by Kunigunde, she is wedded to Count vom Strahl in her place.

One cannot help wondering, in some dismay: What is the point of all this? Clanking armor, clashing swords, the storm beating down on the charcoal burner's hut, hooded Vehmic judges in a ghoulish cave, ghosts under the elderberry bush in broad daylight, prophetic dream vision and sympathetic trance, castle in flames, single combat, sinister plots, beauty produced by cosmetic magic, blindfolded innocence protected by angels and raised to high estate by the discovery of imperial lineage, jubilant marriage celebration—this potpourri of themes from the alchemist's kitchen of the romantics. Is it a mere theatrical fantasy, a tearjerking melodrama, an attempt to achieve popularity at any price? If so, the attempt was successful. *Käthchen* has remained popular to this day—but why?

Undoubtedly, the somnambulistic element, the "night side of nature," reflected an aspect of Kleist's makeup, though here it seems to have taken on undue importance, to have become the very source and inventive principle of the action, while elsewhere—in *The Prince of Homburg*, for example—it has its bearing on the conflict but is largely a matter of atmosphere and character portrayal. Actually, this is also the case with the person of Käthchen, whose otherworldly somnambulism can easily be interpreted as symbolic psychology; her dream vision of cherub and knight can be seen as an intimation of a great love, the chance discoveries that save her beloved from surprise attack and betrayal by the false Kunigunde as the extreme vigilance inherent in such love, the guardian angel's escort through the sea of fire as her "blind" certainty of the course she is taking. All this mystical psychology reminds one of Shakespeare's ghosts as harbingers of doom and embodiments of the murderer's guilty conscience. The medieval trappings were popular in Kleist's day, but it is the character of Käthchen which provides their solid underpinning and which has withstood the ravages of time to this day. Thus, it is no accident that when Kleist speaks favorably of this play, it is always and exclusively in reference to the principal character. She was related to Penthesilea, he said, as plus is related to minus in algebra, they were "one and the same being, but conceived under opposite signs." And elsewhere: she is "the reverse side of Penthesilea, her opposite pole, a being who is just as powerful in her total submissiveness as Penthesilea in her activity."

This analysis owes nothing to romanticism; for that, it is far too excessive, wholly Kleistian, wholly typical of the man who in the presence of death still celebrated the joy "of self-sacrifice, of total self-immolation for what one loves: that is the greatest bliss conceivable on earth, and that, indeed, is what heaven must be made of, if it is true that there is happiness in heaven." This is the theme of *Käthchen*, as Kleist saw it: a feast of self-sacrificing love, of passion which finds its fulfillment not so much in possession of the beloved as in the casting-away of self—an orgy of masochism, whereas Penthesilea was an orgy of sadism. The romantic trappings, the sinister Vehmic court, the shining armor, and finally the revelation of imperial descent, are far less important than vom Strahl's whip; his kicks and his stable, in which Käthchen longs to sleep, are infinitely more significant than the false teeth and artificial bosom of the super-cosmeticized witch. And when Käthchen lets herself be sent into the roaring flames of the burning castle, she does so, not as the victim of a murderous, intriguing rival, but in anticipation of the cruelty of the man she loves: "So be it, then! The little fool won't mind!"

It is this "little fool's" innocence which, despite the perverse psychology, despite Kleist's express striving for popularity, gives the play the dignity that makes for true popularity. Of course, the element of make-believe in this play is deliberate, but it is also naïve; the large cast, with its emperor, archbishop, knight and armorer, nightwatchman and charcoal burner, is not mere pageantry, it also reflects a love of fantastic tales; in this street ballad there is a truly childlike quality, which goes hand in hand with a knowledge of last things.

If, in spite of everything, this "great historical chivalry play" leaves us with something of a bad taste in our mouths, we shall do well to listen to what Kleist himself has to say on the subject: "Up until now, I have been far too much influenced by other people's judgment. *Käthchen of Heilbronn*, in particular, shows many indications of this. The play started out as an excellent invention, and only my desire to make it stageworthy led me to mistakes which I now deplore."

These words were written in the spring of 1811, six months after the play's publication in book form. The intervening months had been taken up with new hopes and new disappointments.

# 21

# DIE BERLINER ABENDBLÄTTER

O N October 1, 1810, the Berlin public was introduced to a newspaper that can be regarded as a precursor of our modern daily press, for it was scheduled to appear every workday afternoon (between five and six), whereas the other leading papers, the *Vossische Zeitung* and the *Spenersche Zeitung*, appeared only three days a week (in the morning). The new paper was cheap, only eight pfennigs a copy, or eighteen groschen for a three months' subscription, and consisted of four pages, numbered consecutively from issue to issue, so that a file covering a whole year could be bound as a book; to make these annual volumes easy to handle, it was printed in a small octavo format, which had the disadvantage of necessitating a certain amount of small and even minuscule type. The *Berliner Abendblätter*, as the new paper was named, was for that time well publicized; posters were put up all over town, and a large press run of the first issue was distributed free of charge. The publisher was Julius Eduard Hitzig, and though the editor was not named, everyone knew—and not only in Berlin —that none other than Heinrich von Kleist was concealed behind this anonymity. Moreover, the most frequent signature to be seen under articles was "HvK." The next most frequent was "AM," identifying the handiwork of Adam Müller.

We are without information about the planning stages of the *Abendblätter*. All we know is that early in September Achim von Arnim, speaking in the name of the editors, asked the Grimm brothers to contribute, and that the paper was discussed at Kleist's meeting with Fouqué on the Wannsee.

It was a ticklish undertaking from the start, chiefly because Hardenberg, with his "pussyfooting policy," could tolerate very little freedom of opinion and virtually muzzled the press. Political publications were subject to the oversight of Foreign Minister Count Goltz, with War Councilor Himly as censor; literary publications to the oversight of Interior Minister Count Dohna, with Police President Justus Gruner as censor. As one might expect, this division of labor resulted in constant friction and jurisdictional disputes, which added to the already difficult situation of newspaper editors.

To this situation Kleist, like it or not, had to accommodate himself, so much so that when Arnim asked Wilhelm Grimm to contribute, Grimm got the impression that this was to be "some pretentious rag." But though restraint would at first be necessary, Kleist's intentions were not at all hazy, as can be seen from his lead article in the first issue, rather transparently titled *Zoroaster's Prayer* (*Gebet des Zoroaster*). In it Zoroaster, with a mind to his future discourse, calls on the deity to imbue him from head to foot "with awareness of the misery in which this age repines and with insight into the baseness, the untruths, the pusillanimity and hypocrisy that are its cause." Thus, under the cloak it was obliged to wear, the new paper was to present an uncompromising critique of existing conditions. Further, it was to be written in as popular a vein as possible and, avoiding one-sidedness, was to present both the pros and the cons and offer a forum to all points of view, provided they were argued seriously and responsibly.

This "adversary" principle was implicit in the personalities of Kleist, the editor, and of Adam Müller, his chief helper, for whereas Müller was archconservative, hostile to reform, and Catholic, Kleist was progressive, in favor of reform, and Protestant—or not even that, for as Nietzsche would have said, when it came to religion, Kleist "had no talent for it." Müller's ultraconservatism has often been blamed for the subsequent difficulties of the *Abendblätter*. This is unjust. If any one thing was to blame, it was Kleist's editorial principle of debate at all costs. Still, the principle as such could be fruitful, as was shown by the controversy over the economist Christian Jakob Kraus (who had died in 1807), under whom Kleist had studied in

Königsberg and whose posthumous writings were now gaining popularity. The Stein–Hardenberg reforms were based on his theories of finance and administration. Müller, as a traditionalist, attacked him; the attack was followed by a pro-government editorial, and this in turn by an article by Arnim in support of Müller. This debate—amounting to a serious and exhaustive discussion of a crucial problem—went on for six weeks.

At first, to be sure, to win the favor of the government and expand circulation, Kleist contented himself with articles of less outspoken and less controversial character, which, however, as Fouqué put it, aimed discreetly at the "patriotic, moral, and artistic betterment of his compatriots." He hoped, through popular appeal, to exert a moral and political force, and to this end tried for a time to make the *Abendblätter* look like an organ of harmless entertainment. In this, he was at first strikingly successful. The *Abendblätter* was read by people of every station, even by the king; the crush at the sales office behind the Hedwigskirche was such that guards had to be posted, and after only ten days it became necessary to move to larger quarters at Jägerstrasse 25. Other papers reprinted items from the *Abendblätter*, for the most part (as usual) without indication of source, and the Berlin correspondents of numerous journals in Hamburg and other cities commented, some favorably, others unfavorably, on the new organ, naming Kleist as the editor despite his closely guarded anonymity.

For all its show of innocence, the modern and almost revolutionary character of the *Abendblätter* could not be overlooked, not only because of its covert political line but also because of what was obvious to all; it was in every sense an organ of current affairs, and in this respect utterly novel. There were no advertisements; each issue included an essay, a kind of leader printed in relatively large type, various shorter contributions, and a number of miscellaneous news items, some printed in almost microscopic type.

The most prominent of these were the police reports, provided daily by Police President Gruner, which brought the more lurid happenings of the day—such as the activities of Schwarz and his gang of incendiaries—to the attention of the Berlin reader with a rapidity he had never so much as dreamed of.

There were also stories on matters of general interest, such as (on October 15) Herr Claudius's balloon ascension. In a day when the local reporter was still unknown, these items were a great novelty, soon to be imitated elsewhere with great fanfare. Other events reported were the opening (not even mentioned in the other papers) of an art exhibition in Berlin at the end of September, and of the Berlin University in October. The foreign news was largely culled from Hamburg papers, because most of it came from France to Hamburg by the sea route, but was skillfully abridged and edited by Kleist.

Lastly, there were short notices in fine print. With their lapidary style, these were models of Kleistian formulation. The following may serve as an example: "Rumor. A schoolmaster is said to have made the original suggestion that the criminal Schwarz, who has been arrested for arson—and who, according to another current rumor, has hanged himself in jail—should be put on display. An admission fee would be charged and the proceeds go to residents of Schönberg and Steglitz whose houses he burned down."

The theater criticism of the *Abendblätter* was most unusual, especially for the unflagging vigor of its attacks on the royal and public favorite, Iffland, who, it was claimed, was guided far more by box-office considerations than by artistic merit in selecting his repertory, which seldom included Goethe and never such moderns as Zacharias Werner. Small wonder that these provocative articles soon became the talk—favorable or unfavorable—of the town. Kleist spared neither sarcasm nor frankness. Why, he asked, wouldn't Herr Iffland attempt a play by Goethe, letting men play the female roles and women the male roles—then the public would fight over the tickets and the management would achieve solvency in a twinkling. And sickened by the pious adulation of the press, he suggested to the critics of the *Vossische Zeitung* (including his onetime teacher S. H. Catel) that to avoid misunderstandings they should publish a declaration to the effect that they were not bribed by the management of Iffland's theater.

He was a remarkable editor. Determined to borrow as little as possible from other periodicals, he managed during the first few months to fill four-fifths of his paper with original contributions. When his fellow contributors did not sign their names, he abridged their pieces and rewrote them so radically, to suit his own taste, that some became to all intents and purposes his work. He cut Fouqué's twenty-eight-page story *Cure* down to two and a half pages, and modified a dialogue on an artistic subject by Brentano and Arnim so radically that it has been included in most editions of Kleist's works under the title *Feelings Aroused by Friedrich's Seascape (Empfindungen vor Friedrichs Seelandschaft)*. Brentano was so offended that Kleist had to ask Arnim to mollify him; the animosity discernible in Brentano's subsequent utterances about Kleist may well be attributable to this little incident.

Even in its treatment of news items, the *Abendblätter* bore the mark of Kleist's personality. In reporting the battles between the English and the French in Spain, the censored press —at variance with the facts—spoke only of French victories. Always on the lookout for ways to circumvent the censorship, Kleist discovered in the Paris *Moniteur* an article reprinted from an English newspaper hostile to the war and boiled it down to one thought-provoking sentence: "In an article dated 9 October, London, the French press observes that even victories are of little use to the English cause in Spain." And with positively Mephistophelean guile he abridged an article from *Le Moniteur*, reporting that all the states of the Confederation had introduced customs duties on colonial products imported from England, and that this measure had had the most fortunate consequences. In Württemberg, for example, prices had risen by half on the day when the decree had been promulgated, so dealing a virtual death blow to the English trade. The *Abendblätter* wrote: "The most fortunate consequences have everywhere been felt: in Württemberg, the price of colonial products rose by half on the day when the decree was promulgated," etc.

It must be admitted that, along with deliberate mischief of this kind, the *Abendblätter* was sometimes guilty of unintentional errors—misdating, reporting of possible events as if they had actually taken place, repetition of reports that had previously appeared. But this is scarcely surprising when we consider that Kleist turned out the whole paper almost single-handed and consulted no one on editorial matters, least of all his publisher Hitzig, who was not a little irritated by Kleist's highhandedness and eccentricity, as for example in December, when an entire issue was devoted to the recently deceased painter Philipp Otto Runge. Undoubtedly, Kleist was overworked, but one piece of good fortune that made things a little easier for him was the presence in the same building, at Jägerstrasse 25, of Rudolph Werckmeister's Readers' Institute, where no less than 174 German and French newspapers and periodicals, as well as the most important recent scientific works, maps, and encyclopedias, were made available.

Nevertheless, the amount of work he did is amazing, especially if we consider that he was not only the sole editor but also by far the most active contributor to the *Abendblätter*. He contributed almost as much as all his other writers together: several lead articles, lesser articles on philosophical and artistic subjects, two short stories and over twenty short sketches and anecdotes, numerous adaptations and translations of foreign pieces, and a number of poems and fables written at an earlier date.

To our knowledge, only two of Kleist's lead articles dealt with political problems of the day. These were discussions of the government's financial policy and most particularly of the taxes levied on luxury articles. Understandably enough, these newly promulgated taxes, which were a vital element in the Stein–Hardenberg reforms, were bitterly opposed by consumers of luxury goods, especially the wealthy nobility. Kleist commented on this reaction in a fictitious letter from one wealthy Junker to another, gleefully telling him how easy it was to circumvent these troublesome duties by a method which—*mutatis mutandis*—is still in common use. This spurious letter was followed by Kleist's suggestion that the Prussian government publish the names of these tax dodgers, who seemed to be indifferent to the common weal, with a notation: "The persons listed above do not pay the tax." Or, Kleist went on, if such a measure struck the government as too draconian, it would have no other course but to expand its staff of tax inspectors and collectors and increase the tax to cover the added expense.

A striking example of Kleist's philosophical writings is *Observations on the Phases of History* (*Betrachtungen über den Weltlauf*), an article barely a printed page in length, in which he takes a skeptical view of the prevailing faith in progress. It is generally believed, he writes, that a civilization develops as follows: from barbarism to a knowledge of virtue, thence to aesthetics, from aesthetics to art, and from art to the highest level of culture. With the Greeks and Romans, however, the exact opposite occurred. "These peoples started with the *heroic* epoch, which is undoubtedly the highest that can be attained; when they had no more heroes of any human or civic virtue, they fashioned heroes in poetry, and when they were no longer able to make poetry, they devised rules for it; when they became confused about the rules, they abstracted philosophy from them; and when they had done that, they became evil."

Even more characteristic and illuminating, because they are more a matter of feeling than of intellectual speculation, are his writings about art. Artistic creation, he insists, requires no special psychic disposition; "common but honest love of play" is quite enough. "The world is a strange place; and the most divine effects . . . are produced by the lowliest and most unimpressive causes." And with striking candor he explains that, similarly in human reproduction, the man who thinks nothing at all but merely gives himself body and soul to the joys of a night of love probably begets the best child, a boy, "who will climb boldly back and forth between heaven and earth and give the philosophers food for thought." In these pieces, Kleist formulates some of the central principles of his theory of art: "For it is characteristic of all true form that the spirit issues from it directly and immediately, whereas imperfect form, like a bad mirror, holds it fast and reminds us of nothing but itself." Or: "It takes more genius to appreciate a mediocre work of art than an excellent one."

The most important of these pieces is the famous essay *On the Marionette Theater* (*Über das Marionettentheater*), which appeared in the *Abendblätter* from December 12 to 15. This essay, as profound as it is playful, develops an insight expressed in Kleist's letter to Rühle of August 31, 1806: "Every primary, involuntary movement is beautiful, and everything that understands itself is crooked and distorted. O reason! Wretched reason!" With these words, the central thesis of the little masterpiece is sketched in; for the marionette combines naturalness with lightness and with the unawareness that saves it from affectation—in contrast to the human dancer, who must rest upon the ground (an undancerly feature), which the marionette barely grazes, and who is usually concerned with the effect he will produce, so that the charm of innocence is gone. Thus (along with the fact that the motive force that pushes and pulls the marionette lies outside it), it is *awareness* that makes the dancer inferior to the puppet.

"We see that in the organic world, proportionately as reflection becomes darker and dimmer, grace becomes more and more radiant and prevalent. —But just as when two lines meet on one side of a point and suddenly, after passing through infinity, emerge on the other side . . . so, too, when knowledge has passed as it were through infinity, grace reappears; thus, it is found in the greatest purity in a human body which has either infinite awareness or none at all, in other words, in a puppet or in a god." This little work has been admired by many persons of discernment. Hugo von Hofmannsthal, for example, writes: "No Englishman or Frenchman or Italian, no one, in fact, since Plato wrote his myths, has produced so pretty a piece of philosophy, so sparkling with intelligence and charm, as Kleist's essay on marionettes."

The two stories of some length that Kleist published in the *Abendblätter* are *The Beggarwoman of Locarno* (*Das Bettelweib von Locarno*) and *St. Cecilia, or The Power of Music* (*Die heilige Cäcile, oder die Gewalt der Musik*). The first is a ghost story, the second the story of a miracle; neither can be numbered among Kleist's strongest works, though of course they are far superior to the usual stories published in newspapers.

*The Beggarwoman of Locarno* tells of an old beggarwoman who spends her days lying in a corner of a room in an old castle. One day the lord of the castle roughly orders her to get up and move to another part of the room. She falls on the way and soon dies of her injury. Years later she avenges herself by haunting the castle. Driven to despair, the lord of the castle, who has other things on his conscience as well, sets fire to his castle and kills himself.

Such punishment for a moment's unkindness seems unduly harsh, compatible neither with Kleist's nor with anyone else's principles. The story itself is a typical fireside ghost story, somewhat reminiscent of the "blotting-paper prince" who had frightened Wieland's servants in Weimar. In it Kleist does not succeed—as Theodor Storm, for instance, does in his tales—in making the unreal seem palpably real.

*St. Cecilia* may have been a melancholy reaction to Hardenberg's decree secularizing church property and dissolving all monastic institutions in Prussia. It is the story of four young iconoclasts, who are restrained from a well-prepared act of profanation when the saint appears and they hear her playing old church music. But as punishment for their wicked intentions they are stricken with a religious madness and condemned to spend the rest of their lives in an insane asylum. They die happy, however, in a state of beatitude.

Apart from Kleist's intense but essentially aesthetic experience of church music in Dresden in 1801, he never, either before or after writing this story, showed any particular leaning toward Catholicism with its cult of saints and miracles; nor does the story convey any profound religious feeling. Yet, for all their weaknesses, the style of the two stories bears Kleist's unmistakable mark: the close-knit syntax characteristic of his prose, its serene but irresistible movement, the unexcelled ordering of his material, and, above all, the effortless but luminous power of his images. In *The Beggarwoman of Locarno*, for example, the reader can almost *see* the sound made by the invisible ghost in its nightly passage through the room, and feel the horror it inspires in the dog. And in *St. Cecilia*, the scene in which the four religious maniacs rise from their table at midnight and bellow the *Gloria in excelsis* has the force of a hallucination.

What seems a weakness in these two stories—the fact that they point to nothing outside themselves—becomes a strength and a virtue in the tales and anecdotes that Kleist wrote for the *Abendblätter*, since they obviously have no other aim than to relate some curious happening. The unexcelled succinctness with which they tell an unpretentious story has won them innumerable imitators down to our own day—one of the not too frequent instances in German literature of a tradition carrying over from one century to another. Prototypes of the modern short story, these sketches present all manner of entertaining material in a few dense and unadorned sentences: the unusual behavior and witty sayings of famous and not so famous persons in unusual situations, incidents that are no less extraordinary for having actually happened, abstruse crimes, coincidences suggesting the workings of a higher justice, ghostly apparitions with comical, terrifying, or fortunate consequences—in short, little odds and ends that are worthy of interest as long as they are not blown up, divertissements, seeds sown, as it were, in the field of memory.

It can hardly surprise us that a newspaper which, apart from its other original qualities, offered such entertaining reading matter should have attracted the attention of the public; what seems more surprising is that its success began to fall off so soon and that by mid-October Hitzig was complaining that the *Abendblätter* threatened him with "appreciable losses." Hitzig was a businessman, he was interested in ideas only as long as they looked profitable. His former employer and teacher Reimer said that "his protestations of disinterest were mere words, they did not really come from the heart," and that he was not an easy man to get along with, "because he is one of those active idlers who bustle about a good deal but accomplish little, and that little not in an orderly way." Since Kleist categorically refused all interference, Hitzig felt that he was being treated with "undeserved distrust," became more and more disgruntled, and attributed the paper's declining popularity to Kleist's choice of material. And indeed, when we consider that Kleist was editing a daily paper, he seems to have set his sights too high. Even Pfuel was later to observe that "he always miscalculated his effects; he confused the general public with his friends, and demanded of the former what could reasonably be expected of the latter; and deep as was his insight into the human soul, people in the mass remained alien and incomprehensible to him."

In reality, however, the loss of popularity in October was a natural consequence of the paper's enormous success; there was no serious danger until the following month, and then it was caused by a political complication.

On November 15 and 16, the *Abendblätter* published Adam Müller's article *On National Credit*, attacking the great financial edict promulgated by the government at the end of October. Hardenberg was so angry that he conceived a lasting grudge—not against Müller, but against the paper that had published his article. He complained to the king, whereupon the cabinet issued an order instructing State Councilor Sack, Police President Gruner's superior, to subject the *Berliner Abendblätter* to strict scrutiny in the future. In an attempt to forestall further trouble, Kleist appealed to Friedrich von Raumer, who in later years won fame as a historian but was then a young councilor on Hardenberg's staff, so influential that he was commonly known as "the little chancellor." On condition that Kleist observe "the strictest discretion," Raumer offered him financial assistance, provided he undertook to pursue an "expedient" policy.

This Kleist declined, for he was no more willing to accept interference from the government than from his publisher. Some agreement, the details of which are unknown to us, seems nevertheless to have been reached, but proved ineffective. An explicit government order obliged Kleist on November 20 and 21 to publish two semi-official replies to Müller's article. It may have given him some comfort to reflect that this was not really incompatible with his principle of editorial balance, but he soon had to recognize that it was all up with the *Abendblätter*'s nonpartisan policy. He was obliged to submit his proofs to the censors, and every article on domestic and foreign policy that displeased them for any reason whatsoever fell victim to their merciless red pencil. "Those two strokes," he wrote

to a contributor, "seem to me like two swords, cutting cross-wise through our dearest and most sacred ideas."
The reason for this unusual severity was that, along with State Councilor Sack, War Councilor Himly, who was also censor to the Foreign Ministry, had gone into action. He had long eyed the "mixed" (partly political, partly literary) periodicals with distrust, because they had in part evaded his control; and now he sent Police President Gruner an order forbidding the *Berliner Abendblätter* and other "popular publications" to carry any political articles whatever. From one day to the next, roughly half the *Abendblätter*'s contributions were suppressed—"almost ten" of Arnim's contributions alone. Kleist's paper had become a kind of government organ without the privileges that would normally have implied.

The public lost interest. Since everything that was deleted by the censors had first to be set in type, the cost of publication rose as the circulation fell. Hitzig belabored Kleist with reproaches, and Kleist felt that considerations of vile greed were driving his publisher to betray him in time of difficulty.

To make matters worse, the loss of political freedom was followed by the loss of another freedom that had nothing to do with politics. In addition to plays, the Nationaltheater produced operettas; the *Abendblätter* had several times come out in favor of a guest singer, a Madame Schmalz, while Iffland favored a Mademoiselle Herbst and was planning to give her a contract. When it was announced that *The Swiss Family* was to be performed, the *Abendblätter*'s music critic, probably Friedrich Schulz and certainly not Kleist, expressly proposed Madame Schmalz for the leading role, affecting ignorance of the fact that the part had already been given to the less suited Mademoiselle Herbst. Taking the hint, some friends of the editors, in particular a group of officers led by Major von Möllendorff, created a disturbance on the opening night (November 21). "There was stamping and whistling."

The next performance was five days later. Iffland had arranged for police protection. The moment the curtain went up, before the singer had even opened her mouth, the trouble-makers began to stamp, boo, clap, and shout "Encore." A police inspector seized a young man, who may have been quite innocent, by the collar and forced him to apologize to Mademoiselle Herbst. The young man's father, a major, convinced of his son's innocence, protested to Police President Gruner, who fined the inspector twenty-five talers and ordered him to beg the young man's pardon. Whereupon Iffland, in a huff, tendered his resignation. The incident had two consequences: Berlin was for a certain time declared off-limits to Major Möllendorff and his group of officers (who proceeded to make merry for several days in Charlottenburg, where they were garrisoned), and theater criticism was from then on confined to the *Vossische Zeitung* and the *Spenersche Zeitung* (which were required to pay a stamp tax for the privilege).

Kleist had tried in vain to forestall this measure with an article expressing surprise over the scandal at the Nationaltheater; and it was of no help to him that *The Liberal*, published by August Kuhn, was likewise forbidden to publish theater criticism. As it turned out, Mademoiselle Herbst was not engaged after all, but that was small consolation. Though Kleist must have approved of his critic's indirect attack on Iffland, he himself had not written a word on the subject, but it was he who took the beating. Loss of the right to run theater criticism brought with it a further loss of circulation and further strain on Kleist's relations with Hitzig. A Berlin boulevard sheet published a parody of the *Abendblätter*, which was ridiculed by other papers as well.

Kleist had to do something, to look for a new publisher and try to get the authorities to repair the harm they had done. This was the beginning of a long struggle with officialdom, in the course of which he came, like his own Michael Kohlhaas, to be regarded as an incorrigible troublemaker.


The beginnings were encouraging. He first called on Police President Gruner, a wise step, for Gruner—lank, lively, witty, flaming red hair, pale face—was probably the only high official in Berlin who was sincerely friendly toward him. Kleist argued convincingly that the political restrictions imposed on him were quite unwarranted, and Gruner promised to put in a word with the chancellor (and perhaps to suggest financial assistance). He kept his word. Under his influence, Hardenberg indicated that he was not disinclined to accord the *Abendblätter* his favor and "some sort of official support." Kleist responded at once, thanking Hardenberg for his promised help, assuring him of his eagerness, once he received explicit instructions, "to enlighten the public fully concerning the wisdom of His Excellency's measures." In conclusion, he asked permission to publish an (appended) statement, mentioning Hardenberg by name and announcing that, from January 1, 1811, on, the *Abendblätter* would regularly report all official communications concerning government measures bearing on the public welfare and security. His letter did not have exactly the desired effect. Hardenberg had no objection to the content of the statement, but he did not want his name to appear in it. Thus, the statement had to be rewritten, and just then the Foreign Minister took a hand, bidding his censor, War Councilor Himly, to send Gruner a new order, urgently recommending "retention of the order to delete all properly political articles"—so rendering the success Kleist had just achieved virtually illusory.

Bypassing Raumer, who vainly assured him that neither he nor his chief had anything to do with the order to Gruner, Kleist obtained an audience with Hardenberg, who proved most affable, advising Kleist to make personal contact with the various ministries and their department heads and promising to intercede with these gentlemen on behalf of the *Abendblätter*. Kleist now regretted his distrust of Raumer and wrote him a letter of apology. In it he mentioned his interview with Hardenberg and reported that the chancellor had "promised" to ask Foreign Minister Count Goltz, Justice Minister von Kircheisen, and others to support him with official news items. This, Kleist concluded, satisfied all his present wishes for the *Abendblätter*, since he wanted nothing more than to maintain an independent position. Indeed, on receipt of a friendly answer from Raumer, he went so far in his endeavor to secure his favor as to submit his own article on the luxury taxes and an article by Müller as well, before having them set in type, and further invited

Raumer to contribute to the *Abendblätter*. After all these concessions one wonders, to be sure, how Kleist could speak of
maintaining an "independent position." He went so far as to
petition the Foreign Ministry to countermand its order forbidding the *Abendblätter* to publish political material, since, as
he alleged, Herr von Raumer wished to discuss certain government measures in its pages and since he, Kleist, could vouch
for the "political inoffensiveness" of Raumer's remarks. All of
which shows that by then Kleist had come to regard his paper
more or less as a government organ.

Concurrently with this seemingly favorable development,
Kleist's relations with Hitzig grew worse and worse. Put off by
Kleist's refusal to consult him in editorial matters, Hitzig seems
to have made two demands: first, that from then on the paper
be distributed on a subscription basis, which would provide a
steady circulation and secure income; and second, that mention
of Hardenberg's sponsorship be made on the masthead. Aware
that the first demand would have been hard, and the second
impossible, to meet, and that the *Abendblätter* was likely to lose
money as a result, Hitzig decided to sever his ties with it. But
since their agreement committed Hitzig until the end of the
year, Kleist regarded him as at least potentially in breach of
contract and therefore refused to pay back certain advances.
Whether they actually went to law, as one would gather from
a letter from Hitzig to Fouqué, it is no longer possible to determine; in any case, their partnership had become untenable.

In great financial straits, Kleist had to look for a new publisher; he first applied to Wilhelm Römer, whom he immediately asked for an advance of fifty talers, and the very same day
to August Kuhn, owner of the Berlin Office for Art and Industry and publisher of Kotzebue's *The Liberal*. Kuhn agreed to
take over the *Abendblätter* as of January 1, 1811, and to pay
Kleist an annual salary of eight hundred talers. The immediate
future of the *Abendblätter* seemed assured. Thereupon Kleist
sent an announcement of his forthcoming issue, with a summary
of its contents, to the *Vossische Zeitung* and the *Spenersche
Zeitung* as a paid advertisement.

This he was probably obliged to do, but it is certain that

nothing could have been more harmful to his interests. The advertisement stating that the *Berliner Abendblätter* was planning to publish official announcements aroused the fear and indignation of the newspaper owners. Voss and Spener immediately lodged a protest with Himly (who had probably advised them to do so) over this "usurpation" by their competitor, arguing that they had been awarded the *exclusive* privilege of carrying government announcements and were authorized to sue for damages in cases of infringement. Actually, since Himly was the censor of the Foreign Ministry, this matter did not come primarily, let alone exclusively, under his jurisdiction; but he did what he could and passed on the complaint to the central administration, in particular to Raumer, "the little chancellor," lending it force with a memorandum to the effect that the complainants deserved special consideration since the stamp tax put a heavy financial burden on them, whereas the *Abendblätter* had proved suspect on several occasions.

In response to these arguments, the chancellery did not withdraw its promise to Kleist, but merely defined it more closely. The *Abendblätter* was authorized to publish political news and articles insofar as they had *previously* appeared in the *Vossische Zeitung* and the *Spenersche Zeitung*. This order, which Himly transmitted to Gruner just a week after the newspaper owners had lodged their protest, dealt the *Abendblätter* the death blow.

Its teeth drawn, it was reduced to a vegetative existence. But about this time, by a strange stroke of irony, the Hamburg *Archive for Art and Literature*, whose Berlin correspondent only a few months before had heaped bitter scorn on the *Abendblätter*, launched a *Hamburgisches Abendblatt*, which resembled Kleist's paper in format, content, and time of publication. As is often the case with plagiarism, it seems to have had more success than the original.

It was no help to Kleist that in January, when a dangerous mood of resistance to the government's reforms was making itself felt, he was once again allowed to reprint three oppositional articles. This well-calculated gesture had no sequel, and the *Abendblätter*'s loss of freedom was reflected in a falling-off in quality. Contributions stopped coming in, Müller contributed less and less, and even Kleist grew discouraged. A comparison between the first and second quarters is illuminating. In Hitzig's day, almost four-fifths of the paper had been made up of original contributions, more than a quarter of them by Kleist himself, and a third by friends. Under Kuhn, not even a quarter consisted of original contributions, the rest was made up of reprints from other papers; Kleist supplied a tenth and his friends a twentieth of the contents. Under these circumstances, the readers lost interest; circulation dropped rapidly and by February had ceased to cover publication costs.

Adam Müller, who was not formally committed to the *Abendblätter*, emerged from the debacle unscathed. Since the opposition was then without an organ, he applied to Hardenberg for authorization to found a new journal. The chancellor declined his proposal but expressed his appreciation by granting the adroit Müller a solatium of twelve hundred talers. Kleist, however, as the responsible editor, found himself in grave difficulty. His contract with Kuhn presupposed the government's agreement to supply official communications; when these failed to materialize, Kuhn claimed that Kleist had misled him with false assurances and failed to live up to their contract. Accordingly, he refused to pay Kleist's salary, demanded considerable damages for publication costs, threatened a lawsuit if he was not given a say in editorial policy, and finally expressed his intention of severing his ties with Kleist and the *Abendblätter* as soon as possible.

Kleist saw no other way out of his dilemma than to remind the authorities of the offers and promises they had made him; no sooner unsaddled, he remounted his Rosinante and set out once again to tilt at the windmills of government. In a letter to Hardenberg, he observed that a semi-ministerial organ like the *Abendblätter* could not hope to survive without the promised help of official news items, that sales had fallen below the norm, that the publisher was withholding his salary of eight hundred talers per annum, demanding three hundred talers in damages, and threatening to sue him for breach of contract. Kleist further pointed out that he had refused Raumer's offer of financial assistance, but must now reconsider, and suggested either that the state finance the *Abendblätter* for the current year or defray his above-mentioned losses of eleven hundred talers.

Hardenberg replied on February 18, 1811, that he was surprised to see the *Abendblätter* referred to as a "semi-ministerial organ," that official communications of government departments were favors conferred on all newspapers without distinction, and that the supposition that he as editor had been offered pecuniary compensation was a misunderstanding: compensation "was never offered you in this connection; I merely stated, at your suggestion, that the government would be glad to assist deserving authors insofar as its means permitted. I am convinced, however, that in the present instance you will not base your claims on the contents and situation of the *Abendblätter*, but will justify them in some other way."

Despite the rejection, a certain note of goodwill is discernible in this reply, and one gets the impression that Hardenberg was not at first disinclined to compensate Kleist in one way or another. Kleist himself, or someone else, must have told him about the honorarium Kleist had lost through the death of Queen Luise. Hardenberg made inquiries, and on February 10, 1811, was informed by Privy Cabinet Secretary Niethe that he was acquainted neither with Herr Kleist nor with the talents or services "which impelled Her late Majesty to assist him so generously"; in any event, he, Niethe, had never paid out a single groschen to Herr Kleist and had no cognizance of a pension, which in view of the queen's constant shortage of funds must be regarded as an unlikelihood . . . though it seemed possible that Her Majesty had helped him in some way, possibly through Frau Marie von Kleist.

It is this communication that leads us to suppose that the so-called queen's honorarium actually came out of Marie von Kleist's own pocket. In any case, it provided Hardenberg with no pretext for helping Kleist, as, to judge by the chancellor's above-cited letter, he might have been inclined to do if Kleist had come to him asking a favor rather than demanding compensation. Indeed, it seems reasonable to suppose that Kleist might well have attained his ends if he had been a little less pigheaded and a little more diplomatic.

But Kleist was Kleist. He attributed (under Müller's influence, it has been thought) the downfall of the *Abendblätter* to a plot instigated by Raumer, who must have denied to Hardenberg that he had ever offered Kleist money. Kleist proceeded to let off steam in a letter to Raumer, threatening that if Raumer failed to convince the chancellor that his demand for compensation was justified, he would publish the entire history of the *Abendblätter* abroad. Raumer replied by return mail that the failure of the *Abendblätter* was due to its contents; that there was no reason to discuss the matter with His Excellency, since enough words had already been wasted; and that Kleist could publish what he saw fit. Kleist turned to Hardenberg, asked him to cease consulting Raumer in his, Kleist's, affairs, insisted once again that money had been offered him in return for editorial complaisance and that the term "semi-ministerial" was quite applicable to a journal which, after being forced to modify its original line, followed the written and unwritten directives of the ministry in all questions of finance and administration, and in conclusion expressed the hope that, in view of the aforesaid, his petition for compensation would be reconsidered in a more favorable light.

The chancellor was irritated by Kleist's stubborn insistence on his rights and his failure to take a hint. Never, he wrote, had anyone tried to buy Kleist; never had Kleist had occasion to decline a government subsidy, and moreover he had no claim to one, "since the *Abendblätter* serves no [relevant] purpose and its failure must be attributed to its worthlessness, for excerpts from political journals that have long since been read, and a few ancedotes, cannot, as you yourself must recognize, lay the slightest claim to a subsidy, nor do they justify the term 'semi-official organ.' " This was an outrageous reversal of cause and effect—as though Kleist had chosen to reprint articles and announcements from the *Vossische Zeitung* and the *Spenersche Zeitung* and had not been forced by the censorship to do so.

And, to top it all, he was made out to be a liar. He had asked Raumer to confirm his contention that he, Raumer, had once offered him money, adding that in the event of a refusal he must demand the satisfaction due to a man of honor under such circumstances. Raumer replied that, wishing to settle the matter once and for all, he had submitted all the letters he had ever received from Kleist to His Excellency, and called on Kleist to do likewise with his, Raumer's, letters. Obviously, it had never occurred to Raumer to commit himself in writing, or to Kleist to keep a written record of any oral commitments; consequently, their correspondence proved nothing and could easily create the impression that Kleist's assertion was unfounded. There was nothing Kleist could do but appeal once more to Raumer's conscience, asking for a direct yes or no within twenty-four hours.

From this point on, we have two contradictory versions of the course of events. According to Raumer, he wrote Kleist a letter in December 1810 denying Kleist's assertion that he had been offered financial assistance; in February 1811, in response to Kleist's appeal to his conscience, he sent his friend Postal Councilor Pistor to Kleist's lodgings, with instructions to obtain the return of the aforesaid letter as evidence or, if Kleist refused to let him have it, to challenge Kleist to a duel on his behalf. Thereupon, still according to Raumer, Kleist had burst into tears, allowed Pistor to copy the letter, and protested that he had "been incited" to act as he had done. Hardenberg had then advised Raumer to be lenient: "Don't waste any more time on the poor fellow! Kleist, you know, once spent several months in the district insane asylum at Bayreuth."

It should be borne in mind that Raumer did not offer this justification of his conduct until half a century later, when all the witnesses who might have corroborated or denied his version were dead, and in the light of the facts available to us, it does not seem very plausible. True, Kleist was overwrought at the time—but it is hard to believe that he burst into tears instead of girding himself for the duel with which he himself had previously threatened Raumer; moreover, there is no other indication that he was in a mental institution at any time; and finally, it seems obvious enough that Raumer's alleged letter denying Kleist's contention would not have disproved it.

Kleist's version of the events was written while the affair was still in progress, and moreover, it is contained in a letter addressed to a person who had every opportunity to check its veracity—namely, the king's brother, Prince Wilhelm of Prussia. According to this letter, Pistor had indeed been sent by Raumer and had appeared at Kleist's lodgings, but "papers" in Kleist's possession had convinced him that Gruner must at the very start have made Kleist an offer of financial assistance. Thereupon, the letter goes on, the chancellor had expressed his willingness to make a statement to the effect that, on closer study of the circumstances, he was inclined to see a certain justification in Kleist's demands for compensation, though they could not be met immediately. Moreover, Pistor had given Kleist to understand that the government would soon favor him with the editorship of an official journal, the projected *Kurmärkisches Amtsblatt.*

Apparently, the chancellery was unwilling to admit, or to have it bruited about, that it employed methods tantamount to bribery; thus, it was agreed in private conference between Kleist and Raumer that, regardless of what arrangements might be concluded later on, no further mention should be made of compensation and that the dispute between the two parties be interpreted as a misunderstanding, without malicious intent on either side. Accordingly, Kleist wrote Hardenberg a letter declaring that since the one thing that mattered to him was to put an end to the chancellor's displeasure, which he had brought upon himself, he requested him most urgently to give ear to Herr von Raumer, to whom he, Kleist, had fully explained the prevailing misapprehensions. Hardenberg replied graciously the very next day that the matter had now been cleared up and that no further apologies or justifications were needed either on Kleist's or on the government's part.

For the moment, both parties were satisfied. The chancellery had a written admission by Kleist that his persistent demands had been based on a misunderstanding; and Kleist was in possession of an oral and, it must be admitted, rather vague promise that he would be compensated for his losses.

Incorrigible optimist that he was, he trusted it. His own upright character led him to trust a gentleman's word and forbade him to suspect a lack of goodwill in his former adversaries. In the meantime, however, he had to live. On top of everything else, a change of personnel at the Police Praesidium at the end of February had deprived the *Abendblätter* of the police reports. It should have been plain to Kleist that, even if this setback were not attributable to pressure from the chancellery, it could easily have been remedied by an order from the chancellery. But the *Abendblätter* was ruined in any case; there was no point in straining the newly acquired favor of the government on its account. If he could only manage to avoid public disgrace and keep Kuhn in line until the end of the first quarter. And in this he actually succeeded, presumably by allowing Kuhn to reprint his story *The Betrothal in Santo Domingo* free of charge in *The Liberal*, thus compensating him to some extent for the expense of publishing the *Abendblätter*.

On March 31, 1811, the *Berliner Abendblätter* ceased publication and Cotta's *Morning Journal for the Cultivated Classes* gave it a worthy obituary: "*The Evening Journal* [*Abendblätter*] has attained the evening of its life and, to the relief of its last long-suffering readers, has gone into retirement."

At about the same time, the chancellery carried out the plan it had hinted at to Kleist and announced the founding of an official journal, the *Kurmärkisches Amtsblatt;* but when Kleist, "passing over the entire matter of compensation," applied for the post of editor "as a mere token of your favor," he was coldly informed that the post was not suitable for him and that if he wished to be employed in the king's civil service, he should submit to the usual regulations. Thus, the chancellery affected to know nothing of any circumstances or direct or indirect assurances giving Kleist a claim to priority over any other applicant for a government post; in short, the chancellery wanted nothing more to do with him.

That was the end of Kleist's battle with the authorities. He emerged battered and empty-handed, except for the futile consolation of knowing himself to be in the right. He wrote to Fouqué: "And now, with contemptible diplomatic guile, they deny all their agreements with me, because they were not put into writing . . . As though a man of honor who has been given the word of a single individual—yes yes, no no—did not set as much store by that word as if it had been framed by a whole tableful of clerks and councilors, and signed and sealed."

In considering the battle of Kleist's *Berliner Abendblätter* with the political establishment, one cannot help thinking of Don Quixote, the simple-hearted fool who supposed that the ideals which triumphed in his brain would also triumph in the world. What adversaries he had taken on! The nobility with their petty, narrow-minded egoism; the reformers with their touchiness and political tergiversations; the government departments with their intrigues and jurisdictional disputes, personal antipathies and misunderstandings; his competitors with their fear and envy; the publishers with their sober business sense. And at every turn he had been led astray by the conviction that he was fighting for an *idea*, to which all men of goodwill would gladly rally.

In all this, he himself was his worst enemy. What he mistook for solid ground under his feet proved to be a morass; with a little clear-sightedness and adroitness, which need not have been synonymous with opportunism, he would have glided over it like Adam Müller. If he had been a better judge of how much freedom of the press was attainable in that time and place, he would not have provoked such antagonism. With a little more tact, he would have had Raumer and Hardenberg on his side, and they would have interceded with other officials on his behalf. With a little more understanding for Hitzig's business worries, he would have taken a word of advice from him now and then. With a little more circumspection, he would not have aroused the fears of competing newspaper owners; he would have curbed his originality just a little, so as not to provoke the bitter gibes and intellectual kleptomania of less gifted fellow journalists . . .

If if if! He was lacking in the practical common sense, the willingness to compromise and conciliate needed for success in worldly undertakings; he was lacking in the easy, well-balanced reactions that inspire sympathy and confidence in all; in practical affairs, he remained a man of the intellect and of art; he was Heinrich von Kleist—there was no help for him.

# 22

## EMPTINESS

FROM March 25 to April 5, 1811, under the title *The Betrothal*, Kuhn's *Liberal* ran Kleist's *Betrothal in Santo Domingo*, a story with so gripping a plot that (unfortunately) young Theodor Körner dramatized it, and so perfect in other respects that it can be put on a level, perhaps not with *Kohlhaas* or *The Marquise of O.*, but most certainly with *The Earthquake in Chile*. Probably inspired by Kleist's imprisonment of 1807 at Fort Joux, where the black leader Toussaint l'Ouverture had died some years before, it is set in Santo Domingo in 1803, when the native general Dessalines led an uprising against Napoleon's attempt to reintroduce slavery. Against this background, Kleist tells a story of his own invention.

The main plot of this intricate, close-knit tale is as follows. An old Negro, animated by a violent hatred of Europeans, uses his mistress and her daughter Toni, a fifteen-year-old half-caste, to lure whites in need of shelter to his house during his absence and keep them there with pretended kindness and near-seduction until he returns with his ruffians and kills them. A young Swiss fugitive from the black uprising appears at the house and is taken in. Lulled into a sense of security by Toni's friendly reception, he tells her the tragic story of how the girl he loved was guillotined during the French Revolution. Toni is strangely moved. Touched by her sympathy and bewildered by the unusual circumstances, he becomes her lover. She now regards herself as betrothed to him. But the cruel Negro returns unexpectedly, and she ties her sleeping lover to her bed—a ruse by which she hopes to save him. She slips out of the house and brings back some whites to set him free, but before she can explain why she tied him, he shoots her for supposed treachery, and then, when he learns the truth, he kills himself. Thus, they fall victim to a passion which in more peaceful times would have brought them happiness.

"Oh, you should not have distrusted me!" These last words spoken by Toni strike a chord that occurs in several of Kleist's works, though in different guises—tragic in *The Schroffenstein Family* and *Penthesilea*, comic in *The Broken Jug*, tragicomic in *Amphitryon*. And the love-rape in a state of semiconscious confusion as well as the sometimes helpful, sometimes destructive intrusion of extrapersonal forces are typically Kleistian motifs, figuring notably in *The Marquise of O.* and *The Earthquake in Chile*.

The historical setting is described more fully in *The Betrothal in Santo Domingo* than in any other of Kleist's tales. The older characters have been shaped once and for all by the barbarous times they live in—only the young, the hero and heroine, are still capable of change. This dominance of the milieu makes the cruelty of the action seem more plausible and less forbidding: on the human plane, it lends measure; on the technical plane, it supports and moderates the movement of the narrative, giving it an even pace and preserving its harmony. Thus, a dramatic element enters into the story, which is also related to drama in its almost perfect observance of the unities of place and time; for, rich and varied as it is, the central action occurs within a few hours in one and the same place, the old Negro's house.

*The Betrothal in Santo Domingo* is one of Kleist's fully successful works. With its depth, its density, and the controlled modulation of its harder and softer tones, it may be regarded as an exemplary short story. Along with Kleist's other tales, it met with ample appreciation even in his lifetime, if we are to believe Brentano, who later, in the carping, condescending tone he often took in speaking of Kleist, declared that some of his works had been "honored beyond their deserts" and that his stories had been "literally devoured."

If the author himself was aware of this popularity, he thought it unworthy of his attention. Neither publication in the popular press nor Reimer's book publication of *The Broken Jug* at Easter 1811 seemed enough of an event to revive his spirits. Nor did he find cheer in the pantomime version of *Penthesilea* performed by the celebrated Henriette Hendel-Schütz in the concert hall of the Nationaltheater on April 23. Kleist attended the rehearsals but did not even mention the production in a letter to Fouqué written two days later, and his only word of acknowledgment to the actress was a brief and coolly polite letter of thanks. On the other hand, it is hard to see how a pantomime of the bloodthirsty but endearing heroine could possibly have yielded anything more than an assortment of ecstatic or teethgnashing grimaces and hectic or moribund gestures, and it comes as no surprise to learn that the audience was not exactly carried away, that the reaction of the local press was lukewarm, and that the out-of-town papers were largely hostile. "The fragment of the play read by Herr Professor Schütz by way of explanation," reported the *Stuttgarter Morgenblatt*, "was boring and repellent by reason of its strained language and crudeness of expression."

At this reception Kleist must have shrugged his shoulders, accustomed as he had grown to the arrogance of the critics, to the vacuous indifference with which his efforts were greeted. His unsuccessful battle to save the *Abendblätter* and his jousting with the authorities had exhausted him. So many words exchanged to no purpose had left him with a bitter taste in his mouth. The tumult of battle gave way to an eerie, menacing silence, which threatened to engulf him. To resist it, to keep his head above water, cost him a desperate effort.

He sat at work in his room on Mauerstrasse, putting the finishing touches to his second volume of stories. He was still working on two short pieces, of which he had published rough sketches some months before in the *Abendblätter*, one entitled *The Newer (Happier) Werther (Der neuere [glücklichere] Werther)*, the other *The Story of a Strange Duel (Geschichte eines merkwürdigen Zweikampfs)*. The first was based on a Berlin news item, the second on an article he had read in a Hamburg magazine. Both, though satisfactory as quick sketches, were in need of his usual slow, thoughtful reworking, if anything substantial was to come of them. But for this he hadn't the time, since he wanted this second volume to be ready for fall publication, and moreover, he would have had to put his whole soul into it, and of that he was then incapable.

His lack of past success and future prospects left him disheartened. He had no doubt of his ability, but he was haunted by the insidious question: What for? From time to time his outlook brightened, as though a sunbeam had burst through a cleft in the dense gray clouds: "Sometimes I feel a breeze from my earliest youth. Suddenly the life that lies barren before me takes on a miraculous radiance, and powers I had thought dead stir within me. At such times I want to follow my heart wheresoever it leads me, taking no heed of anything but my own inner satisfaction . . . In short, I want to imbue my whole being with the thought that, provided a work of art issues in perfect freedom from a human spirit, such a work must necessarily belong to all mankind."

But he was unable to follow his heart, for no sooner arisen, the breeze from his earliest youth died away. Sometimes it seemed to him that a more serene life, if only he could manage it, would easily dispel the dark thoughts arising from the detestable conditions in which he lived. "In that case I might stop writing entirely for a year or more." But how was he to arrive at a more serene life! These illusory hopes, these speculations with which he tried to console himself, are expressed in letters to Marie von Kleist, who had little by little become dearer to him than any other living person. She was able to meet even his most fitful impulse with loving sympathy, though time and again her answer to one ultimate and decisive question was no rather than yes.

The reality surrounding him was hardly such as to encourage hope. There was his room in the house of Quartermaster Müller (as we have seen, not far from the house of Postal Councilor Pistor, where Brentano and Arnim had lodged until a short time before); there were the manuscripts of his stories *The Foundling* (*Der Findling*) and *The Duel* (*Der Zweikampf*), which beyond a doubt he was only too glad to put behind him; there was a joyless present and a future that promised nothing better than a continuation of his present misery.

Pistor had been to see him not so long before and had given him to understand that the authorities felt under obligation to help him out and would soon offer him some sort of post or other assistance. Adam Müller had been granted a solatium amounting to fifty percent more than the editorial fee Kuhn had paid him—was Kleist, to whom the government had binding obligations, to come off empty-handed? Was the silence which had followed the frosty rejection of his last petition really the sole, irrevocable answer to his undeniably justified demands? Suddenly he felt that he could not put up with this state of affairs a moment longer; that he could not sit idle as long as there was any higher jurisdiction with whom he had not yet tried his luck. He would have argued his case before God's own throne, had it been accessible.

As a member of the old nobility close to the ruling family, he saw nothing unusual in writing to the king's brother, Prince Wilhelm of Prussia, setting the whole affair before him in detail. Indignantly, he recalled Hardenberg's suggestion that if he wished a position in the civil service he should submit to the normal regulations: "Since neither the age I have attained nor the position I occupy in the world permits me to accept a post as a subordinate clerk, I fervently beseech Your Royal Highness to offer me your gracious protection against the unkindness and ignominies that have been undermining my peace of mind." Specifically, he asked the prince to intercede with the chancellor to obtain for him either a worthy position in the civil service, compatible with his literary work, or an appropriate solatium.

We do not know how the prince reacted to this letter; more than likely, he gave Kleist to understand that he could not intervene and that Kleist should come to an understanding with the chancellor. That, in any case, is what Kleist tried to do; he ordered a copy of Reimer's special limited edition (printed on vellum) of *The Broken Jug* and sent it to Hardenberg. But in his covering letter, instead of taking the chancellor's hint and invoking poetic merit rather than journalistic claims, he harped exclusively, though politely enough, on the question of compensation, and concluded by repeating his plea to Prince Wilhelm that he be granted either a worthy position or an appropriate solatium.

Hardenberg thought it wise to leave this new importunity unanswered. But the affair had become an obsession with Kleist. In the end he would have forgone personal satisfaction like his Kohlhaas, but to his mind this affair stood for a thousand others, for the fate of truth and justice on earth, and he felt in duty bound to fight it through to the end. He therefore turned to the highest possible authority, the king, and wrote him a letter, respectfully but uncompromisingly relating the whole course of the affair and urging the satisfaction of his rightful claim— either a government post or temporary financial assistance.

Seven years before, in the summer of 1804, when Kleist had appeared in the palace of Charlottenburg after his mad adventure in France, Friedrich Wilhelm III, through his aide-de-camp Köckeritz, had informed him of his poor opinion of him, but had nevertheless admitted him to government service. Kleist's career as a civil servant had come to an end in 1806 with the collapse of Prussia. Kleist, whom Köckeritz had already reproached for writing verses, had become a man of letters, and now, only recently, the chancellor had appealed to the king for support against his seditious *Abendblätter*. True, as Kleist had intimated in his letter, the late queen had had a weakness for him, but Friedrich Wilhelm was hardly the man to show him special favor for that reason. Was he to put his chancellor in the wrong? Wishing neither to make a direct show of favor nor to commit an injustice, he sent Kleist's letter to the competent authority for consideration, and the competent authority was the chancellery, in whose archives it came to light a century later. Whole sentences underscored in red and such marginal notations as "not true," "wrong," show what kind of consideration it received. It is no longer possible to determine whether the chancellery replied to His Majesty that the man's demands were quite unwarranted, but it may be presumed that the king reacted just as Hardenberg had done before him—with silence.

This was *really* the end of the affair; whatever Kleist may have felt, there was nothing more to be done. Injustice was firmly in the saddle.

Turning away from a wicked world, he resumed his work. He made a copy of *The Prince of Homburg* and offered the play to Reimer for book publication, asking for a quick decision, since he wished to dedicate it to the wife of Prince Wilhelm of Prussia, by birth a Princess von Hessen-Homburg and since the death of Queen Luise the first lady of the court. He wrote a fine eight-line dedication, but had no luck with it, for the princess, repelled by a play which sullied the memory of her ancestor with the totally fictitious scene where he describes his fear of death, refused to accept Kleist's dedication. Ten years later, a widely anticipated Berlin production was cancelled by her order. (At the same time, a production planned by the Vienna Burgtheater was likewise cancelled by order of Archduke Karl, on the grounds that such a play could have a demoralizing effect on the army.) Possibly because of the princess's attitude, Reimer decided not to publish the play just then. Kleist sent the manuscript to Marie von Kleist, and in her possession it remained for the present, far from the eyes of the literary world.

While copying *Homburg*, Kleist was also working on a "novel," which, he reported in July, was making good progress and would come to two volumes when finished. Would Reimer, he inquired, give him better terms for it than he had for the two volumes of stories, for which he had paid him a total of a 126 talers and 12 groschen? It was next to impossible, he wrote, to work for such a sum, and reluctant as he would be to publish outside Berlin, he would go back to Cotta if need be. Ferdinand Grimm, a young brother of Wilhelm and Jakob Grimm, who was then employed in Reimer's publishing house, mentions this "novel," "which is said to be very good," but does not make it clear whether he had actually seen it. Apart from Kleist's above-mentioned letter, this vague remark is all we know of this work. The manuscript has never come to light. It was probably among the papers which Kleist burned shortly thereafter.

True, he was working, but work had lost its old fascination;

it merely filled in the time and distracted him from its deathly emptiness. Since the early days of the *Abendblätter*, with their joyous bustle, he had come to be more and more alone. It had begun with Achim von Arnim, whom he had rather neglected, but had always been glad to see; in the middle of March Arnim had married Brentano's sister Bettina and "buried himself alive" with her in the gardens of the Voss palace. Kleist missed him, though he laughed at the bitterness of those friends who couldn't understand that Arnim should prefer solitude with his beloved wife to their wretched company. Brentano himself had gone to Bohemia with Schinkel and had not returned. The Christian-German Dining Club, which he had founded and which Kleist, partly because of its anti-Semitism, rarely attended, seemed to be breaking up. The good Fouqué, who kept sending him cordial invitations, lived far away on his estate, Nennhausen, and Kleist could never summon up the energy for the "complicated" trip.

Early in June, Adam Müller moved to Vienna. That was the hardest blow of all, for it was on his account that Kleist had settled in Berlin a year and a half before. Of all his friends, it was no doubt Müller who best understood his genius. Many a time Müller had taken up the cudgels for him, and in return Kleist not only trusted him implicitly but also mustered the sympathy that enabled him to discern the "essential innocence and goodness" of this brilliant, complicated, and changeable man. Indeed, the two friends would miss each other sorely. All the old grudges between them had died away; two men of stature, struggling to make their way in difficult times, they had learned to do each other justice. Kleist wrote to Marie von Kleist: "Müller's departure has plunged me into loneliness . . . I cannot tell you how touching I find this man's friendship, almost as touching as his love for his wife."

And then it was the turn of Marie von Kleist, whom he loved most dearly of all, to go away. Her exact reasons for leaving Berlin are not known. Possibly it was her ruined marriage, and possibly the state of her health, that made her feel the need of a rest at Gross-Gieritz, the Mecklenberg estate of her friend Frau von Berg, Countess Voss. Her departure meant a painful loss of human friendship and warmth, fatal to a man who had little to attach him to life, no joy, no hope, no real enthusiasm for his work, only habit, as thin and fragile as a spiderweb. It was as though fate had deliberately removed all those who might have saved him from his doom.

And then help seemed to come from an unexpected quarter. The Luisenstift, a girls' school and teachers' seminary, was looking for a lady to direct a new department and offered an annual salary of four hundred talers, in addition to board and lodging. He thought of his sister Ulrike, who, he had heard, was about to found a girls' boarding school at Frankfurt on the Oder.

Ulrike, the intimate of his younger days, had become estranged from him, partly through his fault and partly under the influence of the family, who seem to have "opened her eyes"—that is, convinced her that her insatiable brother would take everything she had and reduce her to beggary if she kept up relations with him. But once an affection had taken root in Kleist, it never died (one need only recall the naïve trust with which he turned up at Müller's rooms after their bitter quarrel). He could not bring himself to believe in this estrangement; his uncertainty about Ulrike's feelings only made him slightly uncomfortable, and that is why his letter asking her if he might look into the position at the Luisenstift seems stiff and formal. This position, he wrote, fell in with his wish to have her permanently near him, though there were "certain obstacles, for one thing, the school regulations," to their living together; assuring her that he would be glad to take all possible steps in this matter, he requested a brief reply, and signed himself "your faithful brother H. v. Kleist." But if Ulrike answered, it was in the negative. She did not come to Berlin.

It was about this time that Friedrich Christoph Dahlmann, who had accompanied Kleist some years before on his trip from Dresden to Austria and who was now living in Denmark, heard that Kleist was having a bad time of it in Berlin and wrote him a letter suggesting that they set up house together in Kiel, where he had just been appointed to a chair at the university. Knowing that the Prussian police opened private mail, he entrusted his letter to a young scholar who was setting out for

Berlin. Unfortunately, the scholar changed his itinerary unexpectedly and, on his return to Denmark, was still carrying Dahlmann's letter. It is by no means certain that Kleist, who had thought the trip to Nennhausen too complicated, would have gone to Kiel. Nevertheless, as evidence of faithful comradeship, Dahlmann's invitation would certainly have buoyed his spirits. But it did not reach him, and his solitude became more and more unbearable.

In mid-August, Reimer brought out Kleist's second volume of stories, consisting of *The Betrothal in Santo Domingo, The Beggarwoman of Locarno, The Miracle of St. Cecilia,* and two new tales, written specially for this volume, *The Foundling* and *The Duel.*

*The Foundling* is the story of a scoundrel. In the course of a business trip to Ragusa, a wealthy Roman merchant finds a ragged little boy of uncertain origin and, when his own son dies of the plague, takes the strange boy home with him. The foundling grows up to be a clever, darkly handsome young man, and the merchant signs over his whole fortune to him as successor to his dead son. Taking advantage of his strange resemblance to a childhood love of his still-young foster mother and of the similarity of their names, the foundling passes himself off as an apparition and, when she falls into a faint, tries to rape her. The merchant returns home unexpectedly and drives the boy out of the house. The wife dies of a fever brought on by the attempted rape. The merchant kills the boy, and after refusing absolution because he wants to join the boy in hell to complete his revenge, he is hanged.

The principal character, with his combination of lust and bigotry, is at best a curiosity, since his villainy, unlike that of Richard III, for example, is utterly unmotivated, while on the other hand he is not, like the hero of Dostoevsky's *The Possessed,* made credible as a demon, who does evil for the sheer love of it. And the story is rendered neither more fascinating nor more plausible by the villain's mysterious points of resemblance with the childhood love, a motif recalling the regrettable fortune-teller episode in *Kohlhaas.* What, in the end, does this story signify? That there is evil in the world and that one day it will show its ugly face? Such a platitude is unworthy of Kleist. True, the tale holds our interest, but only as long as we are reading it, and that is not enough.

*The Duel* is the story of a medieval ordeal by combat. The uncertain outcome of the duel takes on meaning when we learn that on entering the lists both men believed themselves to be in the right. The one who is really in the right is seriously wounded but recovers unexpectedly; the other, who proves to have been the victim of a deception in the affair occasioning the duel, but to have foully murdered his brother, is wounded only slightly but dies a slow and painful death. The story touches on a familiar Kleistian theme—the sanctity and ultimate triumph of trust. But the title and emphasis tend to glorify a medieval institution that can no longer be regarded as anything more than a curiosity. The story, it is true, shows an extraordinary gift of invention; but perhaps the invention is too rich for the underlying idea.

Kleist cannot have been very happy about these two stories. Each of his successful works had been in some sense a fresh start, a lesser or greater conquest in the realms of thought, feeling, and form; these stories represented nothing more than the exercise of a consummate but uninspired craft; in substance they were poor, rehashing themes presented in earlier works: the scoundrel, so much more richly portrayed in Adam, the village judge, and the strange vicissitudes leading up to the ultimate consummation of man's fate, a motif appearing in one variant or another in almost everything he had written, beginning with *The Schroffenstein Family*. And if he compared this second volume of stories with the first, which had appeared the previous year, the conclusion must have been disheartening. The first volume had included *Kohlhaas*, *The Marquise of O.*, and *The Earthquake in Chile*, each in its way brilliant, startling, and powerful; with these, only *The Betrothal in Santo Domingo* could bear comparison, certainly none of the remaining four tales, which were basically no more than blown-up anecdotes.

But even in the unlikely event that he judged these stories less severely, this volume could have afforded him no more effective consolation, no better company than his own shadow, which the lamp cast on the faded walls of his room. From morning to night he sat in that room, where nothing belonged to him; whole days passed without his seeing any visitor who might have brought him news of the outside world. He seldom went out, for he had begun to lose contact with the two or three houses he frequented. In some strange way, every source of cheer had dried up, the life he led since the departure of Müller and Marie von Kleist "was just too bleak and sad."

He wrote to Marie von Kleist describing the misery of his situation. Assuming that she would argue "But what is your imagination for if not to people your solitude with your distant friends?" he replied: "But unfortunate as I am, that consolation is denied me . . . Active as my imagination is in the presence of blank paper, distinct in color and outline as are the figures it brings forth, I find it painfully difficult to imagine what is real. It is as though in the moment of activity my imagination, always organized on a definite pattern, were fettered. Confused by too many forms, I can attain no clarity of inner vision; this object, I keep feeling, is not an object of the imagination: I want to penetrate it with my senses and apprehend its real living presence . . . Life with its pressing, constantly recurring demands comes so often between two beings at the very moment of contact; how much more so when they are far apart . . . In short, Müller seems dead to me now that he is gone, I mourn for him in exactly the same way, and if I did not know that you were coming back, I would feel the same way about you." Perhaps nothing more profound or more instructive (for writers) has ever been written about the splendor and misery, the strength, the weakness, and the unyielding stubbornness of the poetic imagination than these sentences. In the same letter, he speaks of the many "dismal, sorrowful moments, in which consolation is altogether absent."

Was there really nothing to console him? In the meantime, on September 1, 1811, *Käthchen of Heilbronn* was performed in Bamberg at the behest of E. T. A. Hoffmann. This, Kleist probably never knew. What he did know was that ominous clouds were again gathering over the political world. The alliance between Napoleon and Tsar Alexander was breaking up and would soon give way to open hostility. War seemed to be in the offing, and since Prussia could not possibly remain neutral in the event of war between France and Russia, the wildest possibilities were being discussed. Scharnhorst and Gneisenau were appointed to the Council of State, and Kleist hoped fervently to play an active role, this time face to face with the enemy. He therefore applied for reinstatement as an officer, and Marie von Kleist forwarded his petition to the king with a covering letter: "I am not asking the pay of an aide-de-camp for him. He wishes no more than the remuneration of the least of regimental lieutenants and would gladly serve for nothing if he had any resources at all. His sole and entire wish is to die for his country . . . My king, do not forget that a poet of his name was one of our country's greatest heroes, he too a man compounded of indescribable eccentricities, but good and true —let this hero live again in the person of Heinrich von Kleist."

The king, who was not unmoved by this plea from a woman who had been close to his late wife, wrote to Kleist almost immediately: "I acknowledge with pleasure the goodwill underlying your offer of service. True, there is as yet no way of knowing when the eventuality for which you make your offer may materialize; if it does, I shall be glad to bear you favorably in mind . . . Friedrich Wilhelm." And just as graciously, though perhaps even more cautiously, he wrote to Marie von Kleist: "I have written H. v. Kleist, who has made himself known as a writer and is now determined, in the event of war (which God forbid), to fight for his country, a letter giving him hope, should a war occur, but I must add that war does not seem to be as near at hand as some persons and you yourself appear to think."

But Kleist clung to the belief that war was imminent as a shipwrecked man clings to a raft (though with the opposite intention, for he wanted to die). Charlotte von der Marwitz, née Countess von Moltke, former lady-in-waiting to Queen Luise and a friend of Marie von Kleist, lived with her husband on the estate of Friedersdorf in Brandenburg. One day Kleist went to see them. They discussed the political situation, each had his own opinion, and these opinions are recorded in an astonishing document.

Kleist was convinced that war would break out within four

weeks and that if the Prussian army should unexpectedly succeed in crossing the Oder it would be destroyed in a battle to
be fought on October 14; Marwitz believed that before the
Prussian forces could even be mustered, Friedrich Wilhelm
would be crushed by Napoleon but that his army and the
Prussian state would still be in existence on October 14; Frau
von der Marwitz "sensed" that the king's last hour had struck
and that as a result of his eternal indecision, of poor leadership
and the superior power of the French, the Prussian army would
have been decimated in a series of skirmishes by that date. These
three statements, concordant only in their singular pessimism,
were committed to writing and dated "Friedersdorf, September 18, 1811."

On his return to Berlin the following day, Kleist may have
received another letter from the king assuring him of a commission in the army; or perhaps he was only expressing himself
unclearly and referring to the king's previous communication.
In any case, he wrote to Chancellor Hardenberg on September
19, referring to such a commission and asking for a loan of
twenty louis d'or to cover the cost of his uniform and equipment. The chancellery made no reply, skeptically postponing
its decision until the situation should become clear.

The situation was indeed unclear. Of course, Prussia would
have liked to fight, but not without a reasonable chance of victory. It had no intention of serving as a shield to defend gigantic
Russia against all-powerful France. The chancellery wished to
take up the fight on Prussian soil with the Russians as allies.
Tsar Alexander's idea was to lure the French army into his
country, whose vast spaces he wisely regarded as his most
lethal weapon. The two governments could not agree, and the
chancellor's efforts to obtain a firm promise of support from
Vienna and London came to nothing. Since it would be impossible for Prussia to remain neutral in the event of war between Russia and France, the government was obliged willy-
nilly to negotiate an alliance with Napoleon, and such a pact
was actually signed in February 1812. The negotiations were of
course strictly secret, but when it was rumored that Napoleon
was to visit Berlin, everyone could guess what was going on.

It is not hard to imagine the effect of this rumor on Kleist. Undoubtedly, it was he who asked Marie von Kleist to write her letter to Friedrich Wilhelm. His "sole and entire wish" had been to die for his king, "to die the warrior's death" he had dreamed of eight years before in his premature letter of farewell from Saint-Omer. What a splendid opportunity the supposedly impending war had offered to satisfy the death wish that had been with him since childhood! And that opportunity had now been taken away. Fate seemed to be saying to him: Oh no, I will not do it for you. You yourself must make the decision and carry it out. He understood this only too well, and it came to him as a numbing blow. From that time on, he acted like a clock mechanism which, once wound up, must run down before it can come to rest.

Even so, he clung, as though hypnotized, to the notion that the king had given him a commission; he wrote some political articles, took them to Gneisenau, and had a long talk with him —a splendid man whose support might have revived the powers he felt had died within him. But he did not delude himself. All this was *moutarde après dîner*. The repeated disappointment of his hopes had been bad enough, but now things had come to such a pass that he could no longer think of anything worth hoping for.

Marie von Kleist had written to him repeatedly, and every time he tried to answer, the pen fell from his hand. What was there in his miserable life worth communicating to one who loved him? When he finally forced himself to write, he made no attempt to conceal his yearning for death. "I cannot conceive of your returning to me with feelings of undivided friendship until I am dead . . . I would wish you dead if you needed death to make you happy . . . All is bleak and gray in my soul, the future offers not one bright spot to which I can look forward with any joy and hope . . . It is really extraordinary how everything I have undertaken of late has gone to ruin; how every time I resolve to take a firm step, the ground sinks from under my feet." And what of the future? "Should I go to Vienna if I receive the money from Ulrike? And shall I receive it?—I confess that the idea of a trip to Vienna appeals to me no more than the thought of going into the dark night amid rain and snow. Not that the city itself repels me; but it seems sad beyond description to look somewhere else for something which, because of my perverse nature, I have not found anywhere. Still, the connections I might make there could be helpful: perhaps my love of art would revive."

Yes, he had lost his love of art, and that was a death sentence; art was his way of life, he knew no other. Driven by his clockwork, which had not yet run down, he might attempt some other course, but it could only end in new suffering—or death.

It is hard to imagine why he should have expected Ulrike, estranged as she had become from him and his troubles, to give him money. Perhaps the naïve steadfastness of his own feelings led him to suppose that hers, too, had remained unchanged. Moreover, as the above-cited letter shows, he was not thinking very seriously of going to Vienna, but he did believe in earnest that he had been accepted for military service, either as an aide-de-camp to the king or as a company commander, and he could reasonably have felt that his family would regard the need to outfit himself as sufficient justification for a loan. True, apart from his own contention, there is no indication whatever that a commission had ever been granted him, and it is rather frightening that he should have spoken of it when he must at least have suspected that his assertion was unfounded. Lies and subterfuge were not in his character, but perhaps in his urgent plight he imagined that if he had money, happiness would be within his reach. Be that as it may, he realized that this matter could not be arranged by correspondence. Without so much as announcing his visit, he set out for Frankfurt—possibly the worst decision he could have made in his state of mind.

Frankfurt, that old provincial town, had been his "home," the scene of a childhood which in retrospect seemed to him "without joy." There were the narrow streets, the parks, the statue of the *guerrier, poète et philosophe* Ewald Christian von Kleist with his thoughtful, melancholy profile, and there on Nonnenwinkel was the house where, under the eyes of his "most gracious auntie" Massow, he had spent the happiest years of his youth, where in his student days he had built a lectern from which to dispense his stern moralistic pedagogy to the young ladies of his acquaintance, where he had devoted himself to the "education" of his betrothed and mercilessly tormented her with sterile, laborious exercises. All that was dead, buried beneath a decade of glorious and destructive vicissitudes, which had left him exhausted and impoverished.

He rang the doorbell and Ulrike opened. Why was she so dreadfully frightened at the sight of him? Had she banished him so thoroughly from her mind as to take him for a ghost? Did he smile his shy, disarming smile? Had life marked him so horribly? We do not know what words, if any, were exchanged between them. All we know is that he turned around and left the house. The door closed behind him. Aghast at the effect he had produced, he wrote her a short note, probably from a café, explaining that, having obtained a military commission, he wished to ask her financial assistance and adding: "Since, my dear, strange girl, you were so dreadfully frightened at the sight of me, a circumstance which, as true as I live, shook me profoundly, it goes without saying that I abandon this idea entirely, ask your forgiveness with all my heart, and, resolved as I am to return to Berlin this same afternoon, confine myself to the one other wish that was on my mind, that is, to see you once more for a few hours. Can I have lunch with you? —No need to say yes, I take it for granted, I shall be with you in half an hour. Your Heinrich."

Unfortunately, he was as good as his word. As ill luck would have it, Ulrike was not alone but with their sister Auguste von Pannwitz, who seems, under her husband's influence, to have turned Ulrike against their ne'er-do-well brother. The three of them sat down to table in an atmosphere of resentment. All, especially the usually outspoken Ulrike, found it hard to repress their rage. The general tenor, though not the details, of the conversation that developed is known to us. Kleist spoke of his military commission, the sisters were not convinced of its existence, and he had no way of proving it. He seems to have got tangled up in his explanations, and from then on the talk became increasingly unfriendly. A family friend, "old lady Wackern," dropped in and stayed and stayed, but nothing could stop the quarrel, they had too much on their hearts. What had come of all the fantastic promises with which he had wrung money from Ulrike? Nothing but annoyance. Scandalous newspaper articles, a couple of worthless books. Living like a rank bohemian, and even on that level he couldn't support himself. Was he a Kleist or wasn't he? A great name is a responsibility; had he ever tried to live up to it? Could you even call him a member of society?

So that was what his sisters thought of him. An insatiable parasite, to be got rid of as quickly as possible. The three of them parted as irreconcilable enemies. In the silence that followed the dreadful scene, Ulrike may have had qualms: mightn't there be some right on her brother's side? To him, however, the incident with his sisters was the worst of all the humiliations he had suffered, worse than death. To be suddenly made aware of what his supposed dear ones thought of him was a horrible experience, a shock which this defeated, hypersensitive man lacked the vitality and self-assurance to withstand. The harm begun by the cold, stupid, indifferent, malignant world was completed by his sisters. Mortally wounded, he returned to Berlin, to his room on Mauerstrasse, where loneliness stared him in the face and where all hope and all life-giving joy had died within him.

Yet he did not strike others as an object of pity. Sometimes he appeared at the Vogels', listened to Frau Henriette's piano playing, sang chorales with her, or instructed her in military tactics. He also saw Rahel now and then. A few of his notes to her have been preserved and reveal all his old charm: "My dear, why are you so much at large? A woman who knows her best advantage stays at home; that is where she can and should show her full worth. But that is something for you to settle with your conscience. A friend of the family declines to be frightened away, I shall come to you on Saturday, or perhaps sooner, perhaps this very day." Or: "Although my fever was gone, I still felt unwell as a result of it, most unwell; I should have been a poor consoler! But how sad you are in your letter. —There is as much expression in your words as in your eyes. Cheer up; even the best things are not worth regretting!"

But he could no longer summon up the energy for more forthright and intimate communications. From Marie von Kleist, who was still far away, ailing in Gross-Gieritz, he had received four letters since his last and had not sent a single word in reply. She was worried. In a letter to her son, she asked him to find out if Kleist was still in Berlin and to see how he was getting along. Ulrike, she wrote, had given her money to keep for Kleist, and if he was "too miserable," perhaps some of it should be turned over to him at once. Evidently, Ulrike had thought things over and sent Marie money for his uniform and equipment in case it turned out that he really had obtained a commission, but it is also possible that Marie, though anything but well off, had thought up this story as a pretext for sending Kleist money.

If the young man called on Kleist, it is more than likely that he found him in bed; not because he was ill, but because he had taken of late to spending whole days in bed. There he sat, propped up on pillows, pipe in mouth, working on the manuscript of his "novel." When he stopped writing and looked around him and listened to the silence, he might well have heard the words he had written ten years before to his friend Adolphine von Werdeck: "Ah, how empty and bleak and sad it must be to outlive one's heart." That was just what had happened to him. He was still alive, but his heart was no longer in anything he was doing. He had ceased to love his art, and they were vegetating together in a kind of ruined marriage.

# 23

## LIKE TWO JOYOUS BALLOONISTS

THE life Kleist had been leading was barely tolerable as long as the storms and enchantments of creative work could distract him and compensate for a steady flow of disappointments, the cumulative weight of which finally forced awareness that further hope was not only absurd but undignified as well. Not so very long ago he had said: "It is not possible to live without hope." But the last few years had taught him that in his situation the only possible basis for hope was deliberate delusion, and how could a man who had always faced the truth stoop to that? He was not an emotional acrobat; to see himself teetering on a tightrope revolted him. Nor did he possess the gift of balance that true religious faith might have given him; for at the bottom of his heart he was a nihilist, and what sometimes seems Christian in his thinking was in reality a sacred but pagan awe of the world's unfathomable mysteries. Hope and faith were not in his character; he had only his experience to go by, and that was discouraging.

Lack of success had weakened him and blunted his spirit. Works which at the moment of creation seemed bathed in the light of eternity had failed to bring him fame; they had aroused the admiration of a chosen few and the contempt and acrimony of the literary hacks, the indignation of polite society and the bored indifference of the general public. True, like Hebbel, he might have told himself that it matters little if certain people cannot stop talking when they should, that such people are like dogs who go on barking long after the event; but to him it seemed as though all human speech had ceased and only the yelping remained. Kleist had patience in his work, but not when it came to its reception. Impatience may indeed have been his most ruinous weakness. His only defense against it had been sustained creative enthusiasm, and now that was gone.

His ambition, his yearning for fame, was a gnawing hunger that was never sated in his lifetime. But if he were to shift his sights to immortality in a posthumous hereafter, he either had done enough already or would never be able to do enough. Because, for the kind of work to which his talent destined him, he felt that his creative powers were dwindling rather than expanding; his work was tied to the tragic passion and could not aspire to a more balanced harmony than he had attained in *The Prince of Homburg*. His talent was not one to grow old.

Those who wish to outlive the joys of youth must learn to make peace with the world, and of that Kleist was incapable. Time and again, his obsession with truth and justice had been offended. The world had spat in his face. Lies, injustice, blindness to true merit, shabby trickery, baseness of every kind, the forgetfulness of the crowd, the speed with which they reconcile themselves to what they have just termed intolerable—in short, everything that has characterized man and the world down through the ages filled him with nausea. Over the years his skin, instead of growing thicker, had grown thinner, more sensitive, more irritable, too irritable to bear the thousand pinpricks and insect bites of day-to-day life. And all this was exacerbated by his solitude and by the irony of fate which transformed what had attracted him as a favorable opportunity into its opposite the moment he reached out for it. Was the impending Franco–Prussian alliance not indeed the cruelest of ironies, since, if he had actually become an officer, he would now have had to fight for Napoleon rather than against him? The world did not want him as he was, and he did not want the world as it was. There was nothing to be done about that, and his nature both as a man and as an artist compelled him to draw the logical conclusions from unalterable facts. Or rather, he was incapable of not drawing the conclusions, especially if they tended toward his destruction.

For the destructive drive was strong in him, not only as a

counterweight to his equally powerful life drive, but, seen in a
different aspect, as an integral part of it—and that is precisely
what made him a tragic poet. When in this complex of forces
the productive energies flagged or failed, the destructive drive
would inevitably take over, the death wish would become all-
powerful and—by habit, as it were—infect and convert to its
service what was left of the positive energies. If ever a great
artist has "lived dangerously," as Nietzsche was to put it, it is
Kleist; for that was the very essence of his character, he could
not have lived in any other way. His whole life, as we have
attempted to sketch it here, had been dominated by the alternative: either total triumph here and now, or a quick, resolute
death. Even as a boy, he had entered into a suicide pact with
his cousin Carl Otto von Pannwitz, and in his manhood there
was not a single work in which he did not treat explicitly or
implicitly of this alternative, not a single defeat to which he
did not respond with a yearning for self-destruction, not a
single friend of either sex to whom he did not suggest that they
commit suicide together . . . yes, *together*, for death drive and
love were for him inseparable, a longing, as it were, for the
ultimate embrace. And Kleist's distress had never been deeper
or more hopeless than at this moment. All he needed was an
occasion and he would fling himself into the abyss with a shout
of joy that would echo down the century and beyond it.

The occasion did not, and could not, fail to arise, and one is
surprised that so intelligent a man as Pfuel, who knew Kleist
well, should later have spoken of "stupid chance," ignoring the
fact that Kleist had inner resistances to overcome, and could
not have done so without imperative need. We are referring to
Kleist's relationship with Henriette Vogel, who after the departure of Marie von Kleist had little by little taken her place in
his empty life. True, we may speak of "stupid chance" to the
extent that this might not have happened if Marie von Kleist
had stayed in Berlin. Apart from the few women with whom
he maintained a mere nodding acquaintance, there are two with
whom he was still on more intimate terms, Rahel Levin and
Henriette Vogel. If between these two his preference went to
Henriette, it was not because of any intrinsic superiority, but

because of the promising occasion offered by her illness. For her emotional instability (which had at first repelled Kleist) had its source in a real and terrible illness. She was afflicted with a far-advanced tumor of the uterus, which she knew was incurable and which left her no other prospect for the future but steadily increasing pain and a terrible end. Fear of physical torment made her long for a quick and relatively painless death. She freely admitted as much and spoke of it to her husband and to friends in tones of religious exaltation, comparing the limitless glory of a paradise to come to the misery of human life and death. The hushed embarrassment of her listeners, who could not regard death as a fit topic for drawing-room conversation, left her sad and disappointed.

Kleist, for his part, was suffering from an emotional vacuum, which, to their mutual satisfaction, this fear converted into religious exaltation was able to fill only too well. Who will venture to say that the feeling between him and this pale woman in the Empire gown, which he was soon to call love, was not a passion, not a common bond, but only a convergence of two solitudes? Or can it be that just that is love? A love which, unsated by the waters of life, thirsts for those of death? This love was dangerously superior to his love for Marie von Kleist in one respect: its consummation, if it came about, would be irrevocable.

At first, the matter was not mentioned between them; but early in their friendship Kleist's unconscious seems to have played a trick on him: he promised never to deny Henriette anything she wished. And soon she made so little secret of her love that her husband, who was by no means unloving or unloved (Henriette was in the habit of calling him "my darling Vogel"), declared his willingness to release her to Kleist.

The story goes that one day Kleist stood leaning against the piano while she accompanied herself in a song. No sooner had she finished than he cried out: "It's so beautiful I could shoot myself!" She looked up at him, they looked deep into each other's eyes, they did not speak. The story (and we wonder where the person who first told it could have got his information if not directly or indirectly from one of the participants) goes on as follows. Some days later, Henriette mentioned Kleist's cry to him and asked him if he remembered his promise to do anything she asked of him. He confirmed his promise, and she said: "Very good. Then kill me. My sufferings are so terrible, I can't bear to live any longer. Oh, I know you're not likely to do it, there are no men left on earth; but—" "I will do it," Kleist interrupted her. "I am a man of my word."

This story may well be an invention—Peguilhen, for one (of whom we have spoken and shall have more to say), may have felt the need of an explanation to cushion the shock of so sudden and unexpected an event. For suddenly it happened, without the prelude of a loving embrace, which, according to medical testimony, would have been rendered next to impossible by Henriette's condition, quite apart from Kleist's apparent lifelong continence. Marie von Kleist had just returned to Berlin, but she could no longer help—suddenly, intuitively, the decision had been made. The last-quoted note to Rahel, the charm of which betrays not the least suggestion of a last parting, is dated October 24; the first jubilant death message to Marie von Kleist is dated November 9—two and a half weeks had sufficed for them to close their accounts with the world and to solemnize their impending sacrifice in verse and prose offerings addressed to each other. Kleist, for example, wrote a death litany—Berlin, November 1811—for Henriette, twenty lines, consisting of three sentences. Stammering with happiness, it heaps up terms of endearment and praise, and closes with the lines: "Ah, you are my second, better self, my virtues, my accomplishments, my hope, the forgiveness of my sins, my future and my beatitude. O daughter of heaven, O child of God, my advocate, my intercessor, my guardian angel, my cherub and my seraph, how I love you!" And in the same vein, Henriette to Kleist: "My Heinrich, my sweet-sounding one, my bed of hyacinths, my sea of bliss, my sunrise and sunset, my Aeolian harp, my dew, my arch of peace, my darling child."

Madness? No doubt. But what would one expect from a man of Kleist's temperament when a spark of hopeful enthusiasm is kindled in the deepest darkness of despair? Suddenly the whole world is aflame. So it had been in his creative hours, and so it was when not a work of art but a deed was under consideration. Did ever an artist's action prove the truth of his work more strikingly? The personality is obviously the same in both cases, and the resemblance extends even to the method. In the execution of his suicide as in his writing, the wildest exaltation is mingled with the coldest awareness and calculation.

His letters of farewell to Marie von Kleist, to our knowledge the most splendid ever written by anyone in the face of death, are a testimony leaving room for no explanation, no doubt, and no vindication.

[*Berlin, November 10, 1811*]
Your letters break my heart, my dearest Marie, and if it were in my power, I assure you I would alter my decision to die. But I swear to you I cannot possibly live any longer. I am so heartsore, it would hardly be an exaggeration to say that the daylight shining on my nose when I stick it out of the window hurts me. Some people will say I am sick, overwrought, but not you, for you are able to see the world through other eyes than your own. Since my childhood days, in my thoughts and in my writings, I have been in constant contact with beauty and morality and that has made me so sensitive that the most trifling aggressions, to which every man's feelings are exposed by the nature of things here below, are doubly and trebly painful. I can assure you, for instance, that I would rather die ten deaths than once again suffer what I went through on my last visit to Frankfurt, at the luncheon table with my two sisters, especially when old lady Wackern joined us; just let Ulrike tell you about it someday. I have always loved my sisters dearly, in part for their excellent natures and in part for the kindness they have shown me; though I have seldom spoken of it, one of my most fervent and most heartfelt wishes was that my work would someday bring them great joy and honor. I must own that for various reasons it has been dangerous of late to associate with me, and I am all the less inclined to reproach them for drawing away from me when I consider the burden of these times, a part of which

they, too, are condemned to bear; nevertheless, to see un-
recognized the merit to which, be it great or small, I can
surely lay claim, to see myself regarded by them as an
utterly useless member of society, no longer worthy of the
slightest sympathy, is a source of pain to me, and not only
deprives me of the future joys I hoped for but also poisons
my past. —Nor is the alliance the king is now concluding
with the French exactly calculated to attach me to life.
The faces of the people I meet have long repelled me, but
now, even were I to pass them on the street, I would be
overcome by a physical sensation that I prefer not to name
here. True, I no more than they have had the strength to
set the times right; yet I feel that the will which lives in my
heart is different from the will of those who make that
witty remark, so much so that I want nothing more to do
with them. How, if the king concludes this alliance, can
one put up with him any longer? The hour is close at hand
when, if this king is to be the judge, a man will risk the
gallows for loyalty in opposition to him, for self-sacrifice
and steadfastness and all the other civic virtues.

[*Berlin, November 19, 1811*]

My dearest Marie, in the midst of the paean of triumph my
soul has struck up in this hour of death, I must think of you
once more and open myself to you as well as I can; to you,
whose feelings and opinion alone matter to me; everything
else on earth, the general and the particular, I have vanquished in my heart. Yes, it is true, I have been unfaithful
to you, or rather, I have been unfaithful to myself; but
since I have told you a thousand times that I would not
outlive such infidelity, I am proving it now by taking leave
of life. During your absence from Berlin, I exchanged you
for another friend; not, however, if this can console you,
for one who wants to live with me but for one who, sensing that I should be true to her no more than to you, wants
to die with me. My relations with this woman do not permit me to say more. Know only this much, that my soul,
through contact with hers, is now fully prepared for death;

that I have measured all the glory of the human spirit by hers, and that I am going to die because there is nothing more on earth for me to learn or acquire. Farewell. You are the only being on earth I wish to see in the hereafter. Not Ulrike?—yes and no, let her feelings decide. She has not, it seems to me, mastered the art of self-sacrifice, of giving oneself entirely for what one loves; that is the greatest bliss conceivable on earth and must also be the stuff of heaven, if it is true that the people there are happy and gay. Adieu! —Consider, too, that I have found a woman whose soul flies like a young eagle; in all my life I have found no one like her; who understands that my sadness is something sublime, deep-rooted, and incurable, and who, therefore, though she would have ways enough of making me happy on earth, wants to die with me; who is granting me the enormous favor of letting herself be plucked as easily from a situation leaving nothing to be desired as a violet from a meadow; who, for my sake, is leaving a father who worships her, a husband so generous that he has offered to relinquish her to me, a child as beautiful, no, more beautiful than the morning sun; then you will understand that my only jubilant care must be to find an abyss deep enough to plunge into with her. —Again adieu!

[*Stimming's "Jug," near Potsdam, November 21, 1811*] My dearest Marie, if you knew how love and death took turns in crowning these last moments of my life with flowers, both heavenly and earthly, I am sure you would be glad to let me die. Ah, I assure you, I am very happy. Morning and evening I kneel down, something I have never been able to do, and pray to God; now I can thank Him for my life, the most tortured any man has ever led, because He is recompensing me with the most glorious and voluptuous death. Oh, if I could only do something for you, something to attenuate the bitter grief I shall cause you. For a moment I wanted to have my picture painted; but then it seemed to me I had wronged you too much to be justified in thinking that my picture would give you much pleasure. Is it any comfort to you if I say that I would never have taken this friend in your place, if she had wanted nothing more than to live with me? Yes, my dearest Marie, that is the truth; there have been times when I frankly said as much to my dear friend. Oh, I assure you, I love you so much, you are so very dear and precious to me that I cannot truly say that I love my dear, deified friend more than you. The decision that flared up in her soul to die with me has drawn me—with what ineffable and irresistible force!—to her bosom; do you remember that I have several times asked you to die with me?—but you always said no. —A whirl of happiness, such as I never before experienced, has seized hold of me, and I cannot deny that her grave is dearer to me than the beds of all the empresses in the world. —Ah, my dear friend. May God soon call you to a better world, where we shall all embrace one another with angelic love. —Adieu.

It is interesting to note that in these unforgettable letters, whose essential truth must reduce all psychologizing to silence, Kleist for the first and last time addresses this woman he loved so dearly with the familiar "*Du.*" Two of these letters were not mailed in his lifetime. The one dated November 10 was found in a locked trunk in Henriette's home, that of November 21 in a sealed box at the inn where the suicides spent their last night. Kleist left instructions that both were to be given *at the same time* to a certain intermediary for Marie. The underscoring of "at the same time" supports the impression one gains in reading the last letter; namely, that it was conceived as a last farewell and written in the awareness that the suicide was imminent.

At his Mauerstrasse lodgings, Kleist had destroyed all his papers, notes for new works, unfinished works, the manuscript of the "novel" he had mentioned to Reimer, material left over from the *Abendblätter*, and correspondence. If he had not sent a copy of *The Prince of Homburg* to Marie von Kleist, that great work would have been lost forever. In short, he had made a clean sweep, there was nothing more to hold him, the plan stood fast. Originally, they had meant to carry it out in Cottbus, but then a friend of the Vogel family, one Ernst Ludwig Hoff-meister, arrived unexpectedly from Cottbus, and this (for reasons unknown to us) made it necessary to await a more propitious moment, to choose a different site, and to find someone other than the person hitherto envisaged to execute their posthumous instructions, especially in regard to their burial. It seems they knew someone in Cottbus, which had the advantage of being mercifully far away from the persons most directly affected. Where else, not too near and not too far, had they an acquaintance, a friend, whom they could entrust with such a task?

It was just ten years since Kleist and some comrades, gathered on the shore of the Kleiner Wannsee, had discussed the best method of suicide; this was deserted sand and pine country, typically Prussian, barely a mile from Potsdam, and only a few steps from the Berlin highway. He may have had the loneliness and deathlike stillness of this heath in mind when writing the penultimate stanza of his *Last Song* (*Das letzte Lied*): "Where, beneath boughs of evergreen, solitary, silent paths lead to tombstones"; and the austere stillness of the place had occurred to him again a year before when he had invited Fouqué there to celebrate their brotherhood as poets. In all this, there was a kind of predestination, and just as the same images kept recurring in his letters, notes, and literary works, so the thought of this place seems to have come to him time and time again. Moreover, it presented definite advantages; in particular, the loneliness of the place and the presence, at the point where the road divided the lake into the Kleiner and Grosser Wannsee, of a comfortable inn, the New Jug by the Friedrich-Wilhelm Bridge, proprietor Johann Friedrich Stimming; it had been put up in 1790, when the paved Berlin–Potsdam highway was built, and was later to become the busiest hostelry in all Prussia. But in those days and at that time of year hardly anyone went there, although it was within an easy carriage ride from the city. Among their many Berlin friends, it would surely be a simple matter to find someone close enough to them, though not too close, to attend to their last needs. They thought of Peguilhen, who, though barely acquainted with Kleist, was closer to Henriette and was a long-time friend of her husband. Peguilhen was a self-important little man who liked to boast of his prominent friendships and would surely be pleased to play a role in so sensational an affair.

And so it was settled: Peguilhen would be their executor, they would rest and make their final preparations at Stimming's Jug by the Friedrich-Wilhelm Bridge, and take leave of this world on a pine-covered knoll surmounting the Kleiner Wannsee. Henriette informed her husband that she was planning a brief excursion to Potsdam. There is no way of knowing whether Vogel suspected the truth or what he was thinking when he promised to send his carriage to call for her. This conversation must have occurred shortly before her departure, probably the day before, that is, November 19, 1811, and at the same morning hour when Kleist, unannounced and unexpected, appeared at the home of the ailing Frau von Stägemann, the wife of his Königsberg friend. "Forgive me, dear Kleist," she called out to him, "but I can't see you now." Without a word, Kleist turned away and vanished. Later, when the poor woman heard what had happened, she could not forgive herself; it seemed to her that if she had not sent him away he might have spoken out and that awful thing might not have happened.

Her self-reproach was certainly unwarranted; Kleist would not have spoken out, his decision did not belong to him alone and could not have been shaken. The cab had been ordered for the next day, November 20; he and Henriette spent the morning together at Henriette's home. In a mood of macabre gaiety, Kleist thought—as he often had of late—of Sophie von Haza, whom he had once loved, and because of whom he had almost flung Adam Müller, her present husband, off the Elbe Bridge in Dresden. Sophie and Adam Müller—to those names attached a comforting memory of hope, friendship, and joy, of so many wishes and plans, which now lay dead behind him. Moved to send her a last greeting, he sat down at the desk and wrote:

Heaven knows, my dear and excellent friend, what strange feelings, half sad, half joyful, move us in this hour, as our souls rise above the world like two joyous balloonists, to write to you once more, for actually we had decided not to send our friends and acquaintances cards of leave-taking. It must be because we have thought of you in a thousand happy moments, because we have imagined a thousand times how you with your generous nature would have laughed (exulted) if you had seen us together in the green room. Ah, the world is a strange place! —It seems somehow fitting that Jettchen [Henriette] and I, two gloomy, woebegone people, who have always deplored their own coldness, should have come to love each other with all our hearts, and the best proof of it, I feel, is that we are going to die together.

Farewell, our dear, dear friend, and be very happy—it is said to be possible on earth. We for our part wish to know nothing of the joys of this world, we know and dream only of heavenly meadows and suns, in the light of which we shall stroll about with long wings on our shoulders. Adieu! A kiss from me, who am writing this, to Müller; tell him to think of me now and then, and to remain a valiant warrior of God against the diabolical madness that holds the world enchained.—

[Below, in Henriette's hand]

> But how this whole thing came to pass
> I'll let you know another time,
> Today I'm in too great a hurry.

Farewell, my dear friends; in joy and sorrow remember two strange people, who will soon embark on their great voyage of discovery.

HENRIETTE

[And in Kleist's hand]

Set down in the green room, November 20, 1811

H. v. KLEIST

This letter and others they put into a trunk that happened to be in the servants' quarters. Then about noon they drove off in their cab. We owe our knowledge of the ensuing events to the records of the police hearings, which were begun less than forty-eight hours later and completed with German thoroughness. Thanks to them, more is known about Kleist's last day on earth than about any other.

The cab bearing Kleist and Henriette drew up at Stimming's inn between two and three in the afternoon of November 20, 1811. Stimming's wife, Friederike, still a young woman, welcomed the guests. The gentleman, powerfully built, with blue eyes and almost black hair, was wearing a brown coat, a white muslin shirt, a white tie, gray cloth trousers, and high boots; he helped the lady out of the carriage; in alighting, she showed fine cotton stockings and black shoes, fastened with a black ribbon at the ankle.

When the couple asked for two adjoining rooms, Frau Stimming took them to the top floor. The lady went straight to the window, expressed her delight at the fine view, and asked if it was possible to cross over to the far shore of the Kleiner Wannsee in a boat. Frau Stimming said no, there was no boat, but it was an easy walk. The lady then asked Frau Stimming to have two more beds made ready, since they were expecting two friends, who might arrive that same day, or possibly during the night. Meanwhile, Riebisch, the hired man, sent by Herr Stimming, came in and made fires in the stoves of both rooms.

After a while, the guests came down to the supper room and asked for coffee. It was served by M. L. Feilenhauer, the young housemaid. They drank it, stood up, went out, and were seen to disappear across the Wilhelm Bridge. An hour later they came back and paid the coachman, who was unknown in the locality and had waited until then. The carriage drove off in the direction of Berlin. They ordered their evening meal; the little Feilenhauer girl waited on them, but merely took their orders and had no conversation with them. When they had finished eating, they asked for four candles and writing materials, and having obtained them, went to their rooms.

Late that night, Stimming and the others in the house heard them pacing the floor, and the hired man, who was outside, saw them walking back and forth in the candle-lit rooms and occasionally sitting down; they had brought two or three bottles of wine and a flask of rum, and they drank while pondering their testamentary dispositions, which they stated in a joint letter addressed to Peguilhen. The beginning of the letter was written by Henriette: "My esteemed friend: A great test is in store for the faithful friendship you have always shown me. Kleist and I are here at Stimming's on the road to Potsdam, in a state of utter helplessness, or, more specifically, shot dead, and we are counting on the kindness of a friend to confide our mortal remains to the secure fortress of the earth. Try, dearest Peguilhen, to arrive here this evening."

The letter goes on to tell him that he would find a knapsack-like traveling bag and a sealed box full of clothing, books, messages for Vogel, letters, and money. The ten reichstalers in the box should be spent on "a really beautiful *pale-gray cup*, gilded on the inside, with a golden arabesque on a white ground reaching to the edge, and at the top, in a white field, my first name inscribed in what is now considered the most modern lettering"; Peguilhen should order this cup from Herr Meves, the bookkeeper at the porcelain factory, "with instructions to pack it and send it to Louis *on Christmas Eve.*" Henriette also called his attention to a small key that he would find in the sealed box; it belonged to the padlock of her trunk at the house on Behrenstrasse, in which there were more papers and other items requiring his attention.

Then it was Kleist's turn. "I trust, my dearest Peguilhen," he wrote, "that I too may call on your friendship for a few small favors." He had forgotten to pay his barber for the current month; would Peguilhen be so kind as to give him the reichstaler wrapped separately in Madame Vogel's box for that express purpose. As for the traveling bag and those of its contents not required for his burial, let Peguilhen give them to Quartermaster Müller (Kleist's landlord on Mauerstrasse) as a small token of thanks for his friendly hospitality. He signed "H. v. Kleist" and wrote underneath: "Here they say it is the 21st of November, but we don't know if it is true."

In a postscript he gave further instructions for the forwarding of certain letters, one of which Peguilhen would find "here" and the others on Behrenstrasse, in a trunk with a brass padlock, the key to which was in Madame Vogel's box. And to this postscript he added a second, saying that Peguilhen would be reimbursed for the burial costs by his sister Ulrike—who once again had to reach into her pocket for her brother. "Madame Vogel has just told me," he wrote in conclusion, "that the key to the trunk with the brass padlock, which is in the servants' quarters of her house in Berlin and which contains many matters requiring to be taken care of, is here in the sealed wooden box. —I believe I have already told you that, but Madame Vogel insists on my writing it once again. H. v. Kl."

At about four in the morning of November 21, which fell on a Thursday, Henriette descended the stairs from the top story and ordered *one* cup of coffee from the little Feilenhauer girl, who was already up; then Henriette went back upstairs, and the girl, who brought the coffee to her room shortly thereafter, was struck by the fact that she was still wearing the same dress as when she arrived. After that, there was no further sound from the guests' floor. At about seven, Henriette came down again and again ordered coffee. When the girl entered her room with the tray, she was changing her clothes ". . . and she asked me to help lace her up. She was alone in her room. She had removed the handle of the door leading to his room, and when he knocked, she only said she was embarrassed on his account."

First one, then the other would appear in the parlor with some request. Finally they asked for the bill, which Kleist paid and, methodically enough, asked Stimming to return to him receipted. Frau Stimming inquired whether they would be taking their noonday meal at the inn. No, Henriette replied, and Kleist muttered under his breath that they would make up for it at supper. Nevertheless, they took a few cups of bouillon, and Kleist asked if there was someone about who might take a letter to Berlin. Herr Stimming found a messenger, and after exchanging a few words with him, Kleist added to the joint letter to Peguilhen: "The messenger is to be given another 12 groschen." The messenger left the Jug shortly before twelve o'clock, and again the guests withdrew to their rooms.

Then Kleist, unwilling to leave any drop of bitterness in his own heart or anyone else's, wrote his last letter:

Serene and contented as I am, I cannot die without recon-
ciling myself with the whole world, and above all, my
dearest Ulrike, with you. Let me, oh let me retract the
harsh words of my letter to Madame Kleist; you really did
all that was in the power, I will not say of a sister, but of a
human being, to save me; the truth is that there was no
salvation for me on earth. And now farewell; may the
heavens give you a death even approaching mine in joy
and ineffable serenity: that is the most fervent and heartfelt wish that I can summon up for you.

Stimming's near Potsdam, on the morning of my death.

*Yours,*

HEINRICH

At about two in the afternoon, the couple came downstairs
again, went outside, and walked up and down in front of the
house for some time. Stimming stepped outside and they both
chatted with him "most amiably," without showing a trace of
nervousness, fear, or distress. They asked questions about the
neighborhood, the Peacock Islands, for example: was the nearest one accessible? did anyone live there?—and so on. Stimming
explained how to get there, but they said they wouldn't go just
then, no, they would take some coffee, and several times, as
though in passing, they let fall the question: Could the messenger with the letter already be in Berlin? It was then three
o'clock, and Stimming (who thought the letter had been written to order a carriage for their return) said yes, the man ought
to arrive between three and four o'clock. In high spirits they
then strolled out to the yard behind the house, where they could
be heard laughing and joking; Kleist jumped over the side of
the bowling alley and challenged Henriette, to whom he sometimes said "*Sie*" and sometimes "*Du*," to do the same.

Then they appeared in the kitchen, where Frau Stimming
was working. Kleist said two friends were coming for supper,
and "they must eat very well." "Oh no," said Henriette. "Why
bother? They can content themselves with an omelet the same
as us." "All right," said Kleist, and using almost the same words
as a few hours before: "We'll make up for it at dinner tomor-

row." Then Henriette asked Frau Stimming if the coffee they had ordered could be brought "to the lovely green spot" by the lake. What! said Frau Stimming, in this winter weather? Besides, it was too far. Kleist replied that he would gladly pay the servants for their trouble, and asked if she would kindly send eight groschen worth of rum with the coffee? Very well, said Frau Stimming, and in the meantime she would have their rooms done. Oh no, they said, they wouldn't hear of it. "Leave everything as it is." The young lady was carrying a basket carefully covered with a white cloth. It attracted Frau Stimming's attention because she couldn't imagine what was in it— later she understood.

When the guests left the kitchen, she called the hired man's wife, a simple soul, aged fifty (who was illiterate and signed her statements at the inquest with crosses), and told her to take the guests' coffee down to the lake shore. Frau Riebisch shook her head in amazement. Not only was it cold, but a fog was coming up; this was no weather to be drinking coffee out of doors.

Kleist and Henriette, with their little basket, went down to the shore and crossed the bridge to the so-called Summer Path. There they encountered an obstacle. A wheelbarrow full of manure barred their path, and on its shafts sat Riebisch, the hired man, resting. Kleist asked him to move the wheelbarrow out of the way so the lady could pass and tipped him a groschen for his kindness, which left Riebisch with a friendly feeling toward the guests. He moved on with his cart and had hardly crossed the bridge when his wife came toward him. "Did you ever hear of such foolishness?" she asked. "Those two want to have their coffee up there." She was carrying a tray laden with a coffeepot, milk, sugar, and cups and saucers. "They'll make it worth your while," said Riebisch dryly, and left her.

Frau Riebisch headed for the spot that Frau Stimming had indicated to her, a heather-covered knoll with a few tall trees on it. She saw Kleist and Henriette standing side by side at the top, looking down at the Kleiner Wannsee. She went up and set the tray on the ground in front of them. Wouldn't it be possible to have a table and chairs, Henriette asked. Taken aback by such foolishness, Frau Riebisch protested: "But the coffee will be cold before they get here." Henriette made no answer, and Frau Riebisch hurried away. Soon she saw her husband's back ahead of her on the path and called out to him that the guests were now wanting a table and chairs. Riebisch nodded, and together they went to the house. Then he carried the table and she the chairs over the Summer Path to the knoll, and Kleist and Henriette sat down. The Riebisches stood behind them. Kleist turned to Frau Riebisch and said he would like a pencil and please would she ask Herr Stimming how much they still owed him. Since the coffeepot was almost empty, Frau Riebisch waited so as to save herself a trip. Kleist poured himself the last of the coffee and added a bit of rum from the bottle. After drinking it up, he turned to Riebisch, a man in his early forties: "Old father, kindly ask your master to send me back this bottle half-full of rum." "Dear child," Henriette objected. "You've had enough rum for today." Kleist gave in without a murmur. "Very well, dear child," he replied. "If you don't want me to, I won't; never mind, old father, don't bring me anything." Meanwhile, Frau Riebisch had loaded the tray with the coffee things, all except the cup that Kleist still had in his hand; the guests gave her the milk that was left over and she drank it. Henriette pointed her finger, laughed, and cried out: "Look at the milk mustache she's made herself."

They were merry guests, no doubt about it. Riebisch went off with his wife. As he later testified, he saw the two of them "running down the hill toward the lake hand in hand, joking and chasing each other, as if they were playing tag. I'd never seen such a loving couple as those two on the hill. They kept calling each other 'child' and 'dear child.' I can't get over how cheerful they were." They could see them larking on the lake shore and skipping stones over the water. Little by little the colors faded, the air became grayer and darker, the fog thicker, and soon the playful pair paled into leaping shadows.

Frau Riebisch came back with a pencil and the landlord's answer: No hurry about the bill, since they were not about to leave. The guests came sauntering toward her on the hill, the lady held out the remaining cup to her, there was money in it, and she said: "Little mother, here is the cup. Take it, wash it, and bring it back." Carrying the cup with the money she was to bring to Stimming, Frau Riebisch started back to the Jug. She had hardly reached the path when she heard a shot. "Those people!" she thought to herself. "Playing around with a gun . . . Funny I didn't see they had a gun." Fifty steps took her to the Wilhelm Bridge; there she heard another shot; and then it was very still.

Still unsuspecting, she arrived at the inn; she gave Stimming the money, rinsed the cup, and started off again. She came to the hill and started up it, but then she stopped still and stared wide-eyed. At the top of the hill, the lady was lying on her back, deathly pale, and the gentleman was down on his knees in front of her in a strange position. Nothing stirred in the fog round about. Holding back a scream, she shook off her paralysis and ran to the Jug as fast as her legs would carry her, but she did not stop there, she only shouted to the Feilenhauer girl, who was looking out of a window, that the guests had shot themselves, and kept running until she reached the little house where she lived with her husband. "The guests!" she gasped. "They're at the top of the hill, dead." Riebisch didn't believe her at first, but after a moment's hesitation he went with her. The two of them ran to the bridge, across it, and up the Summer Path to the hill, which lay shrouded in fog.

Stimming had just gone out. The women in the house were in great agitation. Remembering how emphatically the guests had refused to have their rooms made up, Frau Stimming went upstairs in the hope of finding a clue to the mystery. The doors on the corridor were locked, and a back door resisted stubbornly—the guests had wedged a chair against it. When Frau Stimming finally got in, she was disappointed in her expectations; apart from the furniture, all she found in the room was a small black traveling bag and a wooden box, both sealed, neither of which could give her the least hint. Then the women, Frau Stimming, her young daughter, and the Feilenhauer girl, followed the Riebisches to the hill by the lake.

At the top of the hill there was a natural pit, about a foot deep and three feet across. Henriette, who had been sitting on the edge of the pit, had slumped backwards and there she lay; she was deathly pale but her eyes were open and the look on her face was one of contentment; she was wearing white kid gloves and her hands were folded over her abdomen. Her fine blue coat was open and her dress of white batiste revealed a small hole ringed with black, barely encrusted with blood.

Kleist was facing her, kneeling between her feet; his left hand hung limply over his left knee; his small round head lay beside Henriette's hip, resting on his right hand, which was still clutching the pistol; the barrel was pointed at his mouth. His teeth were tightly clenched, his lips stained with bloody foam, and his face, as pale as Henriette's, showed the same smiling, contented look. Beside him in the pit lay a second pistol, which had been fired; a third, still loaded, lay on the table that Riebisch had hauled up the hill less than an hour before (it was now shortly after four o'clock). Frau Stimming suddenly realized what the lady had been carrying in her carefully covered little basket. What merry guests they had been! Little more than a day had passed since they had drawn up in their cab; their gaiety had brought life into the house, and now they lay side by side, forever silent, in the fog of a waning November afternoon.

Riebisch was a practical man; realizing at a glance how difficult it would be to put the dead man in his coffin if he were allowed to stiffen in his present kneeling position, he picked up the body and laid it flat on the ground. A soldier who happened to be passing by joined the others. He saw the pistol on the table, examined it, and unloaded it, and Frau Stimming told Frau Riebisch to carry the three weapons down to the Jug in her apron. Finally, Stimming arrived, surveyed the scene, sent the women home, stationed two watchmen on the hill, to make sure the corpses were neither robbed nor otherwise tampered with, and sent a messenger to notify police headquarters at Potsdam.

At about the same time as the shots were being fired by the Wannsee, the suicides' letter reached Peguilhen at Markgrafenstrasse in Berlin. The tone of the letter seemed so "droll" to Peguilhen that on first reading he did not take it seriously; but then he ran to Vogel, who did take the message seriously and was beside himself with horror. The two friends took Vogel's carriage and drove as fast as they could to the Jug by the Friedrich-Wilhelm Bridge, where they arrived at about seven o'clock. They were expected. Three hours before, they were informed, two guests, a lady and a gentleman, who, as Stimming's description made clear, could be none other than Kleist and Henriette, had shot themselves. Vogel, to whom Stimming gave the pistols, the black leather traveling bag, and the wooden box, was shaken with grief and could not bring himself to look at the bodies; he spent the night at the inn in Peguilhen's company.

In the traveling bag and the box, Vogel found Henriette's two farewell letters, which left no doubt that the suicides had been planned. The first letter contained a long list of instructions, requests, and suggestions: which mementos should be given to which friends; where Vogel should have his clothes washed and mended; what to do with some soap Henriette had made (it should be put away and kept for Paulinchen, their little daughter); and "Now, my dear good Vogel, the last request I have to make of you: do not part Kleist and me in death"; and would he please advance the money for Kleist's burial; everything had been provided for and he would be promptly reimbursed.

The second letter, which was dated November 20, 1811, and could have been written either on Behrenstrasse in Berlin or at Stimming's, explained in detail her moral and material reasons for seeking death, and went on: "Kleist, who wishes to be my faithful companion in death as he was in life, will attend to my passage and then shoot himself. Do not weep or grieve, my excellent Vogel . . . My friend's generosity in sacrificing *everything* for me, even his *own life*, and what signifies far more than all that, the *assurance* he had given me that he will carry out *my* wish and kill me, leads me to desire nothing more fervently than that even in death he should not be parted from me. —I am sure, my good Louis, that you will honor the feelings of the most sacred love."

In the sealed box there were two further letters from Henriette to close friends (one of them dated November 22; that is, the following day), Kleist's last letter to Marie von Kleist, and the letter to Ulrike dated "on the morning of my death." It also contained various articles of clothing, keys, money, and two books, a translation of *Don Quixote* and a volume of Klopstock's *Odes*, one of which, *The Dead Clarissa*, is especially marked; the two suicides related it to themselves, and may well have taken the lines

> *Rest be to thee and wreaths of victory, O soul,*
> *Because thou wert so beautiful!*

as an epitaph for each other.

The night passed, the new day dawned: Friday, November 22, 1811. Vogel still could not bring himself to visit the bodies on the hilltop. He asked Peguilhen to cut him a lock of his wife's hair, whereupon Peguilhen crossed the Wilhelm Bridge, climbed the Summer Path "to the spot where the two deceased lay, and immediately recognized Madame Vogel, who was well known to me, as well as v. Kleist." As the husband had instructed in accordance with Henriette's wishes, Peguilhen gave orders that two graves should be dug side by side here, on the knoll where the two had died. He then cut a lock of Henriette's hair and went back to the Jug. Vogel took the lock of hair and listened to his account of what he had seen. Then, still unable to control his grief, he took Peguilhen's advice, got into his carriage, and returned to Berlin alone.

Peguilhen stayed on; he evidently sent a messenger back to Berlin to order the coffins, which arrived a few hours later; he also put himself at the disposal of the authorities. At one-thirty the legal and medical authorities arrived from Potsdam: public prosecutor Felgentreu, town clerk Mevius, forensic surgeon Greiff, and the Teltow district physician, Dr. Sternemann.

First they repaired to the scene of the crime; there the bodies were "inspected" and their identities confirmed by Peguilhen; then, back at the Jug, an "inquest" was held. Not that there was much to inquire into; everything was clear beyond a shadow of doubt, but the officials must have felt that they were doing no more than their duty in disregarding appearances, considering the case as a potential crime, and proceeding accordingly. We are indebted to their thoroughness for the record that enables us to reconstruct in detail the last hours of Kleist's life and the first hours after his death. The hearing to which the four then available witnesses—War Councilor Peguilhen, the Stimmings, and Frau Riebisch, née Haddicke—were subjected went on until late into the night.

First Peguilhen, speaking in the name of the accountant Louis Vogel, declared that Vogel assumed all judicial, medical, ecclesiastical, and other costs contingent on the proceedings; he then submitted Kleist's and Henriette's letters for the record, and set forth the background of the tragedy in detail.

Madame Vogel, he testified, was well known to him. As far back as he remembered, she had always been ailing, overwrought, and subject to religious exaltation; suffering from an intensely painful ailment, diagnosed as incurable, she had longed for the bliss beyond the grave, and time and time again expressed a desire for death. He, Peguilhen, had never really believed her, "for she was a highly cultivated woman, living in a very happy marriage." Then, two years before, Adam Müller had brought Kleist, a man given to similar extravagant ideas, to the house; the two had become close friends, they had spent whole evenings in ecstatic conversation or at the piano, playing and singing hymns, chorales and psalms, and so, little by little, "a spiritual love had been born which, thanks to overheated imagination and extravagant religious notions, had taken on such intensity that they both came to regard the dissolution of their bodies as the supreme happiness."

This statement, along with the farewell letters of the deceased, provided convincing motivation for suicide, while the final preparations and the act itself were fully elucidated by the ensuing testimony of the Stimmings and Frau Riebisch. There being no room for doubt, it was decided to conclude the inquest for the present. The record closes as follows: "Since it is past midnight and the remaining persons are not at present available for questioning, the proceedings are hereby closed. Signed Felgentreu (signed Mevius)." The pedantry with which the first hearing was conducted seems rather excessive when we note that more than a week was allowed to pass before Riebisch the hired man and Feilenhauer the housemaid were questioned, on December 2, 1811. At that time the record of both hearings was read to all the witnesses and given them to sign. (Frau Riebisch, as we have seen, signed with several crosses.)

The medical authorities, however, let no grass grow under their feet. No sooner had they gained a general impression from the police findings at the scene of the crime and the first hearing than they set to work with their saws and scalpels. On November 22, Kleist's body was "carefully" removed to the "tumbledown" peasant hut across from the Jug (presumably the house in which the Riebisches lived); there in the bedroom, by the light of flickering candles, he was "immediately undressed and subjected to a thorough preliminary inspection." When his head was moved, a little blood flowed from his mouth, although the jaws were so tightly shut that they had to be prized open with a kind of jimmy—almost as if Kleist had resisted. In the posterior part of the pharynx, the finger encountered a slight osseous roughness and depression, but the body showed no injuries, only brownish-red spots, such as "are most pronounced in persons dead of asphyxia and apoplexy."

Then the body was opened. "Both lungs in the spacious chest were free from disease," but the right lung was very much distended; when it was cut into, blood flowed copiously and "the imprisoned air rushed out with a hissing sound." The heart and abdomen were found normal; only the liver was "unnaturally large"; when with difficulty it was cut into, a quantity of thick black blood flowed out. The gall bladder was also conspicuously distended and contained a large quantity of thickened gall, whereas the stomach and bladder, which were then cut open, were empty. "After these two cavities were correctly sewed up, the head was opened."

But the head offered a certain resistance—the head saw broke. In the end, however, the brain was laid bare. It "seemed heavy, as though charged with blood." "As for the gray matter, we found it much firmer than usual." But this did not stop the medical gentlemen from cutting into it and removing "from the *globo dextro* a piece of lead weighing three-eighths of an ounce," and establishing that the gray matter was destroyed at this point and the small blood vessels torn.

With this, the doctors' thirst for knowledge was quenched, and they were able in good conscience to draw the following conclusions: "From the carefully executed autopsy and the attendant circumstances as established, it can be inferred with certainty that the deceased v. Kleist placed a loaded pistol in his mouth and shot himself with it . . . Death must have resulted very quickly from gunpowder asphyxia." "We further declare that we found in the deceased an enlarged, indurated liver, a distended gall bladder, and a large quantity of thickened black gall, and further that his gray matter was firmer than usual. On the strength of these indications and in the light of physiological principles, we are led to infer that the deceased was by temperament a *sanguino cholericus in summo gradu* and undoubtedly suffered severe attacks of hypochondria . . . If it is true that this eccentric temperament was accompanied by religious extravagance, it may be inferred that the deceased v. Kleist was suffering from mental illness."

Kleist's body, as "correctly" patched up as was possible after such treatment, was entrusted to Peguilhen, who had it placed in one of the coffins that had been made ready, and "immediately lowered into the ground." Since it was dark night by then, this must have been done by the light of lamps and torches. We can easily imagine such a night burial in the woods, the hushed movements of those present, the groaning of the coffin as it was being lowered, the thud of the first shovelful of earth. No report has come down to us, but his bill shows that a minister was present with his sexton, and that for some mysterious reason he charged twice as much for officiating at Kleist's burial as he did for burying Henriette. Whether he said anything more than prayers over Kleist's grave, we do not know.

Meanwhile, the doctors were busy with Henriette in the tumbledown peasant's hut. In undressing her they were struck by the fineness of her undergarments, which they mentioned expressly in their report. The report stresses the exceptional precision of the fatal shot, which, despite the relatively large size of the bullet, caused no damage whatever to the ribs and which was presumed to have induced almost instant death. The report further states that in examining the thoracic cavity the doctors had found that the left lung was "apparently detached"; in the abdomen they had found everything normal except for the uterus, "the entire tissue of which was so indurated that it seemed to have turned to cartilage." "The head saw having been broken in the autopsy of the deceased v. Kleist," it proved impossible to open the head, but this was not thought to be "absolutely necessary since the *causa mortis* had been adequately established"; there seemed to be no reason to "postulate" a deficient organization of the brain, "since the deceased demonstrated a cultivated mind in all things." The doctors summed up their conclusions as follows: "The deceased Vogel was suffering from an incurable cancer of the womb and chose this easy death for fear of a slow and very hard one."

It was ten o'clock at night when Henriette in her coffin was carried up the hill and found her last resting place in the grave beside Kleist's. A few hours later, the hearing at the Jug was concluded and once again the peace and desolation usual at that time of year descended on the house and the lake shore.

Materially speaking, Kleist left nothing behind him but a few articles of clothing and a black traveling bag.

# 24

## THE ECHO

F RIVOLOUS as it may seem to say so, Kleist's death was his first striking success. The echo of the two shots fired beside the Wannsee shook people out of their lethargy; some obscure instinct told them that this death had meaning, even at a time when human life counted for so little and Napoleon could say to Metternich: "I don't care a fig for a million human lives!" And even today, more than a century and a half later, we have well-nigh forgotten the untold thousands slaughtered in the course of Napoleon's mad struggle for power, while the echo of the shots fired beside the Wannsee still rings in our ears.

Ironically enough, the first recorded reaction comes to us from a source that had made its contribution to Kleist's destruction. His request for a loan of twenty louis d'or was still on file at the chancellery in Berlin. No action had as yet been taken. On November 22—Kleist had not yet been buried—Hardenberg himself wrote on it: "File closed as petitioner v. Kleist is dead as of 11/21/11." If nothing else, this shows us how swiftly the news traveled.

The next reaction is recorded in the Stahnsdorf-Machnow church register: "On (21) twenty-one November (1811) one thousand eight hundred eleven, on the Klein-Machnow heath near the Berlin highway, Bernd Heinr. Wilhelm von Kleist shot Adolphine Sophie Henriette, née Keber, aged 31, wife of Herr Friedrich Ludwig Vogel, accountant general of the Brandenburg Fire Insurance Company and provincial bookkeeper, and then himself, in the 34th year of his life. They were placed in two coffins and buried in one grave at the site of the murder and suicide."

No word has come to us of any death notice inserted in the papers by the Kleist family; nor is he mentioned in the notice sent by Vogel to the *Vossische Zeitung* and the *Spenersche Zeitung:*

> With deepest sorrow I hereby inform all my friends and relatives of the death on November 21 of my dearly beloved spouse Adolphine Sophie Henriette, née Keber.
>
> Her death was as pure as her life. Crushed by the burden of a life of illness, she sought death. In the words which she herself left behind: "Do not weep or grieve, for I am dying a death such as few mortals have enjoyed; accompanied by the most fervent love, I am exchanging earthly happiness for eternal bliss." This must serve to console her old father, my only daughter Pauline, and me for our irreparable loss. I, her deeply afflicted husband, ask to be spared the usual expressions of sympathy. Fr. Louis Vogel.

The quotation from Henriette, which lends itself to more than one interpretation, appears to be an attempt on the widower's part to shield himself from the sensation-mongering gossip aroused by the incident.

And Peguilhen, whom Varnhagen calls an "insignificant, harebrained, thoroughly inferior little man," may have had a similar purpose in mind with the self-important notice he inserted in the *Vossische Zeitung* on the 26th of November and in the *Spenersche Zeitung* on the 28th. Speaking as an intimate of Madame Vogel and as a friend of Kleist, and in his capacity "as executor of the last will of the two deceased," he requested the public to defer passing judgment, since at the urgent plea of his friend Vogel he would soon, before the end of the year in fact, publish a statement concerning "an act unequaled down through the centuries, performed by two persons who were love and purity personified and cannot be measured by common standards."

This embarrassing bit of verbiage seems worth quoting because it gives an idea of the excitement aroused by the suicide. The excitement penetrated to the royal palace, and Friedrich Wilhelm was not pleased. Feeling that the glorification of such a crime would have a demoralizing effect on his people, he arranged for the police president to issue an edict (dated December 6) prohibiting Peguilhen's literary effort. Peguilhen immediately wrote a letter of self-justification to the chancellery, humbly denying any imputation of conduct unbecoming a civil servant. Assuring the chancellor that he would publish nothing further, he commended himself to his benevolent consideration. He was not long under a cloud; on December 31, Hardenberg notes in his daybook: "Aforementioned Peguilhen gives thanks for reinstatement of salary."

Ulrike was neither in Berlin nor in Frankfurt at that time, and she learned of her brother's death through a strange coincidence that recalls a similar though quite innocuous episode in Kleist's life eight years before. She was off on one of her innumerable trips to visit relatives. Headed for Gulben, she stopped in Körlin for the night. At the inn she was kept awake by some people talking in the next room and in spite of herself she began listening. The talk was about a case of murder and suicide. The name of Kleist, a former lieutenant, was spoken and Ulrike froze with horror. It appears that she knocked at the door, questioned the people, and fell into a faint when she heard the details. But the next morning she resumed her journey to Gulben, where she received Kleist's letter of farewell and reconciliation, dated "on the morning of my death."

She never got over Heinrich's death and the circumstances in which she learned of it. Like her younger brother Leopold, she seldom mentioned him and disliked hearing of him from others. "Let's not talk about him. It makes my heart ache." In her presence it was not permissible to mention the name of Goethe, whose help, she was convinced, would have been so decisive, but who had done nothing but harm; nor did she feel any friendlier toward Theodor Körner, who had never had a kind word to say for Kleist, but had dramatized his *Betrothal in Santo Domingo* without so much as mentioning the author, the result being *Toni*, an unspeakable piece of trash, as Ulrike never wearied of saying.

When Kleist's correspondence began to attract interest, she withheld (and induced her favorite niece and sole heir, Frau von Schönfeldt, née von Pannwitz, to withhold) all letters which might in her opinion detract from his reputation or, one cannot help thinking, throw too bright a light on the breakdown of his relations with her and the family. The other members of the family attached no importance to his letters and preserved none of them; for years they continued to feel ashamed of this black sheep and his scandalous death, and it is to be feared that this feeling was shared at least in some degree by Ulrike.

From then on, she lived quietly in the house on Nonnenwinkel, where she and Heinrich had grown up, busying herself with the education of young girls. Toward the end she became mentally ill and was cared for by her favorite niece. She died on February 5, 1849, at the age of seventy-five. After her death, the house on Nonnenwinkel was sold, enlarged, and converted into the Prince of Prussia Hotel. Later it was taken over by the post office, which also acquired the neighboring von Zenge property, and a plaque was put up to inform passers-by who was born and grew up there.

Apart from Ulrike, the relative most deeply affected by the news from the Wannsee was, of course, Marie von Kleist. Since she was still ailing, those about her hesitated to tell her the truth. When at last she learned it, she was torn between grief tempered with pride over "that unfathomable mortal" and a truly feminine hatred of his companion in death. On December 10, 1811, she wrote to her son: "I have lost a friend. How many women can boast of having had one?" And she went on to praise him and defend him: "Heinrich was an admirable man, in most things the most admirable I have ever known. Nowhere else have I seen such innate kindness, love, and gentleness . . . Even if he had never created a single poem, he was by nature a poet. He was the most poetic, the most romantic person I have ever known . . . He was truly a genius, and in a man of that kind there are certain things that defy explanation. But his rectitude, honesty, and integrity were such as to fill me with a horror of all dissembling, all boasting, all calculated behavior."

Peguilhen wrote to her, and to him she repeated: "In Hein-

rich Kleist I lost one who shared in all my joys and all my sufferings. He was the gentlest of companions, the most comforting to my heart." But with an indignation so fierce as to be
almost comical she dismissed the thought that he might have
spoken to that . . . that other woman with the same love, the
same passion as to her—ridiculous! No, he (the most forthright
of men) had never breathed a word of any intimacy with this
Madame Vogel; she had never heard of it, and didn't wish to.

On December 23, 1811, Rahel Levin wrote to Alexander von
der Marwitz: "Kleist's act does not shock me, life was hard on
him, he was true to himself and he suffered a great deal . . . It
pains me to hear of unfortunate mortals drinking their cup of
suffering to the lees . . . I am glad my noble friend—with bitter
tears I call him friend—declined to put up with indignity, he
suffered enough. —None of those who find fault with him
would have offered him ten talers, sat up nights with him,
shown him forbearance—even if he could have let them see
him in his ravaged condition. They would have gone right on
with their eternal calculation: was he or was he not entitled to
this cup of coffee? I know nothing about his death except that
he first shot a woman and then himself. But this much I know:
it takes courage." And to Varnhagen von Ense, her future husband, she wrote on February 27, 1812: "If I were to shoot myself, my friends would be surprised, as they are over Kleist. At
least I have honored his passing by not being surprised."

On November 25, immediately after the tragedy became
known, the publisher Julius Hitzig wrote to Fouqué describing
his "feeling of horror" and concluding: "Peace be to the ashes
of that unhappy man, so rich in heart and mind." But even before receiving Hitzig's letter Fouqué had sent him a poem in
honor of Kleist, which could not, however, be published for
the present because of the royal censorship. "It poured from me
yesterday amid hot tears," he wrote. "My whole soul is afflicted
. . . How strange—these three poets from the house of Kleist!
All so early in their graves, and each, in a manner of speaking,
expressing his times by the manner of his death. The first fallen
in the most glorious of Prussian wars, pious and dutiful to the
last, the second destroyed by wild dissipation even before his

death, the third gone to his grave with philosophical staunch-
ness, with noble if misguided ponderation, one of the most
magnificent suicides of all time." "You know," Hitzig replied,
"Kleist had ceased to be my friend when he departed this
world, but I cannot get over his death." And Fouqué (we do
not know precisely which letters he was speaking of): "Kleist's
parting words make the same impression on me as on you. I
admire their unbending strength, but it shatters me." And
"Serena," his wife, adds: "I have read the dreadful letters.
Dreadful for the icy coldness that pierces the quivering, tearful gaze of life."

The indefatigable Peguilhen had requested information for
his projected obituary from Fouqué as well as Hitzig, and
Fouqué replied: "I am profoundly shaken by the terrible unswerving fortitude with which our Heinrich said farewell to a
life in which so many laurels still awaited him, and so many
loving hearts beat for him. I am at your disposal if there is anything I can do to help you preserve the memory of our noble
fallen friend." And further on: "They are lying side by side
near a lake, in the spot where they fell. In that very place, in
the autumn of the preceding year, the poetic bond between
Kleist and myself was strengthened beyond measure, thanks to
his loving goodwill. And now that splendid man is sleeping his
deep sleep there . . . I cannot think of Heinrich's grave without
groaning inwardly. It is not as I thought at first; for me, every
new report thickens the veil of mystery surrounding his act. I
no longer have an opinion; all I have left is grief over my lost
comrade and the certainty that he cannot have done or even
thought anything base."

Varnhagen von Ense, to whom Goethe imputed the talent
and will "to give our nation literary unity," also felt the greatness of the loss. "How horrified I was at the news of Kleist's
death," he wrote to Rahel. "I had it first from Brentano; Savigny
had written to him about it. Only a short while before, I had
read the second volume of his magnificent stories and rejoiced
in his rich talent. Now it is destroyed. I was shattered. His soul
rose up before me and I had insight into it. The poor man!
What terrible suffering must have gnawed at him to make him

abandon the talent which, in his ravaged life, he regarded as the indestructible talisman of a promised happiness."

But what was the reaction of Adam Müller, who, more perceptive than most, realized that Kleist had nurtured the thought of death "as the spice of a tasteless life"? As a strict Catholic, he was faced with a dilemma; in a private letter, he deplored "our Kleist's terrible end" and complained that Kleist and Henriette had drawn him and his wife "into the sacrilege of their last thoughts." But in the obituary that he published in the Vienna *Sammler* in December 1811, he expressed his feelings about suicide as gently as possible: "It may be said, however, that both their lives were as pure and spotless as they could possibly have been without the higher faith which they denied by their end; further, that Kleist was true, without falsehood or affectation of any kind, and that his act was totally free from the theatrical light which false emphasis and incomprehension have tried to throw on it."

During the following year, he collected material for a more detailed obituary, which, however, never saw the light; but then the *Österreichischer Beobachter*, edited by Friedrich Schlegel, published an article in which Müller defended Kleist against all manner of base attacks: "Perhaps the judgment of his German contemporaries has never been more at fault than when his works appeared: they wanted peace and quiet, cozy comfort, facile sentimentalities. How then could they approve of a writer who, himself incapable of any superficial feeling, had undertaken to prepare the nation for suffering, to fire the hearts of the people with generous devotion to their country and their friends; in short, who had set out with youthful enthusiasm to tear our wounds open even wider."

Here once again we hear the voice of the man who early in 1808 had passionately defended *Penthesilea* against Gentz; despite his moral shock and religious scruples, Adam Müller was back where he belonged—at Kleist's side.

The moral implications, the pros and cons of the double suicide were being discussed everywhere. Typical of the reflections to which it gave rise are the following lines from a letter written by Dresden Appellate Judge Körner to his son in

Vienna: "About Kleist's death: la Chodowiecka has written to
la Piatoli that Kleist did not really love la Vogel but another
woman (not la Hendel). It seems he suggested the shooting
party to her but she wouldn't hear of it. It was only then that
he invited la Vogel to the dance. She already wanted to die because she was suffering from cancer, and so she was willing."
    To which Theodor Körner replied: "Kleist's end did not
surprise me. What I fail to see is how a woman could shoot
herself for love of him. —In this whole incident, I see a clear
expression of the shallow, volatile character of the Prussians."
Most of Körner's fellow writers maintained a discreet silence
for the present—at least in public. This was equally true of
Tieck, who loved Kleist's work; of Arnim, who had meant no
harm in calling Kleist "outspoken to the point of cynicism";
and of Brentano, who since the *Berliner Abendblätter* days had
spoken of him with hypocritical arrogance and, in a misjudg-
ment that would be hard to equal, termed him "boundlessly
vain."
    Among the published reactions, Jung-Stilling condemned the
suicide from a strictly Catholic point of view, while Madame
de Staël, who had previously defended the right to suicide, now
regarded it as a threat to public morality.
    But of course it was in the shallowest waters that the echo
of the shots fired on the Wannsee threw up the stormiest waves.
On November 30, the *Journal for the Fashionable World* published an unsigned article telling how Kleist had been introduced into the house of a Berlin official and his "young, pretty,
and clever" wife. "Between Kleist and the official's wife," the
article went on, "an affair soon developed, which the husband
could not view with indifference. God only knows what family
scenes took place. Be that as it may, the seduced woman decided to go away with her seducer, not in order to live with
him in a different place, possibly because they both felt that
they lacked the necessary means, but in order to die together."
    F. C. Weisser, Cotta's house scribbler, came out with a
wretched article entitled "Public Beatification and Deification
of Murder and Suicide in Germany," but signed himself only
as "—s—." In it he calls Kleist a dishonor to his name, a "flashy

poet, one of the most notorious disciples of the notorious romantico-mystical school," a victim, as it were, of this mysticism and of a literature "which, like a fetid swamp, spawns hardly anything but basilisks."

Indignant at such calumny, the chivalrous Fouqué wrote to the semi-anonymous scribbler, defying him to name himself, but Cotta preferred not to publish the letter. A friend of Fouqué's took the matter up in the Halle magazine *Sabina*, a short verbal duel ensued, and then both sides fell silent. Three years later, an article honoring Kleist, signed "Wa," written by Richard Wagner's uncle Adolph Wagner, appeared in the *Brockhaus Konversationslexikon* (2nd ed., 1815). It was violently attacked by the same F. C. Weisser, who owes his place in the history of literature exclusively to his irreconcilable hatred of Kleist.

The excitement over the dual suicide spread beyond the borders of Germany. Articles were published in the *Journal de l'Empire* and in *The Times* of London. Adam Müller thought the *Times* article the best to have appeared anywhere. All in all, Kleist's death may be regarded as a success such as he had never achieved in his lifetime, an international triumph which, by enriching his legend, may have contributed to his lasting fame.

The excitement had not entirely died down when public interest in Kleist's person was stimulated by an unforeseen event. In June 1812, the manuscript of *The Prince of Homburg* came to light. Marie von Kleist had at last obtained her divorce, and though her husband was declared in the wrong she was left in financial straits. She sent the manuscript to her nephew, Heinrich von Puttkamer, then a student in Berlin, asking him to submit it to Hitzig for publication. Thus, in all innocence, the young man became a connecting link between two of the greatest men of modern Prussia—Kleist, whose "interests" he tried, as it were, to promote, and Bismarck, whose father-in-law he was to become thirty-five years later.

Marie von Kleist's claim, which he conveyed to Hitzig, was well founded, since Kleist had bequeathed her this copy as security for a loan of two hundred talers; she demanded that sum as her fee. Hitzig read the play. He was enthusiastic but felt that two hundred talers was more than he could hope to recover if the play was published in the usual way. He consulted Fouqué, who read it with equal enthusiasm, and they agreed on a counterproposal to put to Marie von Kleist: they would set up a subscription in the hope that one or two hundred persons would contribute a taler, if it were made clear that "the proceeds would be used for a purpose dear to the heart of the author." As an introduction to the book, Fouqué would write a short piece on Kleist's life and death, a vindication such as Cotta had been too cowardly to publish, but for which, now that tempers had had time to cool, the publication of an important but hitherto unknown work offered an excellent occasion. Hitzig agreed to defray the printing costs, provided that the cost of paper was repaid out of the subscription receipts and that he was authorized to print a few hundred copies on special paper.

This was a reasonable solution, calculated to satisfy the interests of all parties. Fouqué got in touch with Marie von Kleist, and if nothing came of the negotiations, historic events were largely to blame, for this was 1812, a year that was yet to witness the Tauroggen Convention between Prussia and Russia, the popular uprising in East Prussia, and the king's proclamation "To my people"; in short, the outbreak of the Wars of Liberation after the destruction of Napoleon's Grande Armée in Russia's ice and snow. Innumerable individual destinies were temporarily or permanently sidetracked. Fouqué went off with the army; Hitzig gave up his publishing house; Chamisso, under suspicion as a Frenchman, fled to the country, where he wrote his *Peter Schlemihl* to amuse Hitzig's children; and for the present no more was said about publishing *The Prince of Homburg*.

But it was not entirely forgotten. Tieck got wind of it, borrowed Marie von Kleist's copy, and was carried away. Like *The Battle of Teutoburg Forest*, *Homburg* was made to order for the martial spirit of the day. Tieck gave readings of both plays at public and private gatherings, so gaining new friends and admirers for Kleist's work. In the course of time, he became so engrossed that he conceived a more ambitious undertaking, and in 1816 wrote to Adam and Sophie Müller with a view to collecting further material.

His letter was answered by Johanna von Haza, Sophie's daughter by her first marriage, who informed him of the so-called Fragments—comprising short notes "full of profound meaning," and the stories *Jeronimo and Josephe* (*The Earthquake in Chile*) and *Michael Kohlhaas*—which, she said, her mother had held in her hands. From Johanna's remarks, Kleist scholars later inferred that these "fragments" were in fact identical with the Magazine of Ideas mentioned by Kleist himself, and that he must have kept it from the time of his trip to Würzburg in 1800 at least until 1807, since before 1807 it could not have included *Kohlhaas*, and since it was then that he had met Sophie von Haza in Dresden.

Another statement by Johanna von Haza has led to still more daring speculations. Eager "to contribute to the glorification of one of the noblest men and greatest authors of our day, a man so little appreciated in his lifetime," she told Tieck about a work entitled *The Story of My Soul*, without which the sum of "Kleist's writings would remain fragmentary, at least for those desirous of knowing him and appreciating him to the full and above all of pardoning his last step." This autobiographical work (for its existence can hardly have been pure invention on the part of Sophie or Johanna von Haza) would undoubtedly have made an important contribution to our knowledge of Kleist, but it was nowhere to be found. According to Johanna, it "was probably lost in the turmoil of his last days." Or possibly—if it was then still in Kleist's possession—he burned it along with his other papers. In any event, it has never been discovered. Some Kleist scholars have concluded that this *Story of My Soul* was the nucleus or first draft of the two-volume "novel" he spoke of to Reimer, his publisher, some months before his death.

After long preparations, Tieck approached Reimer, who in 1821 published Kleist's *Posthumous Writings*, edited and provided with a "biographical-aesthetic introduction" by Ludwig Tieck. Tieck received a fee of fifty talers and a further hundred and fifty talers were set aside for Kleist's heirs.

But in addition to his works and his black traveling bag, Kleist left something else behind him: debts. In 1818 the Court of Appeals set a date by which creditors were to submit their claims. These were to be met from the proceeds of the *Posthumous Writings*, and it is much to be feared that poor Marie and Ulrike received little if anything.

Still, the *Posthumous Writings* sold, and in 1826, only five years after their appearance, Tieck was able to bring out a three-volume edition of *Collected Works* with an expanded introduction. After that, it is true, two decades elapsed before, in 1846, he was able to publish the *Selected Works* in four volumes. But by then there could be little doubt that Kleist belonged to the mainstream of German literature, especially since Tieck in the meantime had been indefatigably promoting the production of his plays, which were now fairly well received.

Tieck's influence was also responsible for the first collection of Kleist's letters: Eduard von Bülow's *Kleist's Life and Letters*, published in 1848. Surviving friends of Kleist—Tieck himself, Rühle, Pfuel, Fouqué, Marie von Kleist, Caroline von Schlieben, Sophie Müller, Wilhelmine Krug, and her sister Luise—contributed letters, and though Bülow's approach to his material was not very scholarly, his effort nevertheless helped to reinforce the memory of Kleist. Other collections of letters followed, edited by Julian Schmidt, August Koberstein, Emil Kuh, and others, and these in turn were complemented by mentions in books of memoirs and recollections such as those by Laun, Varnhagen, Fouqué, Zschokke, Hoffmann von Fallersleben, and Peguilhen. In 1863, Adolf Wilbrandt published the first comprehensive Kleist biography.

A detailed account of the development of the research and literature on Kleist since then is not within the scope of this book. It should be observed, however, that there are many unfortunate gaps in our inventory of Kleist's letters. This is largely the fault of the women in his life. As we have seen, Ulrike, supposedly in the interests of the family, and under her influence Frau von Schönfeldt, her niece, were exceedingly chary of releasing the letters in their possession, and those they did not release must be considered lost. Marie von Kleist instructed her son to burn almost all the letters she had received from Kleist, on the ground that the expression of so great a love was intended not for the world but only for the loved one. And because she thought them "too pessimistic," Wilhelmine (who told Tieck that her "heart would always treasure Kleist") withheld just those letters from the period of their betrothal that would have been most informative.

Once initiated by Tieck with his keen perception and unflagging energy, the triumphant march of Kleist's fame could not be halted. And that makes the story of Kleist's last resting place on earth—with which we conclude the present book—seem all the stranger.

Immediately after the Wannsee tragedy, no one, either among the families or friends of the deceased, thought of erecting even the most modest monument to their memory. The grave mounds, however, were strewn with pine boughs, and in accordance with an old Prussian custom, everyone who happened by added another. In May 1818, six years after their death, Ferdinand Grimm (accompanied by his brother Wilhelm or a friend by that name) visited the site. He has left us a description of it: "From the hilltop, a spacious clearing surrounded by pine trees, one has an open view across the wide sacred lake, taking in the many other wooded hills extending westward almost to distant Spandau, whose pointed church tower can be seen indistinctly. This is probably one of the loveliest and most peaceful spots for miles around. The graves are surrounded by some twenty tall poplars, but except for one I found them all withered; this is because of the sandy soil, in which they seldom thrive; Wilhelm and I removed several of the withered trunks, planted new ones, and tied them all together. Within a short time the saplings formed a wreath and stretched out their hands to one another. It really looked beautiful when we went back and looked. Not a soul had been there, it was so lonely and still; there was no other sound than the song of the chaffinches and titmice, and that, too, was beautiful."

Then for years the site was largely ignored, left to the mercy of wind and weather. Little by little the sand threatened to engulf the dwindling grave mounds. When Eduard von Bülow visited the place in the 1840s, he had a hard time finding them. When he did, it was as though nature had wished to make up for man's indifference—an oak tree had grown up between the two mounds. Bülow wrote newspaper articles deploring this unworthy neglect, and he and Tieck organized a fund-raising campaign. In 1848 a block of unhewn marble, inscribed with Kleist's name and the dates of his birth and death, was erected with the proceeds. The owners of the land, in particular the Stimmings' daughter, agreed to plant shrubs and flowers and take care of the grave.

But little more than a decade later, the site had again fallen into neglect. In 1861, a benefit reading of *The Prince of Homburg* was given in the presence of the Crown Prince of Saxony and his wife. With the hundred talers raised, an iron fence was put up and a second tombstone of white marble (contributing a new variant to the controversy over the date of his birth) was installed:

HEINRICH VON KLEIST

B. 10 OCTOBER 1776

D. 21 NOVEMBER 1811

HE LIVED, SANG AND SUFFERED

IN HARD AND SORROWFUL TIMES,

HE SOUGHT DEATH ON THIS SPOT

AND FOUND IMMORTALITY

MATT. 6:12

Then once again the site was allowed to run down, until finally, in 1885, the Kleist Family Foundation assumed responsibility for it and promised to take care of it in the future. But, if we are correctly informed, it was not until the hundredth anniversary of Kleist's death, on November 21, 1911, that the family overcame its sense of shame over this "useless member of society, unworthy of any sympathy." On that occasion they laid a wreath on his grave. The inscription on the ribbon read: "To the best of his line."

The tombstone was again changed in 1936. The new inscription reads:

HEINRICH VON KLEIST

BORN 18 OCTOBER 1777

DIED 21 NOVEMBER 1811

O IMMORTALITY

NOW YOU ARE

WHOLLY MINE

*Index of Works*

*Index of Names*

# INDEX OF WORKS

## Lost Works